JOHN SCHREINER'S
OKANAGAN
WINE TOUR GUIDE

JOHN SCHREINER'S

OKANAGAN

WINE TOUR GUIDE

whitecap

Copyright © 2006, 2007 and 2010
by John Schreiner
First edition published 2006.
Second edition 2007.
Third edition 2010.

Whitecap Books

EDITED BY Marial Shea
THIRD EDITION EDITED BY Naomi Pauls
COVER DESIGN BY Mauve Pagé and
Diane Yee
INTERIOR DESIGN BY Stacey Noyes /
LuzForm Design
TYPESET BY Mauve Pagé
MAP BY Eric Leinberger
PHOTOGRAPHY BY John Schreiner unless
otherwise specified

Printed in Canada by Friesens

LIBRARY AND ARCHIVES CANADA
CATALOGUING IN PUBLICATION

Schreiner, John, 1936–

    John Schreiner's Okanagan wine tour
guide. — Rev. and updated

ISBN 978-1-77050-014-3

    1. Wineries—British Columbia—
Okanagan Valley (Region)—Guidebooks.
2. Wine and wine making—British
Columbia—Okanagan Valley (Region). 3.
Vintners—British Columbia—Okanagan
Valley (Region). 4. Okanagan Valley
(B.C. : Region)—Tours. I. Title. II. Title:
Okanagan wine tour guide.

TP559.C3S35 2010   663'.20097115
    C2009-906422-7

The publisher acknowledges the financial
support of the Government of Canada
through the Canada Book Fund (CBF) and
the Province of British Columbia through
the Book Publishing Tax Credit.

10 11 12 13 14   5 4 3 2 1

To the deans of Okanagan winemaking.

RON TAYLOR began making wine in 1970 at Andrés, had a role in developing Baby Duck and has reinvented himself since 2000 as a leading maker of fruit wines.

ELIAS PHINIOTIS, after making wine in his native Cyprus, came to British Columbia in 1976 and has made wine at 20 different wineries, from Uncle Ben's to Volcanic Hills.

HOWARD SOON, after a brief stint in a brewery, joined Calona Vineyards in 1980. Besides making the superb Sandhill wines, he continues to mentor other fine winemakers.

CONTENTS

WHY I WROTE
THIS BOOK

THIS THIRD EDITION OF *John Schreiner's Okanagan Wine Tour Guide* comes on the heels of my 500-page third edition of *The Wineries of British Columbia*, which was published last year. It included about 200 profiles, almost double the number in the 2004 edition and five times the number in the first edition of 1994. The ink was barely dry on that authoritative tome before a dozen more wineries surfaced. Hence, a third edition of the *Tour Guide* to bring my readers completely up to date—for now!

I began touring the Okanagan and Similkameen valleys about 35 years ago and have returned there more frequently than to any of the world's other wine regions (and I have visited most of them). Obviously, it is closer to my North Vancouver home than most other regions, but there is much more to the Okanagan's appeal than its accessibility.

First, of course, there are the wines, which have improved steadily and rapidly in the past decade. Bradley Cooper, the winemaker at Township 7 and at his new Black Cloud Winery, made one of his first Okanagan wine tours in the early 1980s as a journalist. He wanted to select a mixed case (12 bottles) of wines to take home, but found only 10 he liked well enough to buy. Today, he observes, you can fill a case with good wine at almost every winery. This is my experience as well. Now, even when I am not researching a book, I travel to the Okanagan and Similkameen

several times a year to taste and stock up on those interesting, limited-production wines that seldom make it to local wine stores.

Just as appealing as the wines is the winery ambiance in the Okanagan. I understood perfectly when Mick Luckhurst, one of the owners of Road 13 Vineyards and a former housing developer, told me there is romance in growing grapes and making wine not always found in other agriculture. If, he said, his vineyards were potato fields, he would be doing something else. It is exciting to hang around with people like Mick, who spend their days seduced by the grape. They are passionate and interesting, proud of what they do and always ready to talk about their wines.

In most of the tasting rooms I have visited, everyone is having fun, especially during wine festival time. During the Okanagan's spring wine festival in 2005, I was lounging on the deck at Jeff and Niva Martin's La Frenz Winery, savouring a glass of Shiraz, when I struck up a conversation with a wine tourist from Seattle. A first-time visitor to the Okanagan, he was visibly impressed by the region's people and wines, and by the scenery, which he acknowledged with a sweeping wave of his arm toward the view of Naramata Bench spread out in front of us. And, he added, the wine prices are so reasonable. I appreciated hearing this from an outsider because some British Columbians, even including a few winemakers, grumble that our wine prices are high when they have not encountered the sticker shock in Washington state's (admittedly fine) wineries.

The scenic and ecological values of British Columbia's wine regions enrich wine touring immeasurably. Peachland's Working Horse Winery is, to the best of my knowledge, the only Canadian winery using draft horses to work the vineyard. The self-guided tour at the Burrowing Owl Estate Winery provides at least as much information on the fragile environment as it does about what happens in the winery. Check out the interpretation centre next to the Nk'Mip Cellars winery—learning about the history of the Osoyoos Indian Band is an enriching experience. The tranquil gardens at the Pacific Agri-Food Research Centre near Summerland offer the perfect spot to relax between winery visits. The Kettle Valley Railway Trail ascends from Penticton and leads along the upper border of the Naramata Bench, providing stunning vineyard panoramas. The Golden Mile Trail on the hills above Tinhorn Creek winery offers breathtaking views of the South Okanagan.

Again and again, you will come across views throughout wine country that are fit for landscapes, postcards and calendars. An image of the beautiful Blue Mountain vineyard south of Okanagan Falls, one of the most photographed in the valley, has been a popular computer screen saver. Many of the wineries, notably Red Rooster and Ruby Tuesday, display and sell the work of fine local artists in their tasting rooms.

Being a writer gives me the opportunity to dig for all manner of information about the people behind the wines. As you read these entries, you will find that most people disclosed their ages and birthplaces. I ask such intrusive questions for good reason. In the Old World, the people running wineries usually come from families that have been doing the same thing for 300 years, give or take a century. This is reflected, in fact, at Summerland's 8th Generation Vineyard, so named because Bernd Schales, one of the owners, is the eighth generation of a Germany wine growing family. (By the time Stefanie, his wife, found out that wine growing goes back 10 generations in her family, the winery had been named.)

Such an extensive background in wine is rare in British Columbia, where Gray Monk's Heiss family are old-timers at four generations. Most of the wineries are run by individuals who came from other careers, as my books reveal. Knowing where these entrepreneurs, growers and winemakers came from, and what inspired them to change occupations, adds texture and colour to winery portraits and enriches the wine touring experience.

There is the familiar story of George and Trudy Heiss, who sold their successful hair salons in Edmonton, planted an Okanagan vineyard and ultimately established Gray Monk Estate Winery. Neighbouring winery Arrowleaf Cellars is run by Josef Zuppiger, formerly an Alberta dairy farmer. Orofino Vineyards' John and Virginia Weber are transplants from Saskatchewan, where he was a teacher and she a nurse. Twisted Tree's Chris and Beata Tolley are formerly of Calgary, where he had a software business and she was a chartered accountant. Another Calgarian, Noble Ridge proprietor Jim D'Andrea, juggles a senior position in a law firm with growing wine. Judy Kingston, owner of the newly opened Serendipity Winery at Naramata, formerly was one of Canada's first specialists in computer law. Silkscarf Winery at Summerland is run by Roie Manoff, a former Israeli fighter pilot, and his family.

One of my favourite stories was told to me by Betty Masscy of Hollywood & Wine Estate Vineyards. Betty and her husband, Neil, a charming retirement-age couple, operate a new Summerland winery. Betty is an accomplished painter; some of her favourite canvasses are displayed around the Massey kitchen, where she told me this story: A male high school teacher once caught her doodling in class, sketching figures of pin-up girls. He detained her after class—and had her sketch more pin-ups for him. The Massey kitchen rang with laughter at her recollection of this original, if vaguely disturbing, approach to discipline.

Why do I put such tales in a wine book? Who, other than a laboratory technician, would find the Brix and the pH of the Masseys' Pinot Gris at harvest as interesting as Betty's story? I am writing for consumers, not technicians. Wine is not a clinical product to be separated from the compelling people who grow it. The art in wine is what attracts both consumers and wine growers. Betty Massey reflected this when she told me, "Right now, my vineyard is my canvas."

GEOGRAPHY
FOR WINE TOURISTS

HERE IS A QUICK GUIDE TO THE OKANAGAN wine country's geography, arranged from south to north, starting with the Similkameen (see map inside back cover). This arrangement assumes entering wine country at the south end, by way of the Crowsnest Highway (No. 3). Reverse the order if entering wine country from the north, by way of the Trans-Canada and Highway 97. Whether you arrive by air in Kelowna or by car via the Coquihalla, you can turn either north or south in the Okanagan Valley depending on where your favourite wineries are located. Alphabetical listings start on page 28. The list of wineries included in each region should also make it easier to plan wine tours.

THE SIMILKAMEEN VALLEY
The Similkameen is a narrow valley, with steep, brooding mountains on both sides and the passive (except during spring floods) Similkameen River in the valley bottom. The wine growing area begins at Keremeos and winds about 30 kilometres (19 miles) south, where the river crosses into the United States. Most of the vines grow on slopes and benches on the north and east sides of the river. The valley gets very little rain or snow, and the persistent wind adds to the desert-like dryness. With just over 100 hectares (247 acres) of vineyard, the Similkameen is dwarfed as an appellation by the Okanagan, which is 20 times the size. Under irrigation, all but the late-ripening vinifera grapes grow here in

a climate marked by 181 frost-free days, more than 2,000 hours of sunshine, blistering summer heat and occasional sharply cold winter days. Numerous other farms dot the valley, growing tree fruits, vegetables and grains. About 40 percent of the farms are organic, perhaps the highest concentration of organic farms in British Columbia. In Keremeos (pop. 1,500), the excellent fruit stands at either end of town are crowded with buyers all season long.

The valley's vineyards and wineries are all between Keremeos and Richter Pass—the low mountain pass near the American border through which Highway 3A undulates on its way to Osoyoos. Grapes have grown here at least since the 1960s on well-drained sand, gravel and rocky soils. Benchland on the east side of the valley, above the highway, provides potential for more vineyards if existing apple orchards are converted.

SIMILKAMEEN WINERIES

CERELIA VINEYARDS & ESTATE
  WINERY
CLOS DU SOLEIL
CROWSNEST VINEYARDS
EAUVIVRE WINERY & VINEYARDS
FORBIDDEN FRUIT WINERY
HERDER WINERY & VINEYARDS

K MOUNTAIN VINEYARDS
OROFINO VINEYARDS
ROBIN RIDGE WINERY
RUSTIC ROOTS WINERY
ST. LASZLO ESTATE WINERY
SEVEN STONES WINERY

OSOYOOS LAKE BENCH

The southernmost vineyards in the Okanagan grow on the Osoyoos Lake Bench. This is one of the narrowest points of the Okanagan Valley—Osoyoos, in fact, is a First Nations word meaning "narrows of the lake"—and one of the hottest. Osoyoos (pop. 5,200), a Spanish-themed lakeside town next to the US border, averages summertime temperatures that are three to five degrees higher than those in Penticton.

This is predominantly red wine country. The most extensive vineyards are those that Vincor International planted in 1998 and 1999 on the sandy slopes on the eastern and northeastern side of Osoyoos Lake, on slopes rising about 60 metres (200 feet) above the valley floor. These have been named Bull Pine, SunRock, Bear Cub, McIntyre and Whitetail, and are now showing up on Jackson-Triggs wine labels. Leading varieties are Merlot, Cabernet Sauvignon, Syrah, Pinot Noir and Canada's first successful Zinfandel block. Whites are also planted, notably Chardonnay, Sauvignon Blanc and Viognier. The bench on the western flank of the valley is perched slightly higher and has a more complex mix of sand, clay and gravel. Reds also dominate plantings here. The Osoyoos Larose vineyard high on the western slope grows only Bordeaux reds, chiefly Merlot, Cabernet Sauvignon and Cabernet Franc. The leading producers that get Osoyoos Lake Bench grapes include Jackson-Triggs, Mission Hill, CedarCreek, Osoyoos Larose, Inniskillin Okanagan and Nk'Mip Cellars.

OSOYOOS LAKE BENCH WINERIES

LASTELLA

NK'MIP CELLARS

OSOYOOS LAROSE ESTATE
   WINERY

TWISTED TREE VINEYARDS
   & WINERY

YOUNG & WYSE COLLECTION
   WINES

THE GOLDEN MILE

If you hike the hills on the west side of the Okanagan Valley south of Oliver, you can still find remains of 19th-century gold and silver mines. That is one reason for calling these vineyards the Golden Mile, even if the distance from Oliver to Osoyoos is 21 kilometres (13 miles). Today the phrase conjures up the salubrious conditions for growing grapes. In contrast to the deep sand of Black Sage Road, which you can see when you look across the valley, the soils here are well-drained clay and glacial gravel. Olivier Combret, whose family came here in 1992 after many generations as winemakers in France, is categorical about this terroir: "The site cannot be questioned in terms of its capability of producing wines. It is always advantageous to be exposed to the sunrise side rather than to the sunset. In many varieties, this produces more flavours." Cool afternoon shadows fall over the vines while the east side of the valley continues to bake for several more hours. Consequently, wineries on the Golden Mile make such white wines as Gewürztraminer and Riesling, plus red wines with bright fruit flavours as well as power.

You should hike the hills if you are reasonably fit and wearing good shoes. The 10-kilometre (six-mile) Golden Mile hiking trail extends along the flank of the mountains above the vineyards. One access point is at the north end, near the kiosk dedicated to Fairview, the long-vanished mining town. Another access point is at the uphill end of Tinhorn Creek winery's vineyard; trail maps are available in Tinhorn's wine shop. The trail provides spectacular views of the Okanagan Valley as well as access to the remains of the mines.

GOLDEN MILE WINERIES

ANTELOPE RIDGE ESTATE WINERY

CASSINI CELLARS

CHANDRA ESTATE WINERY

FAIRVIEW CELLARS

GEHRINGER BROTHERS
   ESTATE WINERY

GOLDEN BEAVER WINERY

HESTER CREEK ESTATE WINERY

INNISKILLIN OKANAGAN
   VINEYARDS

ORCHARD HILL ESTATE CIDERY

ROAD 13 VINEYARDS

RUSTICO FARM & CELLARS

TINHORN CREEK VINEYARDS

WILLOW HILL VINEYARDS

BLACK SAGE ROAD

This is the road to drive if you want to see acres and acres of vines rising up to the low mountains on the east side of the valley. Black Sage Road also shows up on maps as 71st Street. It curls around the eastern side of Oliver (pop. 4,800), finally petering out at Vincor's Osoyoos Lake Bench vineyards, a lovely tour of about 30 kilometres (19 miles). The views over the valley and also of vineyards crowding the road make this one of the Okanagan's most scenic drives.

Winemakers have discovered that these sandy vineyards, in sun from early morning until the end of the day, grow powerful red wines as well as full-flavoured whites. Few places in British Columbia have vines growing in leaner soil. Most vineyards sit on fine and very deep sand deposited a long time ago, when this was the beach of a vast inland lake. In its natural state, the arid earth hosts wiry grasses, tumbleweed and Okanagan rattlesnakes. Irrigation is essential. "It's a really unique little area," Richard Cleave, a veteran vineyard manager, says of Black Sage. "We get very little rainfall, especially during the summer months, when we get less than three inches on average. We have to use very, very few chemicals. We get very few bugs, so we use very few insecticides. It's just a unique area to grow grapes."

In the growing season, the large swing between hot days and cool nights produces grapes yielding wines with ripe fruit but bright acidity, an ideal combination. Although only a handful of wineries are located on or near the road, many premium wineries in other regions use Black Sage grapes, among them Sumac Ridge, Tinhorn Creek and Mission Hill. Domaine de Chaberton Estate Winery, Blackwood Lane Winery in the Fraser Valley and Muse Winery on Vancouver Island (among others) also buy premium Black Sage grapes.

BLACK SAGE ROAD WINERIES

BLACK HILLS ESTATE WINERY	HIDDEN CHAPEL WINERY
BURROWING OWL ESTATE WINERY	(UNDER DEVELOPMENT)
CHURCH & STATE WINES	JACKSON-TRIGGS VINTNERS
DESERT HILLS ESTATE WINERY	LE VIEUX PIN
DUNHAM & FROESE ESTATE	OLIVER TWIST ESTATE WINERY
WINERY	PROSPECT WINERY

QUINTA FERREIRA ESTATE	SILVER SAGE WINERY
WINERY	STONEBOAT VINEYARDS
SANDHILL WINES	

OKANAGAN FALLS

This compact vineyard region, with twisting back roads well worth exploring, includes landscapes of legendary beauty. The vineyard at the Blue Mountain winery, where rows of vines rise and fall with perfect precision toward a hazy blue horizon, is a favourite with photographers despite the recently erected electrified bear fence. The netted vines at Noble Ridge and the rocky vineyard at Wild Goose are equally photogenic.

The region is midway between Oliver and Penticton: each of those communities is 21 kilometres (13 miles) distant from the quaint village of Okanagan Falls. Many visitors take a break from wine touring to have ice cream at the legendary Tickleberry's, which challenges you to remember when "that ice cream cone was the center of your whole world."

The soil types vary so dramatically that some vineyards grow fine Burgundy grapes; others succeed with Alsace whites and still others with Bordeaux varieties. This is a wine tourist's paradise, with every style of wine available, from sparkling to icewine. See Ya Later Ranch's Hawthorne Mountain Vineyards boasts the highest-elevation vineyard (536 metres/1,760 feet) in the South Okanagan, with an unusual northeastern exposure. This comparatively cool vineyard produces some of the finest Gewürztraminer and Pinot Gris in the valley. As well, the heritage home serving as See Ya Later's wine shop and tasting room offers an incomparable view over the Okanagan Falls region.

OKANAGAN FALLS WINERIES

BLUE MOUNTAIN VINEYARD	SEE YA LATER RANCH
& CELLARS	AT HAWTHORNE MOUNTAIN
MEYER FAMILY VINEYARDS	VINEYARDS
NOBLE RIDGE VINEYARD	STAG'S HOLLOW WINERY
& WINERY	TANGLED VINES ESTATE WINERY
	WILD GOOSE VINEYARDS

SKAHA LAKE

Twisting but scenic, Eastside Road is the shortest route from Penticton south to Okanagan Falls (about 20 kilometres/12½ miles). It is just being discovered by wine tourists, who usually drive the longer but faster Highway 97, west of Skaha Lake. One winery has just opened on the west side of the lake in picturesque Kaleden, which has several good vineyards.

Currently four exceptional wineries are open along the road. The vineyards here all have good western exposure and benefit from the effect of Skaha Lake. Even though the lake is relatively shallow (maximum depth is 55 metres/180 feet) and small, with only 30 kilometres (19 miles) of shoreline, Skaha tempers the climate and extends the ripening season in late autumn.

In earlier times, one of Canada's larger peach orchards operated on the benchland between the lake and the cliffs to the east. Peaches are notoriously tender. It is an axiom that grapes will flourish wherever peaches grow. The constraint to this viticulture region is the narrowness of the arable bench, which backs against silt and clay cliffs. The Skaha Bluffs southeast of Penticton at the end of Valleyview Road, which rise to 80 metres (260 feet), are popular with rock climbers.

SKAHA LAKE WINERIES

BLASTED CHURCH VINEYARDS

KRĀZĒ LEGZ VINEYARD AND
  WINERY

PAINTED ROCK ESTATE WINERY

PENTÂGE WINERY

NARAMATA BENCH

Thanks to superb growing conditions and the remarkable landscape, Naramata Road has plentiful wineries, making it the hottest winery address in British Columbia. Vineyards along the road have been selling for double the price of vineyards in, for example, California's long-established Mendocino County. Why? Well, first, not much land is available. Second, wine tourists can easily move from one superb winery to the next on what is the Okanagan's most concentrated route of fine wine. The distance from Penticton to Nichol Vineyards, just north of Naramata, is a mere 12 kilometres (7½ miles).

Okanagan Lake tempers the climate, meaning no vine-killing winter temperatures, few late spring frosts and a very long autumn that brings grapes to optimal ripeness. Merlot and other Bordeaux reds grow well here, along with elegant Pinot Noir, peppery Syrah, full-flavoured Pinot Gris, Sauvignon Blanc, Riesling and Viognier. The bench on the eastern shore of the lake is a narrow strip of land that drops down from what is left of the Kettle Valley Railway (a good walking and biking trail) to the rugged lakeshore bluffs. The vines are bathed in sun from mid-morning to the end of the day. The views from many tasting rooms take the breath away. Several wineries offer good bistro-style dining for those who wish to linger in this superb setting.

NARAMATA BENCH WINERIES

ACES WINE GROUP

BLACK CLOUD WINERY

BLACK WIDOW WINERY

D'ANGELO ESTATE WINERY

ELEPHANT ISLAND ORCHARD
  WINES

FOXTROT VINEYARDS

HILLSIDE ESTATE WINERY

HOWLING BLUFF ESTATE WINES

JOIEFARM

KETTLE VALLEY WINERY

LA FRENZ WINERY

LAKE BREEZE VINEYARDS

LANG VINEYARDS

LAUGHING STOCK VINEYARDS

MARICHEL VINEYARD

MISCONDUCT WINE COMPANY

MISTRAL ESTATE WINERY

NICHOL VINEYARD & ESTATE
  WINERY

POPLAR GROVE WINERY

RED ROOSTER WINERY

RUBY TUESDAY WINERY

SERENDIPITY WINERY

SOARING EAGLE ESTATE WINERY

SPILLER ESTATE WINERY

STONEHILL ESTATE WINERY

SYNERGY WINERY & VINEYARDS

THERAPY VINEYARDS

TOWNSHIP 7 VINEYARDS &
  WINERY

VAN WESTEN VINEYARDS

ZERO BALANCE VINEYARDS

SUMMERLAND AND PEACHLAND

When developer John Moore Robinson founded Summerland in 1902, he advertised it as "Heaven on earth, with summer weather forever." That salubrious climate also accounts for Summerland's significant agricultural hinterland, seldom explored by visitors. Highway 97 sweeps by on the eastern side of Giant's Head. This stubby extinct volcano overshadows the quaint town (pop. 11,000) whose Tudor-style architecture is mirrored in the Sumac Ridge winery.

For many years Sumac Ridge was the community's only winery. Its monopoly on winery visitors was enhanced by its location right on the highway 23 kilometres (14 miles) north of Penticton. Recently more wineries have opened, mostly on the western side of Giant's Head, which features good southeastern-facing slopes for grapes. The bucolic countryside, with twisting valley fingers extending deep into the mountains, is worth exploring (you might even find the buffalo farm). Between Summerland and Peachland (another 23-kilometre drive), most of the vineyards cling to steep slopes running down toward Okanagan Lake and are not visible from the highway. The exception is Greata Ranch, whose majestic spread of vines and red-roofed winery occupy a postcard-perfect plateau just below the highway. Vineyards on the hillsides above Peachland await discovery by wine tourists who venture off the beaten path.

Most of the vineyards in this area share cool-climate grape growing conditions. Expect to find good Pinot Noir, Chardonnay, Pinot Gris, Pinot Blanc and Gewürztraminer.

SUMMERLAND AND PEACHLAND WINERIES

BONITAS FAMILY ESTATE WINERY	HOLLYWOOD & WINE ESTATE
DEEP CREEK WINE ESTATE &	VINEYARDS
HAINLE VINEYARDS ESTATE	SILKSCARF WINERY
WINERY	SLEEPING GIANT FRUIT WINERY
DIRTY LAUNDRY VINEYARD	SONORAN ESTATE WINERY
8TH GENERATION VINEYARD	SUMAC RIDGE ESTATE WINERY
FIRST ESTATE CELLARS	THORNHAVEN ESTATES WINERY
GREATA RANCH ESTATE WINERY	WORKING HORSE WINERY

THE SLOPES OF MOUNT BOUCHERIE

Just a 20-kilometre (12½-mile) drive south of Kelowna's urban sprawl, the Mount Boucherie wine region's best vineyards continue to hold off the pressure of land developers. Although all but one of the wineries here also have vineyards in the South Okanagan or the Similkameen, they husband these precious slopes. Bathed in the reflected light from Okanagan Lake, Mount Boucherie vineyards are well suited to delicate premium varieties like Pinot Noir and Riesling. Quails' Gate, which practises some of the best viticulture in the valley, even succeeds with Merlot and Cabernet Sauvignon.

The Stewart family, owners of Quails' Gate, have grown grapes here since the mid-1950s. They began planting even before the floating bridge was built across the lake at Kelowna in 1958, replacing ferries and rail barges. The most mature vines at Quails' Gate include a block of Maréchal Foch planted in 1969.

Such old blocks are the exception; most vineyards on these slopes have been replanted since 1990 with premium varieties. Some of the steeper slopes have been given over to palatial homes, whose owners are drawn by stunning views over the lake. Arguably the best lake view from any of the wineries belongs to the Mission Hill winery, perched on the brow of the mountain, some 130 metres (426 feet) above the surface of the lake.

MOUNT BOUCHERIE WINERIES

BEAUMONT FAMILY ESTATE
  WINERY
KALALA ORGANIC ESTATE
  WINERY
LITTLE STRAW VINEYARDS
MEADOW VISTA HONEY WINES

MISSION HILL FAMILY ESTATE
MT. BOUCHERIE ESTATE WINERY
QUAILS' GATE ESTATE WINERY
ROLLINGDALE WINERY
VOLCANIC HILLS VINEYARD &
  CELLARS

KELOWNA AND LAKE COUNTRY

This region extends from Kelowna to Lake Country, about 27 kilometres (17 miles) north, and beyond to Oyama. It is a region for history lovers. The Okanagan's first vines were planted in what is now East Kelowna, at an Oblate mission founded in 1859 by a French priest named Charles Pandosy. The restored mission buildings are now a heritage site on Kelowna's Benvoulin Road, worth a visit even though the mission never had a commercial vineyard. Wine grapes have been cultivated on the nearby southwest-facing slopes since the 1920s.

Compared to the South Okanagan, the Kelowna area features cool growing conditions favourable to such white varieties as Riesling and Pinot Gris and reds such as Pinot Noir. Tantalus Vineyards and St. Hubertus have Riesling vines that were planted in the late 1970s; these now produce remarkably intense wines.

Another piece of history is the old Calona Vineyards winery, which sprawls untidily across three hectares (7½ acres) near downtown Calona. This is British Columbia's oldest continually operating winery (established in 1932). Those who venture into the rooms behind the Calona wine shop will find a small collection of artifacts—like a 1930s Champagne bottler—and photographs from the bygone era of early Okanagan wine production. Another essential stop in Kelowna is the British Columbia Wine Museum on Ellis Street in downtown Kelowna and the archives in the nearby Kelowna Library.

Many of the Lake Country vineyards, which date from the 1970s, are on the eastern shore of Okanagan Lake, benefitting from the light and heat reflected from the lake on the long summer afternoons. The restaurants at Summerland Pyramid Winery and at Gray Monk offer captivating views over the lake, while CedarCreek's restaurant provides vineyard views and the restaurant at Raven Ridge overlooks the city.

KELOWNA AND LAKE COUNTRY WINERIES

ANCIENT HILL VINEYARDS & WINERY	CAMELOT VINEYARDS ESTATE WINERY
ARROWLEAF CELLARS	CEDARCREEK ESTATE WINERY
BOUNTY CELLARS	EAST KELOWNA CIDER COMPANY
CALONA VINEYARDS	EX NIHILO VINEYARDS

GRAY MONK ESTATE WINERY	ST. HUBERTUS & OAK BAY
HOUSE OF ROSE VINEYARDS	ESTATE WINERY
INTRIGUE WINES	SPERLING VINEYARDS
PARADISE RANCH WINES	SUMMERHILL PYRAMID WINERY
PELLER ESTATES	TANTALUS VINEYARDS
RAVEN RIDGE CIDERY	THE VIEW WINERY & VINEYARD

VERNON AND SALMON ARM

Although this region is about 120 kilometres (74½ miles) north of Kelowna, access to wineries is easy from either the Trans-Canada Highway or Highway 97. The wine touring signs that have gone up beside highways in recent years direct a burgeoning number of visitors to these and other wineries.

Grape growing this far north succeeds only where microclimates are unusually favourable or wine growers are unusually determined. In Vernon, vineyards are planted on steep slopes whose southern pitch creates even more frost-free days than Black Sage Road. The northern arms of Okanagan Lake also help to moderate the climate. Closer to Salmon Arm, the vineyard at Larch Hills, with the highest elevation in British Columbia (700 metres/2,300 feet), grows grapes on a steep, south-facing slope but, without a lake anywhere near, only the earliest grape varieties succeed. Winters are chill at this elevation, but the heavy snowfall dumps an insulating blanket on the vines. The Salmon Arm area has enough precipitation that generally vineyards are not irrigated. Several vineyards have been planted around the shores of Shuswap Lake, and several growers have future wineries under consideration. Nearly all northern wineries turn to Okanagan vineyards to source varieties, such as Merlot, that will not mature this far north.

VERNON AND SALMON ARM WINERIES

EDGE OF THE EARTH VINEYARD	RECLINE RIDGE VINEYARDS
GRANITE CREEK ESTATE WINES	& WINERY
HUNTING HAWK VINEYARDS	THE RISE CELLARS
LARCH HILLS WINERY	(UNDER DEVELOPMENT)
OVINO WINERY	

THE KOOTENAYS

Fruitvale, the name of a small town just east of Trail, hints that grapes can be grown in the Kootenays. This region has a considerable history of successful tree fruit production, with a climate in which early to mid-season grape varieties will thrive. In the words of a provincial tourism brochure, "This is the warm side of the Rockies."

The word "Kootenay" has Aboriginal roots. In the language of the Ktunaxa First Nation, the word quthni means "to travel by water," a reference to the many rivers in this scenic region.

The Kootenay region stretches along Highway 3 from Grand Forks on the west to Creston on the east, and from the US border north to about Nelson. In microclimates throughout this area, grapes and other fruits are grown. Additional wineries are under consideration. There has been a small but promising vineyard trial at Grand Forks, and Heron Ridge Estates Winery, a blueberry winery, is proposed for Thrums, a tiny community north of Castlegar.

KOOTENAY WINERIES

BAILLIE-GROHMAN ESTATE
   WINERY
COLUMBIA GARDENS VINEYARD
   & WINERY

SKIMMERHORN WINERY
   & VINEYARD

THE
WINERIES

PHOTO BY RICHARD ROSKELL

ACES WINE GROUP

This winery has a concept unique to Okanagan wineries, flowing from owner Holger Clausen's passion for Texas hold'em poker. Born in Summerland in 1969, he took up poker at university, even wagering some of his student loans at cards.

He had become interested in wine at his family's table. When a dinner guest waxed poetic about his hostess gift, a bottle of Sumac Ridge 1982 Gewürztraminer, Holger challenged his father to a chess game with the wine going to the winner. Holger still has that bottle, still unopened.

"When I turned 21 and was legal to drink, I toured the Napa Valley," Holger says. "That's really when I fell in love with the industry. I have been there several times since." On the same trip, he also took in the casinos at Las Vegas. "The bright lights and the big city, that got me." Meanwhile, he worked in the forest industry before launching a company operating grape harvesters here and in Australia in 1999.

His passions have come together in Aces Wine Group. Noting how popular Texas hold'em has become on television and in casinos, he conceived of wines with labels aimed directly at the poker crowd. It is primarily poker players who would appreciate the special significance of wines with such names as Pocket Aces, Pocket Kings and Pocket Queens. "What is true to the poker world is true in the wine world," Holger says. "Every year Mother Nature deals the vineyards and the winemakers a different hand. Poker players are dealt a different hand all the time as well."

Like any good poker player, Holger is placing his bets carefully. Initially, he has not tied up his cash (or that of his silent partners) in a winery or vineyards. Instead, he has sourced top-quality grapes from various Okanagan growers, and Jason Parkes, his consulting winemaker, is making the wines at another winery. The wines, all packaged in luxury-weight bottles with playing card motifs, are sold primarily from the winery's website, and are often limited to the exclusive Aces wine club.

MY PICKS

Aces turned heads with its first release, a $95 Syrah from 2007 called Pocket Aces Syrah, a wine as bold in flavour as in price. That was followed with an impressive Cabernet-based red (Pocket Kings Red) and a fine Chardonnay (Pocket Queens Chardonnay).

OPENED 2009

1309 Smethurst Road
PO Box 40
Naramata, BC V0H 1N0
W www.aceswine.ca

WHEN TO VISIT
Wine shop to be established on the Naramata Bench in future

HOLGER CLAUSEN

ANCIENT HILL VINEYARDS & WINERY

This splendid Robert Mackenzie–designed winery overlooking Kelowna International Airport returns viticulture to where it began in the North Okanagan when the Rittich brothers planted grapes near here in 1930. Natives of Hungary, Eugene and Virgil Rittich concluded that vinifera grapes could be grown successfully and wrote a book (British Columba's first wine book) on how to grow grapes and make wine. Periodic severe winters doomed those pioneering trials in the Ellison district, as it was known.

The modern-day pioneers are Richard and Jitske Kamphuys (rhymes with "compass"), who came from Holland in 1992 and bought an apple orchard. Richard, who was born in 1963, completed an advanced economics degree at the historic Erasmus University in Amsterdam before deciding he wanted a rural lifestyle for himself and his family.

He considered growing grapes as soon as he and Jitske, a former doctor's assistant, bought the orchard, but was put off by general pessimism at that time about the future of BC wineries. The previous owners, encouraged by the Rittich trials, planted grapes on the hillside in 1944, but abandoned the vineyard when the hard 1949–50 winter killed many of the vines and even some apple trees. About 40 of those ancient vines, probably Okanagan Riesling, still survive.

When apples became unprofitable, Richard and Jitske replaced the orchard in 2005 with 27,000 vines over about six hectares (15 acres). They have chosen mid-season-ripening varieties: Pinot Gris, Gewürztraminer, Lemberger, Zweigelt and Pinot Noir. The biggest block, about a quarter of the vineyard, is Baco Noir, a red French hybrid that is notably winter hardy. "We are a lot closer to the North Pole here than in Europe," Richard notes. Given his planting choices, today's better understanding of viticulture and generally warmer winters, he should succeed where the Rittich brothers and their disciples failed 60 years ago.

RICHARD AND JITSKE KAMPHUYS

With consultant Christine Leroux as winemaker, Ancient Hill launched with about 1,000 cases in the 2009 vintage. Richard and Jitske (and their daughter, Gaby) plan to build to 3,000 cases, supplementing their own vineyard harvest with purchased grapes.

OPENED 2010

4918 Anderson Road
Kelowna, BC V1X 7V7

T   250.491.2766

W www.ancienthillwinery.com

WHEN TO VISIT
To be established

MY PICKS

No wines were available for tasting as this was written, but Christine Leroux's considerable experience at other wineries is the promise of good wine here.

ANTELOPE RIDGE ESTATE WINERY

In 2006 the French family behind this winery, originally known as Domaine Combret, surprised their peers by changing the name to Antelope Ridge. They had two reasons, the first being to eliminate the endless confusion between Domaine Combret and Langley's Domaine de Chaberton, whose founder was also French.

"We have to remember that Canada is not a traditional wine country," winemaker Olivier Combret says. "The people have absolutely no clue as to what the word *domaine* means. In 2002, I said, that's it, we've got to do something here. I decided to change the name. 'Domaine Combret' means 'the house' or 'the estate of Combret,' which is my family name." It is a family with a wine tradition that goes back 10 generations. Olivier, who was 21 when his family moved to the Okanagan in 1992 to make wine, represents the first generation to make New World wines.

And that was the second reason for the name change: Olivier wanted to underline the major change in wine style on which he has embarked. The wines of Domaine Combret were generally made in the French style. The award-winning Chardonnay wines, for example, were crisp and dry like Chablis. The Riesling was as austerely dry as anything from Alsace. The Antelope Ridge wines, especially the red wines—which, unusually, are aged in Appalachian oak—are big and bold, like so many New World reds. "My wines before were complex, but you can say they were like rough diamonds, and now the diamonds are shaped," he says.

The winery here is remarkable for being the first gravity-flow winery in the Okanagan, designed by Olivier when he was just a green wine-school graduate. The winery's three levels drape over the hillside in such a way that gravity, not pumps, moves the wine most of the time. Here the wines are made only from the estate's 17 hectares (42 acres) of vines, which grow serenely on fine southeastern slopes on a plateau

high above the valley. A small vineyard already grew here when the Combrets arrived from France and found what they still regard as one of the finest vineyard sites in the Okanagan. Aside from Chardonnay, the vineyard is dedicated primarily to red varieties, including Cabernet Sauvignon, Cabernet Franc and Gamay.

OPENED 1994
(AS DOMAINE COMBRET)

32057 #13 Road
PO Box 1170
Oliver, BC V0H 1T0

T 250.498.6966
1.866.TERROIR (837.7647)
(toll free)

W www.anteloperidge.com

WHEN TO VISIT
By appointment

MY PICKS

The first Antelope Ridge reds included an impressive Cabernet Franc and an equally good Cabernet Sauvignon. But the star was a blend of the two called Equilibrium, a dense and concentrated red built to age with elegance.

ARROWLEAF CELLARS

Named for the Okanagan's familiar springtime flower, Arrowleaf Cellars came about because Josef Zuppiger's five children did not care for milking cows. Originally dairy farmers from near Zurich in Switzerland, the Zuppigers moved to an Alberta dairy farm in 1986. When it became clear that his children wanted to do something else, Josef bought this 6.5-hectare (16-acre) North Okanagan vineyard in 1997. Josef had also grown fruit in Switzerland, and he figured that managing a vineyard would not be much different from an orchard.

After selling grapes for a few years Josef concluded the family was more likely to prosper with its own winery. The decision was made easier when son Manuel, born in 1976, enrolled in Switzerland's top wine school. He graduated in 2001 and showed enough promise to land a practicum with Grant Burge, a leading Australian winemaker, before returning to Arrowleaf.

Sixty percent of Arrowleaf's production, about 7,500 cases a year, is white wine. The reason: the original owner of the Arrowleaf vineyard, who planted vines in 1986, put in white varieties exclusively, including the prized Alsace clone of Gewürztraminer, along with Bacchus, Pinot Gris and Auxerrois. The last variety has since been dropped in favour of more Pinot Gris, a wine much more in fashion. For Arrowleaf's reds, Josef planted Merlot and Zweigelt and signed a long-term lease on a nearby Pinot Noir planting. Gradually, the winery's volume of reds is rising.

The winery, whose tasting room sparkles with Swiss tidiness, is nestled on a plateau at the edge of the vineyard, with an excellent view from the winery's picnic benches of Okanagan Lake to the west. Even more appealing than the view are the wine values. The unpretentious Zuppiger family charges reasonable prices for wines that could sell for more.

JOSEF AND MARGRIT ZUPPIGER

MY PICKS

The excellent reserve wines are released under the Solstice label. They include a Chardonnay, a Pinot Noir and two red blends. The rest of the portfolio is also very reliable. The steal here is the inexpensive Bacchus, a light, refreshing white with lots of spicy fruit. The Gewürztraminer is one of the Okanagan's best, while the regular Pinot Noir is probably the best example of this varietal under $20.

OPENED 2003

1574 Camp Road
Lake Country, BC V4V 1K1
T 250.766.2992
W www.arrowleafcellars.com

WHEN TO VISIT
Open daily 10:30 am – 5:30 pm
from May 1 to November 15

BAILLIE-GROHMAN ESTATE WINERY

During years of vacationing here, Calgarians Bob Johnson and Petra Flaa developed such an affection for the Creston Valley that they bought a cherry orchard, only to discover how hard it is for weekend farmers to sell cherries. They had a better idea when they saw former fruit growers Al and Marleen Hoag build the Skimmerhorn Winery, Creston's first. A case of wine has a longer shelf life than a case of fresh cherries. In 2006 Bob and Petra bought a property right next door to Skimmerhorn and planted vines, and in 2009 they built a spacious winery to process their first vintage.

A former technology manager, Petra now runs the 5.8-hectare (14½-acre) vineyard with skills acquired from University of Washington correspondence courses and Al Hoag's counsel. Pinot Noir comprises two-fifths of the vines. The rest of the vineyard is planted to Pinot Gris, Chardonnay, Sauvignon Blanc and Schönburger, along with 250 Kerner plants for icewine.

Born in 1958 in Red Deer, Bob is a reservoir engineer with Sproule Associates, a consulting firm he joined in 1984. Long interested in wine—he and Petra have been members of the Opimian Society—Bob made wine at home with kits for a number of years before becoming a serious collector. But he has neither the time nor the desire to become a professional winemaker; in any event, he is more interested in marketing the 3,000 to 5,000 cases the winery eventually plans to produce.

When the winery advertised for a winemaker, no experienced Canadians applied. "At this time, no Canadian winemaker wants to come to Creston because it is not in their career," Petra says. Like Skimmerhorn, this winery has looked to New Zealand, recruiting Dan Barker, the owner and winemaker of the Moana Park Winery in Hawkes Bay. Full of youthful energy (he was New Zealand's Young Winemaker of the Year in 2003), Dan is prepared to spend the southern hemisphere's

PETRA FLAA

off-season making wine in the northern hemisphere.

Like Skimmerhorn, Bob and Petra's winery is named for a Kootenay area pioneer, William Baillie-Grohman. He came in 1882 with Teddy Roosevelt to hunt trophy mountain goats. Impressed with the area's farm land, he organized a British syndicate to divert the Kootenay River and settle colonists on the drained land. The scheme ultimately failed when a lawyer made off with investment funds, but Baillie-Grohman's colourful story deserves to be remembered.

OPENING PROPOSED 2011

1140 27th Avenue South
Creston, BC V0B 1G1
T 250.428.8768

WHEN TO VISIT
To be established

MY PICKS

Wines are not yet available for tasting, but Dan Barker's track record should inspire confidence.

BEAUMONT FAMILY ESTATE WINERY

You might wonder why there are musical staves on the Beaumont labels and a guitar in the tasting room. Long before Alex Lubchynski grew grapes for a living, he played and sang with weekend bands in Alberta, one of which was called the Twilighters. An excellent singer and guitar player, Alex now often turns Beaumont's tasting room into a lively hootenanny.

Both Alex and Louise, his wife, were born in Alberta and were farmers there before coming to the Okanagan in 1990 to build houses. Her hometown was Beaumont, which inspired this winery's name. The couple decided to return to farming in 1995 when they bought an orchard in the Lakeview Heights district near Westbank, promptly replanting with vines. This was the first of the three organic vineyards they now run in what is a fairly residential neighbourhood. No doubt the neighbours appreciate that the Lubchynskis avoid vineyard chemicals.

"We did not want the kids to be near the chemicals," Louise explains. Daughter Alana, now the winemaker, was born in 1987 and had already learned how to drive the tractor by the time she was eight. "I have always done work in the vineyard," Alana says. Finding that a bit repetitious, she began studying business at Okanagan College. However, a conversation with the winemaker at Tantalus Vineyards set her on a new career path. She switched to the college's winemaking courses, and her parents, who had been selling all their grapes, began developing the family winery. Alana added to her practical skills by doing vintages at two small Okanagan wineries and working in a Kelowna wine store as well as doing the 2008 vintage at an Australia winery and the 2009 at a New Zealand producer. She returned to Australia (Xanadu Winery in Margaret River) for the 2010 crush.

The Lubchynskis continue to sell most of the fruit from their three vineyards, cautiously keeping the winery small until they develop a fan base for the vinous music they now make.

MY PICKS

Attractions here, besides Alex's fine voice, are wines with Pinot Noir, Gamay Noir, Gewürztraminer and Pinot Gris, all moderately priced and organically grown.

OPENED 2008

2775 Boucherie Road
Kelowna, BC V4T 2G4
T 250.769.1222
W www.beaumontwines.ca

WHEN TO VISIT
Open daily 10 am – 6 pm
May 1 to October 31

ALANA, ALEX AND LOUISE LUBCHYNSKI

BLACK CLOUD WINERY

Bradley Cooper's goal of establishing his own winery was accelerated when one of his winemaking clients ran out of cash and offered to pay him with wine. Beginning with the 2005 vintage, Brad made three vintages for Stone Mountain Vineyards, an Okanagan Falls project that never opened. (It failed after the principal's Arizona real estate business collapsed.) In lieu of payment, Brad received 80 cases of unreleased, unlabelled 2006 Pinot Noir that he had made.

Audralee Daum, his wife and business partner, was unimpressed. "She said, 'Great, just as things get going, another black cloud comes over,'" Brad recalls. They seized on that remark for their winery's name, bought another 200 cases from Stone Mountain and also bought grapes to make Black Cloud Pinot Noir in 2008 and 2009, along with a blended white. By selling the wines directly, and by word of mouth, they are building Black Cloud and growing into a vineyard and winery of their own (or with a partner). "I already like going to work on Monday mornings, and I'd like to make it even better," Brad says.

Born in New Westminster in 1958, Brad is a journalism graduate of Langara College. After several years as a writer and photographer with community newspapers, he switched careers to work in restaurants, where he became wine savvy. In 1997 he started working in the wine shop at Hawthorne Mountain Vineyard, then became a cellar technician and took Okanagan College's first winery assistant course. He honed his skills by working the 1999 vintage at Vidal Estate in New Zealand and the 2000 icewine harvest at Stonechurch in Ontario. In 2002 he left Hawthorne Mountain for the winemaking team at Mount Baker Vineyards in Washington state but returned to the Okanagan in 2003, joining Stag's Hollow Winery. Two years later he became the winemaker for Township 7 Vineyards & Winery. As well, he has consulted to several wineries.

His experience at Vidal, a large winery compared to most Okanagan boutiques, shaped Brad's view on what he wants to do with a winery. Employees at large wineries become specialists. Brad is a generalist and Black Cloud will produce 2,000 cases a year at most. "I am interested in having a hand in everything," he says. However, he leaves marketing to Audralee, a children's counsellor who has also worked in various Okanagan wine shops and has plenty of thoughts on running a tasting room in the future.

MY PICKS

The debut Pinot Noirs show that Brad Cooper has an affinity for a variety he has admired for more than 25 years.

OPENED 2009

1510 Reservoir Road
Penticton. BC V2A 8T3

T   250.490.7314
     250.488.2181

W www.blackcloud.ca

WHEN TO VISIT
By appointment. There is no tasting room.

BRADLEY COOPER

BLACK HILLS ESTATE WINERY

In recent years, almost everything has changed at Black Hills except for what made this a cult winery from day one: Nota Bene, Alibi and the other consistently excellent wines created here by the founding partners and continued by the new owners.

Black Hills was launched in 1996 when two business couples from Vancouver—Senka and Bob Tennant and Susan and Peter McCarrell—bought a 14-hectare (35-acre) property on Black Sage Road and planted 36,000 vines. Croatian-born Senka, formerly a retailer with a degree in botany, had Washington state winemaker Rusty Figgins coach her (mostly by telephone) in making her first vintage in 1999. Coolly self-confident, she dubbed that blend of Cabernet Sauvignon, Merlot and Cabernet Franc Nota Bene, a Latin name meaning "take notice." Consumers do take notice, scrambling eagerly for their annual allotments of Nota Bene. Made exclusively from grapes grown at the estate, Nota Bene's production now is capped at 4,000 to 4,300 cases a year, roughly half of the total output at Black Hills.

The original winery here, a homely Quonset hut, did the job until 2006, when it was replaced with a new winery that nests among the vines at the base of a very steep driveway. The year after Black Hills occupied the new facility, the McCarrells decided to retire. The winery was purchased by a group of 265 investors that calls itself Vinequest Wine Partners Limited Partnership. Graham Pierce, then the winemaker at Mt. Boucherie, was recruited as the general manager and senior winemaker, taking over from Senka, who left in September 2008. (She and Bob, not ready for retirement, are developing a boutique vineyard and winery on the Naramata Bench.)

Vinequest, whose investors include Hollywood actor Jason Priestley, has brought a theatricality to Black Hills, and not just by opening the tasting room far more often than the original owners did. In 2008 the winery contributed a barrel of Nota Bene (containing about 300 bottles

GRAHAM PIERCE

of wine) to a charity auction and set a Canadian record, selling the barrel for $19,000. The winery also organizes an annual winter weekend of ski and snowboard racing at an Okanagan ski resort. Called the Winemaker's Cup, it is primarily for (but not limited to) winemakers and others working in the wine industry, fostering a camaraderie that is all too rare.

OPENED 2001

30880 71st Street
(Black Sage Road)
RR1 Site 52 Comp 22
Oliver, BC V0H 1T0

T 250.498.0666

W www.blackhillswinery.com

WHEN TO VISIT
Open Saturdays by appointment only, if not sold out

MY PICKS

Try everything, if you can. The full-bodied Nota Bene has had a cult following since the first vintage in 1999. The same is true for Alibi, a blend of Sauvignon Blanc with a dash of Sémillon, and for Sequentia, a dessert Sauvignon Blanc. In the 2005 vintage, Black Hills made Canada's first Carmenère (a red made notable by wineries in Chile). More recently the winery has added an excellent Chardonnay.

BLACK WIDOW WINERY

In the summer of 2000, while looking for a getaway cottage with a few vines, Dick and Shona Lancaster saw this property on Naramata Road. At three hectares (7½ acres), it was bigger than what they were looking for, but, with producing vines and a panoramic view of Naramata Bench and the lake, it was too good to turn down. "Classic up-selling," Dick says of the realtor. "And as soon as we got a vineyard, the goal was to set up a winery."

Born in Toronto in 1953, Dick was raised in Montreal, picking up an interest in wine from his father, Graham, then Air Canada's food services manager. Dick began making wine from wild grapes while still in high school. A three-month tour of European wine regions in 1976 sealed that interest. In Vancouver, where he and Shona lived until moving to the Okanagan a few years ago, Dick was an award-winning home winemaker for more than 25 years.

You could call Dick a polymath, given all the skills he has acquired. Starting out in biology, he earned a master's degree. Disillusioned by the lack of well-paying jobs, he took a real estate course, then sold cars and became district manager for a leasing company. Then he got a master's degree in business administration and finally qualified as an accountant. From 1992 until 2008, he was a vice-president with Imasco, western Canada's largest stucco manufacturer. Naturally, Black Widow's gravity-flow winery, which Dick designed, is finished in tawny-hued stucco. "How can I not use stucco?" he says with a laugh.

The vineyard already had Gewürztraminer, Pinot Gris and Schönburger when the Lancasters bought it. In 2001 they added Merlot and a bit of Cabernet Sauvignon, selling grapes to Kettle Valley Winery until launching Black Widow in 2006. "We like wines that have some real flavour and character to them, and that comes from really ripe grapes," Dick says. Targeted production is 1,200 cases a year.

SHONA AND DICK LANCASTER

The winery is named after the indigenous desert-dwelling spider that is, fortunately, so shy it is seldom seen. The insect should be avoided because the bite (which only the females give) is highly venomous.

OPENED 2006

1630 Naramata Road
Penticton, BC V2A 8T7
T   250.487.2347
W www.blackwidowwinery.com

WHEN TO VISIT
By appointment

ACCOMMODATION
Two bed-and-breakfast units

MY PICKS

The winery's signature red is Hourglass, a bold Merlot/Cabernet blend. The Gewürztraminer and the Pinot Gris, both finishing dry, are packed with flavour. Oasis is a lovely aromatic blend of Schönburger, Gewürztraminer and Muscat. The winery's delicious dessert wines include a delightful Dessert Schönburger, a fortified Schönburger called Mirage and a port-style Merlot called Vintage One.

BLASTED CHURCH VINEYARDS

The most original event at the Okanagan's fall wine festival is the free-spirited "Midnight Service" at Blasted Church. A professional gospel choir fills the cellars with spirited hymns while guests wash down southern soul food with the vineyard's best wines. The service only begins after the early evening wine tasting in nearby Penticton and it ends well after midnight, with guests being bussed back to their hotels. This irreverent take on worship reflects the flair that Chris and Evelyn Campbell brought to the business when they bought this winery in 2002, after careers in hotel management and then accounting.

The winery had opened two years earlier as Prpich Hills, named for Croatian-born grape grower Dan Prpich, who dug the cellar into a hill on the vineyard, topping it with a log-cabin tasting room overlooking Skaha Lake. The Campbells hired consultant Bernie Hadley-Beauregard to create a new name. Blasted Church was inspired by how the movers took apart a church in 1929 while relocating it to Okanagan Falls from the abandoned mining town of Fairview. They loosened the nails in the heavy timbers with a small dynamite charge. Until recently the church has served a congregation in Okanagan Falls.

The Campbells retell the tale through caricature labels on wines bearing such names as Hatfield's Fuse, named for Harley Hatfield, the man who lit the dynamite fuse. They have visited other local stories, such as with the wine called The Dam Flood. This blend of Lemberger, Pinot Noir and Syrah was inspired by the failure of an Okanagan Falls dam (apparently built by the hapless Harley Hatfield) in 1936 and again in 1944.

Now producing about 10,000 cases a year from its 17-hectare (42-acre) vineyard (and with some purchased grapes), Blasted Church defined its wine styles through a succession of winemakers. Langley native Richard Kanazawa, the current winemaker, briefly played rugby

in Japan before starting his wine career at Domaine de Chaberton. Professionally trained in Australia, Richard makes powerful but also polished wines.

MY PICKS

The winery makes a rare example of Chardonnay Musqué, from the lovely aromatic clone of Chardonnay. Bestseller Hatfield's Fuse is another delicious aromatic white. In fact, all the wines here are tasty. The reserve wines are released under what the winery terms its Revered label. My favourites include the Malbec/Syrah blend, the Merlot, all the whites and the rosé.

OPENED 2000
(AS PRPICH HILLS)

378 Parsons Road
RR1 Site 32 Comp 67
Okanagan Falls, BC V0H 1R0

T 250.497.1125
   1.8.SPELLBOUND
   (1.877.355.2686) (toll free)

W www.blastedchurch.com

WHEN TO VISIT
Open daily 10 am – 5 pm in summer and fall. By appointment at other times.

RICHARD KANAZAWA

BLUE MOUNTAIN VINEYARD & CELLARS

Most of Blue Mountain's elegant wines are allocated to a cult following of consumers and restaurateurs. That is one reason why the wine shop is only open by appointment. But even those without an appointment (and it is not hard to make one) should drive down Allendale Road far enough to take in the much-photographed postcard view of the 30-hectare (74-acre) vineyard with its south-facing slopes undulating toward Vaseux Lake—taking care not to touch the electrified bear fence while viewing the vineyard.

The winery's name was prompted by the occasional blue haze on the mountains in the distance. Winery owners Ian and Jane Mavety began growing hybrid grapes on this idyllic spot in 1972. When demand for hybrids ebbed in the 1980s, they decided, after a European wine tour, to convert to Burgundy and Alsace varieties for dry table wines—a daring move at a time when most other Okanagan wineries made primarily sweet German-style wines.

Initially the Mavetys made wine with the aid of a French-trained consultant from California. Subsequently their son Matt earned a winemaking degree in New Zealand and joined the family business. Having gained a knowledge of biodynamic viticulture, he persuaded his father, already a believer in sustainable viticulture, to adopt biodynamic practices where practical. Even if the edgy methodology sounds weird (stags' bladders buried in compost, for example), it is used widely to foster balanced vitality in vineyards.

Blue Mountain's annual production, about 12,000 cases, is disciplined. About a quarter comprises Champagne-method sparkling wines. The portfolio is completed with two reds (Pinot Noir and Gamay) and three whites (Chardonnay, Pinot Gris and Pinot Blanc). The winery's first Sauvignon Blanc, from vines planted in 2007, is awaited eagerly. The reserve tier wines bear striped labels and the others have cream labels.

Blue Mountain consciously keeps the alcohol content of its wine around 13 percent when many of its peers release wines with one or two percent more. This is achieved by picking the grapes before they are too ripe, while the fruit still retains the piquant acidity that brightens the flavours—"the essence of what the Okanagan Valley has to offer," Matt says. His father asserts that the wines not only have more vivid flavour but are better with food than heavier, more alcoholic wines.

OPENED 1992

2385 Allendale Road
RR1 Site 3 Comp 4
Okanagan Falls, BC V0H 1R0

T 250.497.8244

W www.bluemountainwinery.com

WHEN TO VISIT
By appointment

MY PICKS

In a word, *everything*. The Striped Label wines, more intense on the palate, are built for longer aging. Above all, Blue Mountain is one of the Okanagan's leading producers of sparkling wine and of delicately finessed Pinot Noir.

IAN MAVETY

MATT MAVETY

BONITAS FAMILY ESTATE WINERY

Much of the Okanagan's beauty is revealed only as you get off the main roads. Lawrence Hopper's Bonitas winery bears that out. Just north of the Sumac Ridge winery, Bonitas is not visible from the highway but is perched at the end of winding McDougald Road, which drops sharply down toward the lake. Lawrence built a gleaming white Mediterranean home here in 1994 and wrapped a three-hectare (7½-acre) vineyard around it three years later.

The winery building echoes the design of his 465-square-metre (5,000-square-foot) home. Postcards are made with vistas like this. "We have a pristine view," Lawrence says. The property has 300 metres (984 feet) fronting on the lake, nearly all in its natural state. An admirer of the Spanish language, Lawrence originally called the property Hijas Bonitas—"beautiful daughters"—in honour of his daughters, Chelsea and Teira. He dropped Hijas (pronounced EE-ass) when his visitors had trouble with the pronunciation.

A lean, wiry amateur golfer who has an indoor driving range in his office, Lawrence was born in Cobden, Ontario, in 1954 and raised in Edmonton in a single-family home, the oldest of nine children. His mother was a hairdresser—"and she taught us a good work ethic," he says. Lawrence started his career as a millwright in Fort McMurray, then became a brewery salesman. He admits that beer was long his favourite beverage.

Lawrence has lived in the Okanagan since 1986, attracted by the valley's lifestyle. He sells industrial lubricants for a big Texas oil company, carefully organizing his travels so that he is home in March to prune vines, in June to spray and in October to pick his grapes (Pinot Gris, Gewürztraminer and Merlot).

He has relied on consultants for winemaking, notably Bradley Cooper of Township 7. Beginning in the 2008 vintage, the Bonitas cellar also has accommodated an emerging Pinot Noir project for Krimo Souilah, a Napa-based wine barrel salesman. An Algerian-born winemaker, Krimo decided the Okanagan could be another Napa after he started selling barrels here in 2003. His four-hectare (10-acre) vineyard in nearby Summerland is planted only to Pinot Noir and might be a future winery site.

MY PICKS

Start with Gewürztraminer (the most recent vintage) and rosé. The 2006 Merlot is big and bold and the Pinot Noir is robust.

OPENED 2008
(AS HIJAS BONITAS)

20623 McDougald Road
Summerland, BC V0H 1Z6

T   250.494.5208
    1.866.534.4527 (toll free)

W www.bonitaswinery.com

WHEN TO VISIT
Open daily 11 am – 5 pm April through October

RESTAURANT
Lorenzo's . . . On the Lake

LAWRENCE HOPPER

BOUNTY CELLARS

Not many wineries will fill orders for custom-labelled wines, because designing labels for as little as two or three cases of wine is a nuisance. But Ron Pennington, the nimble marketer who runs Bounty Cellars, embraced this as an opportunity. He found a short-run labelling machine in the United States, hired a graphic designer and turned Bounty Cellars into the go-to winery for corporate clients and anyone else needing personalized labels.

Born in Medicine Hat in 1962, Pennington, who has a degree in chemistry, got his marketing acumen during a long career with Canada Safeway. In 2001 he and his wife moved to the Okanagan for family reasons and quickly fell in love with the valley. He started a marketing company, then partnered with an Internet company and soon had a client list that included wineries.

As Pennington tells the story, the idea for Bounty Cellars arose when he took Alan Marks, then the winemaker for Summerhill, a Pennington client, on a tour of his offices in an industrial mall not far from Kelowna's airport. Marks observed that the sprawling two-level building would be suitable for a commercial winery. Pennington and his partner, pharmacist Wade Rains, launched Bounty Cellars in 2005. His model, Pennington says, is that of a French *négociant*.

Bounty buys wine from other producers—both VQA wines and wine imported from the United States. If required, Todd Moore, the current winemaker, blends wines into unique Bounty wines, although Pennington keeps the option of naming the original producer on the label. Bounty also produces its own wine from purchased grapes and contemplates its own estate wines in its 10-year plan. Until that happens, Bounty, which currently has no tasting room, sells all its wines (priced $15 to $25 a bottle) directly to restaurants, private-label clients and wine stores.

RON PENNINGTON

MY PICKS

Bounty's well-made VQA wines, available through the VQA wine stores, include Gewürztraminer, Pinot Blanc and Cabernet Sauvignon. Bounty also offers excellent wines under the Osoyoos Lake Bench designation that are produced on the Washington side of Osoyoos Lake.

OPENED 2005

7 – 364 Lougheed Road
Kelowna, BC V1X 7R8

T   250.765.9200
    1.866.465.9463 (toll free)

W www.bountycellars.com

WHEN TO VISIT
No wine shop

TODD MOORE

BURROWING OWL ESTATE WINERY

The original boxy winery here has evolved into what could be taken for a small Tuscan palace, with echoing barrel cellars below ground and a stubby bell tower overlooking the vineyards. The elegant country inn was added in 2006. The effective self-guided winery tour at Burrowing Owl revolves around the tower, with windows that look into the working areas of the winery. The picture boards inside the tower teach visitors about the ecosystem as well as wine.

While tourists get to stroll the winery at their own pace, there is always a chance of encountering one or more members of the Wyse family, proprietors of Burrowing Owl. Jim Wyse, a former Vancouver property developer, and his wife, Midge, live near the winery. Chris Wyse (Jim and Midge's oldest son) and his sister, Kerry, now do hands-on management of winery operations.

The sandy slopes Jim Wyse planted in 1993 constitute a fragile environment, husbanded carefully by Burrowing Owl. The winery and its 55-hectare (136-acre) vineyard are on the northernmost tip of the Sonoran Desert. Many creatures living in the area struggle to survive, including the owl after which the winery is named. The winery's sensitive farming practices aim to protect and foster the species with which it coexists. As an example, when native rattlesnakes are found in the vineyard, they are relocated, not destroyed. Wine sales and tasting room fees generate conservation funds, including a program to re-establish the endangered burrowing owl.

A premium producer since its first vintage in 1997, Burrowing Owl makes up to 30,000 cases a year. About a third is allocated for Internet sales, another third for wine stores and restaurants, and the final third for Burrowing Owl's wine shop. Older vintages no longer available anywhere else remain on the Sonora Room's wine list, accompanying what is arguably the best food of any South Okanagan restaurant.

MY PICKS

Count me among fans of Burrowing Owl wines, including the sumptuous Syrah, the classy Meritage, the plump Merlot, the full-bodied Cabernet Franc and the tasty Cabernet Sauvignon. Both the Pinot Gris and the Chardonnay invariably show polished elegance.

OPENED 1998

100 Burrowing Owl Place
Oliver, BC V0H 1T0

T 250.498.0620
   1.877.498.0620 (toll free)

W www.bovwine.ca

WHEN TO VISIT
Open daily 10 am – 5 pm
Easter through October or
by appointment

RESTAURANT
The Sonora Room
Closed during winter

ACCOMMODATION
Guest house with 10 luxurious
rooms and one large suite

CHRIS WYSE

CALONA VINEYARDS

Calona Vineyards is the diamond in the rough on any Okanagan wine tour. Easy to find, the winery occupies several city blocks within walking distance of downtown Kelowna. The winery is steeped in history and looks it. The tasting room has the comfortable ambiance of a barrel cellar and delivers a great wine touring experience.

Calona is British Columbia's oldest continually operating winery. It was launched by Giuseppe Ghezzi, an Italian winemaker, backed by a group of Kelowna investors led by grocer Pasquale "Cap" Capozzi. The bland original name was Domestic Wines and By-Products. A province-wide competition in 1936 was won by a Fraser Valley resident who suggested Calona, claiming the prize of $20 and a case of wine.

By the 1960s Calona's products, including fortified fruit-flavoured wines sold in gallon jugs, had a following across the country. The inspiration was the E & J Gallo winery in California: the Capozzi family boldly copied many of Gallo's best ideas (right down to bottle shapes), to the point of inviting the Gallo brothers as investors. The deal nearly happened. Who knows how the Okanagan wine industry would have developed if the world's largest family-owned winery had taken a piece of it? Since the Capozzi family sold it in 1971, Calona has had several owners. Andrew Peller Ltd. acquired the winery in 2005.

You can still buy wines that made Calona famous in an earlier era, including Schloss Laderheim, a Germanic white that was once Canada's bestselling wine. Today, however, Calona is carving out a reputation with VQA wines crafted by Katie Dickieson, an Ontario-trained winemaker who joined winemaster Howard Soon's team in 2008. The wines, featuring original art on the labels, are appealing for their vibrant fruit flavours—and also for their affordability.

MY PICKS

Calona's Artist Series wines are among the Okanagan's best values in VQA wines, especially the Pinot Gris, the Pinot Blanc, the Gewürztraminer, the unoaked Chardonnay and the Pinot Noir. The spicy Sovereign Opal, an exotic Calona exclusive, is a unique white made from a variety developed in the 1960s at the Summerland research station. Calona's icewines—Ehrenfelser and Pinot Blanc— are first class.

OPENED 1932

1125 Richter Street
Kelowna, BC V1Y 2K6

T   250.762.3332
    1.888.246.4472 (toll free)

W www.calonavineyards.ca

WHEN TO VISIT
Open daily 9 am – 6 pm
June through September,
9 am – 5 pm (to 4 pm on
Sundays) October through May

KATIE DICKIESON (PHOTO COURTESY
OF CALONA VINEYARDS)

CAMELOT VINEYARDS ESTATE WINERY

R.J. Young was ahead of his time when he planted a hectare (2½ acres) of Maréchal Foch vines on this property in 1974. Unable to get a winery contract, he soon pulled them out and planted apples. After R.J. died in 1996, son Robert took over the family farm. He and Denise Brass, his wife, kept growing apples until 2006, when their crop no longer covered packing house handling charges. Vines replaced the orchard in the next year: 2.4 hectares (six acres) of Pinot Gris, Riesling, Gewürztraminer and Pinot Noir. The original plan was just to sell the grapes, but, perhaps reflecting on R.J.'s experience, the couple chose to develop their own winery.

The venture is something of a retirement project, even if both are about 10 years from retiring. Robert, who was born in Quesnel in 1961, and Denise, who was born in Britain, have been Air Canada flight attendants for about 20 years. They usually work together on the same international flights, on schedules that allow them time to deal with the vineyard between trips.

Neither is a winemaker, but that shortcoming resolved itself through remarkable good fortune in the summer of 2008. They learned that winemaker Ann Sperling needed a licensed winery in which to make the debut wines for her family's Sperling Vineyards winery, only 10 minutes down the road from Camelot. Robert and Denise quickly invited Ann to use Camelot until Sperling licensed its own winery, and they engaged her as their winemaker. Ann, who was born in Kelowna, started her winemaking career in British Columbia before moving to Ontario in 1995, where she has helped launch several outstanding wineries.

Camelot was the name once given to a family home by Robert's father. The couple have embellished the medieval theme by installing a round table in the tasting room and by adding other touches of King Arthur's time, among them a sword embedded in a stone. The suit of armour in

ROBERT YOUNG AND DENISE BRASS

the wine shop is a well-crafted replica that Denise secured for $650 at an auction. "We had seen a genuine one from England," she says, a bit wistfully. "They were going for about £5,000."

MY PICKS

Camelot opened with excellent Pinot Gris, Chardonnay, Merlot and Syrah.

OPENED 2009

3489 East Kelowna Road
Kelowna, BC V1W 4H1

T   250.862.8873

W www.camelotvineyards.ca

WHEN TO VISIT
Open 11 am – 5 pm Thursday and Friday, 11 am – 4 pm weekends June through November, and by appointment

CASSINI CELLARS

As a 30-year-old immigrant to Canada, Romanian-born Adrian Capeneata set out to make a new life with astonishing hustle. "I have that entrepreneur thing," he says. "I see something and I'll go for it." While perfecting his language skills in Montreal, he held down as many as three jobs at the same time. These included buying used cars at auction, repairing them and reselling them.

His family in Romania had farmed grapes, but Adrian credits his interest in wine to restaurant jobs he had in both Romania and Canada. "I had a chance to discover the food that goes with the wine," he recalls. "I discovered the taste and the romance of the wine." However, when he moved to Vancouver, it was to sell and then manufacture and service equipment for fitness clubs. That led to making props for movie sets, then building houses. After an Okanagan vacation in 2000, he conceived the idea of developing a vineyard of his own.

"I see myself in the vineyard," he says, waxing romantic during one interview. "I like the whole package. I like the Okanagan. I like the vineyards. I see myself walking the dog in that vineyard in a few years." Late in 2006 he purchased a lavender farm beside Highway 97, south of Oliver, now the site for his winery. After selling the lavender plants (another example of his entrepreneurial instincts), he planted 2.2 hectares (5½ acres) of vines (Merlot, Cabernet Franc and Pinot Gris) in the spring of 2007. Next he secured consultant Philip Soo as his winemaker and purchased grapes for Cassini's initial vintages.

Adrian brought his con brio style to the design and construction of the winery, an eye-catching Tuscany-styled building that wine tourists should find irresistible. Once inside, visitors discover a tasting room with a 10-metre (33-foot) tasting bar long enough to accommodate 25 or so tasters. "I can put in another bar on wheels, depending on the need, so that people are not frustrated from waiting," he says. Large

ADRIAN CAPENEATA

windows on each side of the tasting room afford views of the barrel room and part of the winery's production area so that visitors can, as Adrian puts it, "see the magic."

Adrian had planned to call the winery Crazy Horse Cellars until he encountered copyright objections from wineries with somewhat similar names. So he used Cassini, a name already employed for some of his other businesses. It was the surname of his Italian-born grandfather.

OPENED 2009

32056 Highway 97
Oliver, BC V0H 1T0

T 250.483.4370

W www.cassini.ca

WHEN TO VISIT
Open daily 10 am – 6 pm
May to October

MY PICKS

Pride of place here belongs to a powerful and generous red blend called (what else?) Maximus. The other wines are also delicious, including the Syrah, Merlot, Pinot Noir, Chardonnay, Pinot Gris and Viognier.

CEDARCREEK ESTATE WINERY

With its gleaming white Mediterranean architecture, the CedarCreek winery belongs in the Greek islands, except for the wine. One of the Okanagan's leading Pinot Noir producers, it also does so well with other varieties that it was named Canada's winery of the year in a national competition in 2002 and again in 2005. The 17.4-hectare (43-acre) estate vineyard, much of it visible from the shaded Vineyard Terrace restaurant, is planted with Pinot Noir. Rows of Chardonnay, Riesling, Gewürztraminer, Pinot Gris and one of the Okanagan's earliest Merlot plantings run with military precision up the steep hillside behind the winery. The winery also gets grapes from its Greata Ranch vineyard across the lake, where CedarCreek has a small second winery. The big Bordeaux reds and the Syrah wines made by CedarCreek come from two recently planted vineyards at Osoyoos.

Uniacke, as it was originally known, one of the first estate wineries, struggled for recognition in the 1980s at what was then perceived to be the wilderness end of Lakeshore Road. In 1986 Senator Ross Fitzpatrick, the son of an Okanagan fruit packer, bought the property for its apple orchard. Captured by the romance of wine, he replaced all the apple trees with vines. With a talented winemaker, CedarCreek soon received favourable reviews. Judges at the Okanagan Wine Festival struck an unprecedented platinum medal for the winery's 1992 Merlot Reserve. Today CedarCreek's top wines are labelled Platinum Reserve.

Only about 10 percent of CedarCreek's production, which totals 40,000 cases a year, is Platinum Reserve. Gordon Fitzpatrick, the senator's son and the winery president since 1996, believes that the winery's expensive top tier should be exclusive. In 2009 CedarCreek eliminated its mid-tier range to focus its portfolio. This was a boon to consumers as the winery, by devoting most of its ever better quality grapes to its affordable basic tier, began offering wines that clearly overdeliver.

GORDON FITZPATRICK (PHOTO BY ALBERT NORMANDIN)

MY PICKS

Everything, including the scrumptiously fruity Ehrenfelser, now a cult favourite. The Platinum wines, including elegant Pinot Noir, rich Chardonnay, complex Meritage, Merlot and Cabernet Sauvignon— and an extraordinary Malbec—are wines to be cellared for 10 to 15 years.

OPENED 1980
(AS UNIACKE)

5445 Lakeshore Road
Kelowna, BC V1W 4S5

T 250.764.8866
   1.800.730.9463 (toll free)

W www.cedarcreek.bc.ca

WHEN TO VISIT
Open daily 10 am – 6 pm May through October; 11 am – 5 pm November through April

RESTAURANT
Vineyard Terrace
Open daily 11:30 am – 3:30 pm mid-June to mid-September

CERELIA VINEYARDS & ESTATE WINERY

Logger David Mutch, who grew up in the Similkameen Valley, is a farmer by avocation. For some years he and Peggy, his wife (a nurse), satisfied that vocation by growing hay, until learning from a television program that they could do far better with a vineyard. In 2005 they bought a derelict orchard near Cawston and began planting vines. When they realized that, in Peggy's words, "we had bitten off more than we could chew," they enlisted other family members not only to grow grapes but also to develop a winery.

David's brother, Dennis, and Dennis's wife, Roxanne, moved from Edmonton and built a home near the winery. Now retired from operating a business that maintained lumber manufacturing plants, Dennis also planted vines and agreed to be the winery's president. David's daughter, Megan, returned to the Similkameen Valley from Alberta with husband Corey Witter, an oilfield worker, and their children. Megan, who was born in 1983, had worked as a pharmacy technician before becoming a full-time mother. Now part of the family winery, she has taken Okanagan College's winemaking course and is being mentored by Cerelia's consulting winemaker, John Weber, who operates nearby Orofino Vineyards.

On adjoining properties owned by David and Dennis, 5.6 hectares (14 acres) of vines have been planted—Cabernet Franc, Merlot, Chardonnay, Pinot Gris, Gewürztraminer and Orange Muscat. With grapes purchased in 2008, the winery was able to open the following summer with a modest quality of Chardonnay and Pinot Gris. The reds—Cabernet Sauvignon, Cabernet Franc and Merlot—spent an extra year in barrel before the winery's formal grand opening in 2010. The Roman numerals on the labels relate to the winery's name: Cerelia is the harvest festival for Ceres, a Roman goddess of agriculture.

Cerelia's tasting room is in a heritage house attached to a new winery, deliberately large enough that a bistro and bed-and-breakfast accommodation can be added later.

MY PICKS

The debut Chardonnay and Pinot Gris wines are fresh and crisp, made in an uncomplicated fruit-forward style.

OPENED 2009

2235 Ferko Road
Cawston, BC V0X 1C2

T   250.499.8000

W   www.cerelia.ca

WHEN TO VISIT
Open 10 am – 5 pm
Friday through Monday,
and by appointment

MEGAN MUTCH

CHANDRA ESTATE WINERY

Dave Dhillon seems too mild-mannered and soft-spoken to have been a prison warden and a 30-year veteran of the Canadian corrections system. "I found the field very, very challenging," he says, in what is clearly an understatement. "And then I got into another one which is even more challenging. Wine is even more complex."

Born in India in 1939, Dave was trained as a teacher when he arrived in Canada in 1965, only to find that the teaching post he had lined up was already filled. Needing work, he applied for a correction officer's job at British Columbia Penitentiary in New Westminster (now demolished). "To be honest, I did not know what penitentiary meant," he admits. "I thought being an officer is a big thing." Fortunately for Dave, his interviewer spotted what he was really trained to do and steered him to a teaching post at the Prince Albert Penitentiary. Once he got through the first brutally cold winter there, he was on his way to a successful career, rising through the ranks as a warden and ultimately becoming regional director general before retiring in 1996.

When the usual retiree pursuits of consulting and travelling bored him, Dave, who had already partnered with a friend in an Okanagan wine-related business, turned to establishing a vineyard and winery of his own. "I thought it can't be any more complex than inmate behaviour," he says with a laugh. A colleague in the corrections service was a wine enthusiast, firing Dave's interest. "Even now he sends me literature," he says. "He was quite a motivator for me."

Early in 2005 Dave bought a four-hectare (10-acre) property not far from Oliver. Two-thirds was already planted (Merlot, Pinot Noir, Lemberger and Chardonnay); he planted Malbec and Sauvignon Blanc in the remainder. To underline the organic farming methods here, Dave initially named the winery Ecovitis. His daughters, Summer and Kiren, both with marketing experience, said the name sounded like a detergent, and they suggested Chandra, the Hindi word for "moon." The name evokes eastern mysticism, and reflects the Dhillon family's culture. Dave believes it also suits the vineyard's organic practices. "People used to plant and harvest according to the moon," he notes. "The moon played a great part in agriculture."

MY PICKS

Pinot Gris, Isis (Blaufränkisch), Halo (Merlot) and Red Fusion, a unique Zweigelt/Michurinetz blend. All of the labels allude to the moon.

OPENED 2008

33264 121 Street
Oliver, BC V0H 1T0

T   250.485.4081
    1.866.777.4081 (toll free)

W   www.chandrawinery.com

WHEN TO VISIT
Open daily 10 am – 6 pm
May 1 to October 31,
and by appointment

DAVE DHILLON

CHURCH & STATE WINES

By developing or leasing 44.5 hectares (110 acres) of vineyard in the South Okanagan, Church & State Wines has become a force in the region while remaining Vancouver Island's largest winery. Most of the winery's grapes now are processed in a leased packing house close to its Okanagan vineyards. An Okanagan tasting room is under development, complementing the wine shop at Church & State's Saanich winery.

The original 20,000-case winery was opened as Victoria Estate Winery in 2002 by a group of investors. Unfortunately the wines were not nearly as impressive as the building. The venture was sliding toward failure in the fall of 2004 when former tax lawyer Kim Pullen took it over. Born in Victoria and the owner of the Sidney Marina, Kim has a knack for turning businesses around. Previously he had built a fish farming company into a business with annual sales of $25 million before selling it in 2002. He had just come back from an extended cycling vacation in Australia when he bought the winery.

Kim especially liked the science behind aquaculture and he finds parallels in the science behind wine. "What you have to add in wine-making is the black magic that Bill has," Kim says. He is referring to Bill Dyer, who was the consulting winemaker at Burrowing Owl from 1997 to 2004. Kim snapped him up in 2005 when Bill, who is based in the Napa Valley, expressed a desire to keep making Okanagan wines. In 2009 Jeff Del Nin, another Burrowing Owl alumnus, joined as the on-site winemaker in Church & State's Okanagan facility. A native of Thunder Bay, Jeff has a master's degree in chemistry and after working with an Australian developer of synthetic corks, he got an enology degree at the University of Adelaide.

Since the 2006 vintage the winery has crushed nearly all of its grapes in the Okanagan rather than risk the loss of quality that can result from shipping grapes halfway across the province before dealing with them.

JEFF DEL NIN

KIM PULLEN

The winery still maintains a 4.5-hectare (11-acre) vineyard of Pinot Noir and Pinot Gris around the Saanich winery, primarily for making sparkling wine.

The bar is deliberately high at this winery. A few years ago, Kim set 87 points as the minimum score that his wines had to achieve to go forward. Since then, Church & State wines have racked up numerous awards. The debut 2005 vintage of the winery's $50 flagship red, Quintessential, won three silver medals, a gold and a double gold (and best of class) at five different California competitions.

OPENED 2002
(AS VICTORIA ESTATE WINERY)

31120 87th Street
Oliver, BC V0H 1T0

T 250.498.2700

W www.churchandstatewines.com

WHEN TO VISIT
Open daily 11 am – 6 pm May 1
to October 31

SAANICH WINERY
1445 Benvenuto Avenue
Brentwood Bay, BC V8M 1J5

T 250.652.2671

MY PICKS

Quintessential, of course (I scored it 91). Other excellent wines include the Coyote Bowl Vineyard Merlot and Syrah, the Hollenbach Vineyard Pinot Noir, the Chardonnays and the Sauvignon Blancs. Don't miss the winery's budget-priced Church Mouse wines.

CLOS DU SOLEIL

The world's best-known wine marathon is the Marathon du Médoc, a run that includes wine tasting stations. Perhaps it was competing there in 2002 with his wife, Bonnie Henry, that confirmed Spencer Massie's determination to open a winery of his own four years later in the Similkameen Valley.

His interest in wine began long before that. Born in 1961 in the BC coastal community of Alert Bay (his father was an air traffic controller), Spencer joined the Canadian Navy in 1979 as an officer trainee. During a vacation five years later, he backpacked through the French wine country. He soon took over ordering wines for the ship's mess and he even led on-board port tastings. He retired from the navy in 2000 as a lieutenant commander and, having acquired a master of business administration degree, set up a business incubator firm in Toronto. He moved that business to Vancouver in 2005 when Bonnie, a physician, was recruited for a senior medical post there.

Spencer then began looking at vineyard property in the Okanagan and, even though he had made wine as an amateur, sought a winemaking partner. Impressed by a bottle of Josephine, the flagship red from Herder Vineyards, Spencer enlisted Lawrence and Sharon Herder to help launch Clos du Soleil. With Lawrence's help, Spencer acquired a four-hectare (10-acre) orchard property near Keremeos in 2007. That summer, all but a small corner was planted to red and white Bordeaux varieties. "I love everything classic French," Spencer says. "My family roots go back to Normandy." Lawrence made the initial vintage before handing over winemaking duties to consultant Ann Sperling. Coincidentally, Kelowna-born Ann and Spencer were classmates in high school.

While Spencer and Bonnie are the public faces of this winery, there are three other couples partnering in Clos du Soleil: Ottawa-based Gus Kramer, a former naval colleague, and Lisa Underhill; Peter and

Andria Lee, a Vancouver business couple; and Calgarian oil executives Leslie Le Quelenec and Sue Lee.

MY PICKS

Production is tightly focused on the model of Bordeaux. Clos du Soleil White is a Graves-style Sauvignon Blanc while Clos du Soleil Red is a blend of Merlot, Cabernet Sauvignon and Cabernet Franc.

OPENED 2008

2568 Upper Bench Road
Keremeos, BC V0X 1N4

T 250.499.2831

W www.closdusoleil.ca

WHEN TO VISIT
Tasting room not yet open

SPENCER MASSIE, ANN SPERLING AND LESLIE LE QUELENEC (PHOTO COURTESY OF CLOS DU SOLEIL)

COLUMBIA GARDENS VINEYARD & WINERY

The aptly named village of Fruitvale, just east of Trail, offered the clue years ago that, since fruit has long been produced in the Kootenays, grapevines might also thrive. This was confirmed by the late Tom Bryden and Lawrence Wallace, his winemaking son-in-law, when they planted 2.4 hectares (six acres) of vines on a farm 16 kilometres (10 miles) down the Columbia River valley from Trail. Columbia Gardens was the first winery in the Kootenays. Two more have opened since.

The Bryden family have lived on this 20-hectare (50-acre) farm in the Columbia Valley since the 1930s, growing a range of products from vegetables to hay. In the 1990s Lawrence began researching the potential of grapes. Various trial plantings showed which varieties could succeed here, where the summer is hot but the season is shorter than in the Okanagan. The reds in the vineyard are Maréchal Foch and Pinot Noir. The white varieties are Gewürztraminer, Auxerrois and Chardonnay. As well there are small plantings of Kerner, Siegerrebe and Schönburger. This gives Lawrence useful blending options. Columbia Gardens' signature wine, in fact, has turned out to be an off-dry white called Garden Gold, a tasty blend of Auxerrois, Chardonnay and Gewürztraminer.

A plumbing and heating contractor by trade, Lawrence is a winemaker by avocation. He makes his wines with the winery's own grapes as well as with purchased fruit. From the start Columbia Gardens has submitted its wines to the VQA panel. The VQA sticker on the bottles quietly makes the point that good wine can be made in the Kootenays.

The understated charm of the Columbia Gardens wine shop, where Tom's son, Kevin, often presides, surprises first-time visitors, who do not expect a tasting room with sophisticated décor this far off the wine touring route. The shop is a comfortably appointed log house with a patio deck for wine tasting and picnic lunches in fine weather.

LAWRENCE WALLACE

MY PICKS

Maréchal Foch is the backbone for three wines here: the premium Maréchal Foch Private Reserve and two blends, Station Red (with Pinot Noir) and Kootenay Red (a blend of several vintages of Foch). Garden Gold and Gewürztraminer are popular white wines. The Station Road Rosé, made from Pinot Noir, is refreshing.

OPENED 2001

9340 Station Road
RR1 Site 11 Comp 61
Trail, BC V1R 4W6

T 250.367.7493

W www.cgwinery.com

WHEN TO VISIT
Open daily 10 am – 6 pm
mid-April through September,
and by appointment

PICNIC AREA

CROWSNEST VINEYARDS

Crowsnest Vineyards is a taste of Germany in the Similkameen. Here you can wash down a plate of bratwurst or a huge Jaeger schnitzel with a fruity glass of Samtrot, a red made from an obscure German grape (the name means "red velvet"), while chatting with a member of the Heinecke family, owners of the winery since 1998. Olaf Heinecke, the patriarch of the family, was born in Leipzig. After a career as a developer in Germany, he came to the Okanagan. Crowsnest was a struggling winery producing only 500 cases a year, almost all white, when Olaf bought it.

The entire family has been marshalled to turn Crowsnest into the Similkameen's largest winery, now making 6,000 cases annually, almost half of it red wine. Sabine, Olaf's wife, keeps an eye on the restaurant, housed in the Landgasthof, the cozy inn that the winery added in 2005. Son Sascha, with a diploma in hotel management, presides over the tasting room with professional warmth. Clad in a white apron, he bakes remarkable bread daily in a wood-fired oven. Some visitors believe Crowsnest is worth a visit for the bread alone, never mind the wines.

Daughter Ann, who has a German winemaking diploma, makes the wines. The portfolio includes Merlot and Pinot Noir from the winery's own vineyard (5.5 hectares/13½ acres), and an Old Vines Foch and the Samtrot, both from purchased grapes. The most acclaimed white is the unoaked Chardonnay Stahltank (the German word for the steel tanks in which the wine is aged before being bottled). Crowsnest also releases wines labelled Barcello Canyon, a name drawn from the nearby canyon that pierces the mountain range between the Similkameen and Okanagan valleys. The gravel road through the canyon is open in summer, but savvy locals advise driving it only with a sturdy vehicle—or with a rental car.

MY PICKS

I like the uncomplicated freshness of the Chardonnay and Riesling. I also like the complexity of Barcello Canyon Cuvée #3, a dry blend of Auxerrois, Pinot Gris and Chardonnay. Among the reds, my favourite is the Crowsnest Merlot.

OPENED 1995

2035 Surprise Drive
Cawston, BC V0X 1C0
T 250.499.5129
W www.crowsnestvineyards.com

WHEN TO VISIT
Open daily 10 am – 6:30 pm
April 1 to December 24

RESTAURANT
Country Inn and Restaurant
Traditional Bavarian cuisine

ANN HEINECKE

D'ANGELO ESTATE WINERY

This winery has one of the most strategic locations on the Naramata Bench: guests staying at the bed-and-breakfast units here find themselves within walking distance of half a dozen wineries. And they can take a break from wine touring by hiking the scenic Kettle Valley Railway Trail, which swings just past the winery.

Sal D'Angelo, who runs a winery called D'Angelo near Windsor, Ontario, that opened in 1989, has been attracted to the Naramata Bench since he started vacationing here in the early 1990s. He has a rare condition of the nervous system called Guillain-Barré syndrome that is far less trying in the dry Okanagan than in humid Southern Ontario. Not that he has ever let the condition hold him back: during one four-hour treatment for the paralyzing ailment, he landed a $1,100 wine order from the doctor.

Born in Italy in 1953, Sal grew up in Canada in an immigrant home where his family made wine each fall. "I grew up with the smell of fermenting grapes," he says. He became a science teacher but began to plant grapes in 1983 on his Windsor-area property, opening a winery six years later. During an early Naramata vacation, he presented one of his Ontario reds to Hillside Estate Winery founder Vera Klokocka with the cocky assertion that the Okanagan was not suited to growing big reds. She produced a Cabernet Sauvignon (she was the first in the region to make this varietal). Sal then changed his mind and starting considering the Okanagan.

Since 2001 Sal has acquired an entire peninsula on the eastern bluffs above Lake Okanagan, only minutes north of Penticton. He planted about three hectares (7½ acres) initially and he is gradually tripling his plantings. Not afraid to be original, Sal was the first in the Okanagan to plant Tempranillo, the leading red variety in Spain. He also planted red Bordeaux varieties and some Pinot Noir and intends to add

SAL D'ANGELO

Viognier, Sauvignon Blanc and Chenin Blanc. The winery is in a metal-clad barn on the property and the wine shop is on the ground floor of the family home. Longer-term plans call for the building of a gravity-flow winery.

MY PICKS

The flagship wine is a red blend called Sette Coppa, which means "seventh measure." The wine takes its name from the nickname of Sal's great-grandfather, Donato, who talked the local flour mill into keeping every seventh measure as payment for grinding his grain—when other villagers were being assessed every sixth measure. Look for the Tempranillo and the Tempranillo icewine.

OPENED 2007

979 Lochore Road
Penticton, BC V2A 8V1

T   250.493.1364
     1.866.329.6421 (toll free)

W www.dangelowinery.com

WHEN TO VISIT
Open 10 am – 6 pm Monday through Saturday and 11 am – 5 pm Sunday May through October, and by appointment

PICNIC AREA

ACCOMMODATION
Vineyard View Bed & Breakfast
(chalet and three suites)

DEEP CREEK WINE ESTATE & HAINLE VINEYARDS ESTATE WINERY

Walter Huber anointed this winery with tradition when he announced that the wines are made in accordance with his family's wine purity law of 1856. This echoes the famous Bavarian beer purity laws of 1516, and perhaps it is no coincidence that Walter was born in Munich, in 1959. He came to Canada in 1980 to run his family's fishing resort in Northern Ontario. Eleven years later, he bought land above Peachland, developed a vineyard near Deep Creek, and was about to open his own winery when, in 2002, he bought the Hainle family's winery.

It had its own tradition. Canada's first icewines were made here in the early 1970s by the late Walter Hainle and his German-trained winemaker son, Tilman. After a rare bottle of the 1978 icewine, the winery's first commercial vintage, was stolen from Walter's truck, he considered insuring his remaining bottle for $1 million. In the true German tradition, Hainle icewines have always been made in treasured small volumes. The largest production was in 2003 to celebrate icewine's 25th anniversary in Canada. The volume was a mere 7,200 bottles, each containing only 200 millilitres (seven ounces) of precious wine. The hallowed Hainle name remains on the winery's icewines and on some new table wine releases.

As one would expect, the new owner has put his own stamp on the winery, elevating Deep Creek as the winery's primary name and pricing some of the wines aggressively. No Okanagan winery has had as many wines priced over $100 a bottle. In the curious psychology of wine marketing, that increased his sales of $40 and $60 wines. The average sale in this wine shop is $59. For consumers on a budget, there is usually at least one wine under $20, several under $30—and generous pours of others at the tasting bar.

This winery has embraced the Zweigelt varietal like no other Okanagan winery. The grape, Austria's most important red, is named for Professor

WALTER HUBER

Fritz Zweigelt, the Austrian who bred the variety in the 1920s. Conceding that the grape's name is a challenge to English speakers, Deep Creek has created a "Z" series for some of its Zweigelt blends. For example, Z2 initially was Zweigelt and Cabernet Sauvignon, while Z3 blended Merlot, Zweigelt and Pinot Noir. Whether on its own—as in the winery's rich estate-grown Zweigelt—or in a blend, Zweigelt is a grape worth tasting.

Deep Creek produces about 5,000 cases a year, most of it from 10 hectares (25 acres) of its own organic vineyards. In 1995, when the winery was still known just as Hainle, this was Canada's first winery to win organic certification for its vines.

OPENED 1988
(AS HAINLE VINEYARDS)

5355 Trepanier Bench Road
Peachland, BC V0H 1X2

T 250.767.2525
   1.800.767.3109 (toll free)

W www.hainle.com

WHEN TO VISIT
Open daily 11 am – 5 pm
May through October; 11 am –
5 pm Monday through Friday
November to April

MY PICKS

The Zweigelt varietals and Z blends (except for a fine rosé) are boldly oaked reds. The estate Pinot Noir, the Viognier and the Cabernet Sauvignon are all attractive wines. Lovers of older wines will be drawn to the library wines here, including the mature dry Riesling.

DESERT HILLS ESTATE WINERY

Twin brothers Randy and Jessie Toor, born in 1964 in the Punjab, India, spent summers working in Okanagan vineyards after coming to Canada. Having acquired a taste for the land, they bought a 10-hectare (25-acre) apple orchard in 1988 on Black Sage Road, one of the Okanagan's best vineyard areas. Discovering that only apples of middling quality can be grown on Black Sage, they switched to grapes (mostly Bordeaux reds) in 1995. Their sponsor was Langley's Domaine de Chaberton, which needed a reliable supply of red grapes to supplement the white varieties in its own vineyard. In 2005 the brothers snapped up a mature six-hectare (15-acre) vineyard nearby on Black Sage Road that is densely planted with Cabernet Sauvignon and Merlot.

Although they continue to sell grapes to Domaine de Chaberton, the demand for their own wines is driving them to increase production to 10,000 cases, five times the volume with which they began. "It was a little dream to start a small winery," Randy says. The tasting room is still in a modest building next to the vineyard, at the end of a short but grand driveway. Behind it is a large addition (241 square metres/ 2,600 square feet) built in 2005 on top of a barrel cellar, all to house the extra tanks and new equipment required for the winery's growth.

The brothers, who clearly like big reds, have added Zinfandel to their portfolio by grafting that variety onto a small parcel of Gamay. That decision, Randy says, was triggered when he was swept away by a Zinfandel he tasted in a fine restaurant.

MY PICKS

The wine to ask for, if it is not sold out, is the Syrah, which is remarkable for intense nutmeg spice in both the aroma and the taste. Also worth seeking out are the Mirage (a Meritage blend), the Gamay, the Chardonnay and the Pinot Gris.

OPENED 2003

30480 71st Street
(Black Sage Road)
RR2 Site 52 Comp 11
Oliver, BC V0H 1T0

T 250.498.1040

W www.deserthills.ca

WHEN TO VISIT
Open daily 10 am – 6 pm April
through October; 10 am – 5 pm
November to March

JESSIE AND RANDY TOOR

DIRTY LAUNDRY VINEYARD

This winery set a new benchmark for slightly outrageous labels in 2009 when it released a red wine called Bordello. The gold-medal wine is a Bordeaux blend (Cabernet Sauvignon and Merlot), and the label extends the whimsical romp that began in 2005, when the winery changed its name from Scherzinger Vineyards to Dirty Laundry.

The winery was started a decade earlier by a former Bavarian wood-carver named Edgar Scherzinger who, on retiring in 2001, sold it to protegés Ron and Cher Watkins. To refresh the winery's image, Ron and Cher enlisted Bernie Hadley-Beauregard, the Vancouver marketer whose earlier successes included turning Prpich Hills Winery into Blasted Church Winery. His research subsequently uncovered the tale of a former Chinese railroad labourer who opened a laundry in Summerland a century earlier. It became know as the "dirty laundry" after it was turned into the front for a bordello.

Dirty Laundry was an instant hit; wines were sold out in a matter of weeks. Needing to expand the tiny winery quickly (it was making only 2,000 cases a year), the Watkins first looked for partners and then sold the winery in the fall of 2006 to a group of Albertans headed by Fort McMurray lawyer Bob Campbell. The lawyer has had a long love affair with Summerland, having owned a country house on the lake since 1977. He had just planted a vineyard nearby, with a winery in mind, when he was able to buy Dirty Laundry.

Production was tripled in 2007 while the new owners developed additional vineyards around Summerland. Dirty Laundry now is supported by 14 hectares (35 acres) of vineyards operated by its owners, one of which includes a site for a larger future winery. The plantings are heavily tilted to Gewürztraminer and Pinot Noir, signature varietals made by consultant Philip Soo.

The entertaining strategy of edgy "wink wink, nudge nudge" labels continues to catch the fancy of wine tourists. The winery's oak-aged Private Reserve Chardonnay was not selling well until the label was changed to Naughty Chardonnay, with a disingenuous explanation that oak can be "knotty." The winery's bestseller continues to be its Woo Woo Vines Gewürztraminer, probably because a little touch of sweetness goes well with intimations of naughtiness.

MY PICKS

The top wines are spicy Gewürztraminers with equally spicy names: Madame's Vines, Woo Woo Vines and Threadbare Vines. Hush, as the rosé is called, is tasty. The 2007 Bordello, the first release, is firm and should be decanted or cellared a few years more.

OPENED 1995
(AS SCHERZINGER VINEYARDS)

7311 Fiske Street
Summerland, BC V0H 1Z2
T 250.494.8815
W www.dirtylaundry.ca

WHEN TO VISIT
Open daily 10 am – 5 pm
April 1 to October 31, 11 am – 4 pm Monday to Friday
November through March
and by appointment

PICNIC AREA

PHILIP SOO (PHOTO COURTESY OF DIRTY LAUNDRY)

DUNHAM & FROESE ESTATE WINERY

Think of the owners of this winery as, in Crystal Froese's words, "the perfect foursome." Crystal's husband, Kirby, is a winemaker and she is a marketing whiz. Their partners are grape grower Gene Covert, general manager of Covert Farms, and his wife, Shelly, who is skilled in administration and accounting. They combined their talents in 2006 to launch a winery on one of Oliver's most famous farms. The Dunham half of the winery's name comes from Gene's grandmother's maiden name.

Covert Farms was established half a century ago on the plateau just south of McIntyre Bluff by George Covert, a Californian who came to the Okanagan to grow tomatoes, onions, tree fruits and, ultimately, grapes. The vineyard was large enough in the early 1980s that a mechanical harvester was tested (with questionable results, for the early harvesters mangled the vines). Except for six hectares (15 acres) of table grapes, vines were pulled out in 1988 and were not replanted until 2005, when the perfect foursome decided to start a winery.

Born in 1971, Gene Covert, grandson of the farm's founder, joined the family business after getting a degree in physical geography. Shelly, an Edmonton-born teacher, runs the farm's market, selling organically grown produce directly to the public. Born in Moose Jaw in 1970, Kirby Froese has gone from serving wines at the Banff Springs Hotel to making wine in Australia, Chile and California and for several Okanagan producers, including Hawthorne Mountain and Red Rooster. Also a Moose Jaw native, Crystal has her own marketing company, whose clients include the annual Covert Farms Festival of the Tomato each September. It was she and Shelly who prodded their husbands to harness their skills in a winery.

Since 2005 Gene has planted nine hectares (22 acres) of wine grapes, including the five Bordeaux reds, Zinfandel, Syrah, Pinot Blanc, Sémillon and Sauvignon Blanc. Because they could easily turn farm buildings into a winery, the partners launched with purchased grapes, making 500 cases of wine. In full production, the vineyard should support 5,000 cases a year.

MY PICKS

The top red and white blends are released under the Amicitia label, Latin for "friends." The winery also has made its mark with Pinot Blanc, Pinot Noir and Merlot.

OPENED 2006

38614 107th Street
(Secrest Road)
Oliver, BC V0H 1T0

T 250.498.9463

W www.dunhamfroese.ca

WHEN TO VISIT
Open daily 11 am – 5 pm
May 1 to May 9 and July 1 to
October 31, and by appointment

GENE COVERT, CRYSTAL FROESE, SHELLY COVERT AND KIRBY FROESE

EAST KELOWNA CIDER COMPANY

A visit to the East Kelowna cidery, surrounded by apple trees, is a step back in time to an era when Kelowna was a community of orchards, not condominiums. This pastoral suburb still has the historic apple orchards, although for how much longer might be a question. The value of Red Delicious apples is so low that packers in one recent year did not pay for the apples but billed growers for handling them. David and Theressa Ross, who own a 3.6-hectare (nine-acre) apple orchard here, add value to their crop by making cider.

The driving influence, however, was David's interest in hard (alcoholic) cider. "Ever since he was 12, he has been concocting mixtures of moonshine, and that kind of stuff, just for the pure enjoyment of doing it," Theressa says of her husband. Now a logger, David was born in 1969 and grew up on this orchard, which has been in his family since his grandfather bought it in 1942. Ross Hard Apple Cider, the cidery's main alcoholic product, has a photograph of Grandfather Ross on the label.

Theressa, a hard-working young mother, has become an accomplished cider maker with a remarkable talent for improvisation. Rather than pressing the crushed apples, she extracts the juice by spinning the pulp in a converted dairy centrifuge and on the spin cycle of several washing machines. The only time this does not work well is when she makes ice apple cider. The sugar-saturated juice is extracted but the frozen pulp remaining in the spinners has to be practically chiselled out.

The Rosses grow dessert apples for cider. They do not care for the bitter taste that classic cider apples yield. The ice cider—the apple cider world's answer to icewine—is made with Golden Delicious and Braemar apples left on the trees to freeze naturally. Theressa contends that naturally frozen apples contain more sugar than artificially frozen apples because trees going into hibernation feed extra sugar into the fruit still hanging on them. "Yum, yum," she says of the taste of these apples, which she has picked in temperatures as low as −20°C (−4°F). She produces such small quantities of the golden nectar that ice cider is available only at the cidery.

MY PICKS

The Hard Cider is refreshing and, with about six percent alcohol, not too intoxicating.

OPENED 2003

2960 McCulloch Road
Kelowna, BC V1W 4A5
T 250.860.8118

WHEN TO VISIT
Open 9 am – 2 pm Tuesday to
Thursday, and by appointment

THERESSA ROSS

EAUVIVRE WINERY & VINEYARDS

Dale Wright and Jeri Estin, busy with their careers in Saskatchewan, only began visiting BC wine country after Trina, their daughter, moved to the Similkameen Valley. "We got to know all the wineries around here," Dale says. "We would tour around the valleys and go home with half the truck full of wine for the winter until we could come back in the spring." Soon their Regina wine cellar was stocked almost exclusively with BC wines.

Born in the Saskatchewan village of Rouleau in 1949, Dale, a professional geologist, has run his own oil well drilling company since 1984. Jeri, who has an education degree, is a college-level teacher and counsellor. They came to wine as consumers, having dabbled in making country wines and kit wines, until they learned that their increasingly refined palates enjoyed BC wine, including wines made by Herder Vineyards.

However, when they began looking at wine country property, it was retirement they had in mind, until they discovered that Lawrence and Sharon Herder, who were moving to a different Similkameen property, had their original Cawston winery for sale. Dale and Jeri liked the new house and also the potential of an equipped winery and a one-hectare (2½-acre) vineyard half planted to Gewürztraminer; the other half has now been planted with Pinot Noir. By the time they concluded their negotiations with the Herders, Lawrence had agreed to make the debut wines for EauVivre in 2007. "Before you knew it, we became Sharon and Lawrence's apprentices," Dale says and laughs. Kaleden-born Spencer Kelly, a food science graduate from the University of British Columbia, became EauVivre's winemaker after an apprenticeship at the Herder winery. In 2010 he left to enrol in the wine program at Fresno State University.

Dale and Jeri conceived their winery's unusual name. "We thought it would indicate something vague, the ungraspable," Jeri says poeti-

JERI ESTIN AND DALE WRIGHT

cally. Dale, a down-to-earth geologist, explains that "it is just a slang term for *water of life*."

MY PICKS

The winery launched with a powerfully spicy Gewürztraminer, an austere Chardonnay, an elegant Pinot Noir and a classic Cabernet Franc that is full of spicy berry flavours and chocolate.

OPENED 2009

716 Lowe Drive
Cawston, BC V0X 1C2
T   250.499.2655
W www.eauvivrewinery.ca

WHEN TO VISIT
To be established

SPENCER KELLY

EDGE OF THE EARTH VINEYARD

Although this winery, which Russ and Marnie Niles opened in 2002, is only six kilometres (less than four miles) from the highway, the scenic but twisty country roads create the perception that it is off the beaten path. Russ met that perception head-on in renaming the winery in 2009. "By the time people get here, they think they have gone off the edge of the earth," he says, chuckling.

Hunting Hawk Vineyards, the winery's original name, was sold along with Hunting Hawk's second winery, which Russ and Marnie operated for several years at the O'Keefe Ranch near Vernon. The city, which runs the ranch, declined to renew the winery lease. Under new owners, Hunting Hawk moved to a vineyard near Salmon Arm.

After four years of stretching himself between two wineries, Russ sounds relieved at having reduced the stress in his business. "This has become fun," he says. "This has become a lot of fun." Born in Victoria in 1957, Niles is the former editor of the now defunct *Vernon Daily Times*. He was drawn to wine as one of the original minority partners in Vernon's Bella Vista winery, since closed. He launched his own winery after the closure of the *Daily Times*.

At the same time the owner of the local flying club alerted him that an aviation website had posted a job offer. Russ began writing for www.AVweb.com and eventually became editor of what he says is the world's largest general aviation website, with 200,000 subscribers. He also edits *Canadian Aviator* magazine and pilots his Cessna 140 around the Okanagan.

Russ relies on purchased grapes (such as Merlot, Pinot Noir, Pinot Gris and Gewürztraminer) as well as those from his own 1.2-hectare (three-acre) vineyard. He is particularly enthusiastic about Maréchal Foch, grown in both his vineyards and by any neighbours he can talk into it. "I just happen to love the grape," he says. "It makes fabulous

RUSS NILES

red wine." But when marauding wasps wiped out his ripe Foch in 2009, he replaced the fruit with Osoyoos-grown Syrah, making a fleshy red with that variety instead. Meanwhile he has developed aggressive tactics to combat wasps in the future.

MY PICKS

How can you not sample the Foch when the winemaker is so enthusiastic about it? The rest of the portfolio changes to reflect the winemaking opportunities that come Russ's way. During a recent visit, the tasting room included an excellent Pinot Gris, a nicely oaked red blend called Mostly Merlot and an organic Pinot Noir Icewine, a winemaking first for Russ. The wines are also vegan.

OPENED 2002
(AS HUNTING HAWK VINEYARDS)

4758 Gulch Road
Spallumcheen, BC V0E 1B4

T 250.546.6743

W edgeoftheearthvineyard.com

WHEN TO VISIT
Open daily noon – 5 pm Easter to Canadian Thanksgiving, and by appointment

8TH GENERATION VINEYARD

The name of this winery celebrates the eight generations of the family of winemaker and co-proprietor Bernd Schales who have been wine growers. However, it could also be called 10th Generation. The Frank family of Stefanie Schales, Bernd's wife, recently learned that their wine growing history in Germany is at least 92 years longer than that of the Schales family. The Franks confirmed this in 2009 when research in some church archives in Germany found that the family has grown grapes since 1691.

Bernd and Stefanie brought the family tradition to the Okanagan in 2003. Bernd, born in 1972 and trained at Weinsberg, had spent 9 or 10 years managing a vineyard for his family's Weingut Schales in Flörsheim-Dalsheim. With Bernd's father and two uncles already in the business in Germany, the young couple struck out on their own, canvassing opportunities in South Africa, New York state and Ontario before being seduced, during a vacation, by the Okanagan's beauty. They bought an established four-hectare (10-acre) Okanagan Falls vineyard with a breathtaking view of Vaseux Lake.

Bernd's family sent him off to Canada with his grandfather's antique wine press, which was a godsend in the 2007 vintage. That summer, Bernd and Stefanie shelved their original plans to attach a winery to their Okanagan Falls home when they were able to buy the building previously housing the highway-side Adora winery just south of Summerland. The building was empty (Adora moved its equipment elsewhere), and Bernd moved urgently to order new equipment because the grapes were ripening quickly. His grandfather's press, he discovered, was good for yet another vintage. "We never thought that we would use it and it actually did a pretty good job," Stefanie says.

The 2.4-hectare (six-acre) vineyard that came with the Adora purchase grows Syrah, Pinot Noir and Pinot Meunier, complementing the Riesling, Chardonnay, Pinot Gris and Merlot grown at Okanagan Falls. That enables Bernd to make fine estate-grown wines for tasting and sale in the very well-located wine shop.

MY PICKS

The generations of experience in German wine country show in the fine Rieslings, whether dry, off-dry or late-harvest. Bernd also has a nice touch with Pinot Gris, Chardonnay and Pinot Noir Rosé. Best of the solid reds is the Syrah.

OPENED 2007

6807 Highway 97
Summerland, BC V0H 1Z9
T   250.494.1783
W www.8thgenerationvineyard.com

WHEN TO VISIT
Open daily 10 am – 6 pm
May through October,
and by appointment

BERND, HELENA, PHILLIP, STEFANIE AND JOHANNA SCHALES (PHOTO BY TARA MORRIS)

ELEPHANT ISLAND ORCHARD WINES

Elephant Island has raised the bar for fruit wines since Del and Miranda Halladay launched this winery. They retained as winemaker Christine Leroux, whose entire training and experience had been in making grape wines. As a result, Elephant Island's fruit wines take the measure of grape wines any day. There are dry wines to go with food, sparkling wines for celebration, iced apple wines made just like icewine, and fortified wines with cherries or currants standing in superbly as port. Most of the wines are made only with undiluted juice. "I know that it's a pretty common practice with fruit wine production to use water," Del says. "What better way to dilute flavours and dilute wine? We're doing everything we can to use the pure fruit and that's it."

This winery is pleasantly tucked away amid the orchard that Miranda's grandparents bought years ago as a summer retreat on the Naramata Bench. The serene and shaded patio behind the wine shop is still a great spot for a picnic. The winery's singular name memorializes a family legend. When Catharine Chard Wisnicki, an architect and Miranda's grandmother, designed the house, her husband, Paul (an engineer), scoffed that it was designed purely "for the eye." Having already been told the property would be a white elephant, she responded by calling the house Elephant Eye-land.

The fruit wines owe a debt to Paul Wisnicki, who had considered distilling fruits before his death. Del and Miranda started this enterprise with some of his fruit wine recipes. Miranda, born in Powell River in 1973, is a geologist. Del, born in Victoria in 1972, went to Loyola College in Maryland on a lacrosse scholarship. He earned a marketing degree and a spot on a professional American lacrosse team. Playing lacrosse, from which he retired in 2007, provided a "good part-time job" during the winter months as the winery became established.

The couple research continually to identify fruits suitable for wine. "For instance," explains Del, "for our apple wine I tested over 30 varieties

DEL HALLADAY

MIRANDA HALLADAY

of apple and made wine and blends until we settled on our apple blend, with three varieties." Their marketing includes publishing cocktails and practical recipes that complement their wines on their website, all leavened with the same good humour that reigns in the wine shop. What's the benefit of matching fruit wines with dessert? "The wine cancels out all the calories in the dessert," they suggest.

MY PICKS

The pear wine, light and delicate, is a favourite of mine with a salad course. The Little Prince, a crisply dry sparkling apple wine, is made by the traditional Champagne method. The winery's tasty dessert products include the Stellaport, the Cassis and the immensely popular Framboise. You need to get on the mailing list for these.

OPENED 2001

2730 Aikins Loop
RR1 Site 5 Comp 18
Naramata, BC V0H 1N0

T 250.496.5522

W www.elephantislandwine.com

WHEN TO VISIT
Open daily 10:30 am – 5:30 pm
May 1 to October 31, and by
appointment

PATIO PICNIC AREA

ACCOMMODATION
The Tree House rental suite

EX NIHILO VINEYARDS

"Creating something from nothing"—one translation of Ex Nihilo from Latin—succeeds best if you hitch your wagon to a star. This winery debuted in 2008 by enlisting the Rolling Stones (yes, the rock band) as a partner in a brand of icewine called Sympathy for the Devil, the title of one of the band's most famous songs. Seldom has a new Okanagan winery opened with as much publicity.

Jeff and Decoa Harder, who run Ex Nihilo, got the idea of linking up with the Rolling Stones in California. Jeff's younger brother, James, who has a wine company in Napa, took the couple to a VIP dinner there where one of the wines carried the band's signature red tongue and lips as a label. When Jeff dug further, he discovered Celebrity Cellars, an outfit that links celebrities to consumer products like wine. It took some doing, but eventually Jeff convinced Celebrity Cellars and the band to put the "tongue and lips" logo on a Canadian icewine. "Our gift to the wine world is icewine," Jeff believes.

Jeff was born in Edmonton in 1964. A burly entrepreneur who formerly owned a pleasure boat manufacturer, he got his first taste of the consumer beverage business as a partner in an apple cider venture in the late 1990s. Decoa, who was born in Innisfail, Alberta, in 1973, is a former skiing instructor with a marketing education who took up selling wine for Quails' Gate and then Mt. Boucherie. "I woke up one morning [in 2003] and said, 'Jeff, we have to find land,'" she recalls. In 2004 they bought their four-hectare (10-acre) property, formerly an orchard, which sits on a bench overlooking the Arrowleaf Cellars winery. Three years later they planted Pinot Noir, Pinot Gris and Riesling—the latter with icewine in mind. Their 697-square-metre (7,500-square-foot) winery was built in 2009. Previously the Ex Nihilo wines were made at the Mt. Boucherie Estate Winery, some of whose winemakers continue to work with Ex Nihilo.

DECOA AND JEFF HARDER

The other partners in Ex Nihilo are Alberta livestock dealers Jay and Twila Paulson, high school friends of Jeff's. Among other things, they contributed Ex Nihilo's mascot, a fibreglass bull. It was inspired by bronze scuptures of animals at Napa's Cliff Lede Vineyards, whose owners are friends of the Paulsons. "*We* aren't quite at the bronze cow stage," Jeff says with a laugh, acknowledging that Ex Nihilo is just getting started.

OPENED 2008

1525 Camp Road
Lake Country, BC V4V 1K1

T 250.766.5522

W www.exnihilovineyards.com

WHEN TO VISIT
Consult website

MY PICKS

The Merlot is super-extracted. Night is a fine Bordeaux blend. A recent vintage of the winery's excellent Riesling won a gold medal at the Riesling du Monde competition in France. The Pinot Gris is delicious. Of course, the Pinot Noir and Riesling icewines make it on their own merit but are even more appealing to collectors of Rolling Stones memorabilia.

FAIRVIEW CELLARS

It may surprise those who relish the wines from Fairview Cellars that owner Bill Eggert does not consider himself a winemaker. He insists that he is a grape grower. Just don't ask him how he grows his grapes. "My wine is made in the vineyard and it is the vineyard secrets I keep to myself, not the winemaking secrets," he says.

His secrets occupy a 2.4-hectare (six-acre) plateau overlooking the first tee of the Fairview Mountain Golf Club and two smaller plots south of Vaseux Lake (midway between Okanagan Falls and Oliver). The Fairview vineyard, which he began planting in 1993, is dedicated to Merlot, Cabernet Sauvignon, Cabernet Franc and a row of Syrah. "I honestly don't want to waste my land on whites," he says. Since 2005 he has purchased Sauvignon Blanc to make Fairview's one white. The Vaseux Lake properties were purchased in 2008 and planted the following year to Pinot Noir. This marks Bill's first foray into making wine with Burgundy grapes.

Born in Ottawa in 1957, Bill is the son of a mining engineer. He developed his passion for grapes on his uncle's Niagara vineyard and moved to the Okanagan in 1983 after failing to talk his uncle into switching from Concord grapes. Here he became so adept at vineyard management that, in recent years, he developed and taught short courses on the subject at Okanagan College.

Bill's wines (he is in fact a pretty good winemaker) are a lot like Bill: bold direct wines that don't beat around the bush. He calls his big Meritage "The Bear." A wine writer once referred to him as a madcap winemaker, so Bill blended Merlot and the two Cabernet varieties and called it Madcap Red. Expect to find at least one irreverently christened wine in the tasting room. A recent red blend, this one Cabernet-dominated, was called Two Hoots, primarily for the pair of owls that nest on Fairview's property every year. In 2004 he teamed up with

Olivier Combret of Antelope Ridge to make two barrels of a red blend called Two Thumbs Up. It was the first $100 table wine from an Okanagan winery.

That pricing, however, is not typical of Bill. Most of Fairview's wines, which collectors and restaurants snap up quickly, sell at prices between $20 and $40. And Bill, being a straight shooter, has been known to roll back prices in a weak vintage. However, given his farming skills, weak vintages are few and far between.

MY PICKS

The Fairview wines are bold, sturdy in structure and capable of aging very well. The Cabernet Sauvignon, Cabernet Franc, Merlot and The Bear Meritage are appealing. The Syrah/Cabernet blend is delicious.

OPENED 2000

13147 334th Avenue (Old Golf Course Road)
Oliver, BC V0H 1T0

T   250.498.2211

W www.fairviewcellars.ca

WHEN TO VISIT
Open 1 pm – 6 pm Monday through Saturday May to October, unless the SOLD OUT sign is up

BILL EGGERT

FIRST ESTATE CELLARS

You would be hard-pressed to find a winery with a more tangled history. This was the first winery to be licensed (in 1978) when new estate winery regulations came down in British Columbia, an achievement honoured in the winery's current name. The first owner, Bulgarian-born Marion Jonn, was larger than life: he launched grandiloquently as Chateau Jonn de Trepanier. (The winery is located on a short street just off the end of Trepanier Bench Road.)

Barely a year after opening, Jonn sold the winery to Bob Claremont, formerly a winemaker at Calona. He changed the winery's name to Claremont and ran it until 1986, when the business slipped into receivership.

The third owner was Croatian-born Goldie Smitlener, who did not drink but who was a shrewd real estate operator. The winery was named Chateau Ste. Claire and drifted along indifferently as Smitlener negotiated with potential buyers. It was taken over in 1998 by Gary Strachan, now an Okanagan winery consultant, who coined the First Estate name. Unfortunately, Strachan did not have the finances to turn the rundown facility around; it reverted back to Smitlener and her partners in 2000 and closed for several years.

Finally Frank Silvestri purchased and reopened the winery in 2004. Born in Italy in 1948, Silvestri operates RemWan Carriers, a Calgary trucking company. True to his Italian heritage, however, he had long nurtured the ambition to own a winery. Now he divides his time between Calgary and the vineyard, where he makes the wine. The day-to-day vineyard operations and the wine shop (with décor unchanged from Claremont's days) were looked after by his parents, Alf (who has since died) and Fleana. Although they had lived in Canada since 1954, both had that special gusto Italians have for the wine grape. "We were born in wine," Fleana told me, laughing. "In Italy, nobody is drinking water."

The primary varieties in the seven-hectare (17-acre) vineyard are Maréchal Foch, Gewürztraminer and Gamay. Some of the vines are survivors of those that the original owner, Marion Jonn, began planting in 1973. Silvestri recognizes the virtue of mature vines by making an Old Vines Foch, with his debut vintage in 2002.

OPENED 1979

5078 Cousins Place
Peachland, BC V0H 1X2
T   250.767.6465
W www.firstestatecellars.com

WHEN TO VISIT
The winery had a TEMPORARILY
CLOSED sign in 2009

MY PICK

The Old Vines Foch is a hearty, full-bodied red with vanilla aromas and the round texture that comes from being well aged in American oak.

FORBIDDEN FRUIT WINERY

Only a kilometre or so from the highway, this winery is a secluded refuge at the end of a narrow and sometimes winding road. Owners Steve Venables and Kim Brind'Amour, organic fruit growers here for 25 years, keep most of their 57-hectare (141-acre) property as an untouched ecological sanctuary. The public only began exploring this Similkameen gem after the couple opened a guesthouse in 2001, followed by an art gallery and then the winery.

Steve and Kim are self-described members of the "back to the land" generation. Steve was born in Victoria in 1952 and grew up in Indiana, where his father was deputy coroner. After two years studying science in college, he returned to the Okanagan to work in orchards. In 1977, he purchased the Sumac Road property, then raw land. Kim was born in Hull in 1963, the daughter of a market gardener; she formerly operated a health food store in Keremeos.

Their nine-hectare (22-acre) orchard is dedicated to tree fruits, including an astonishing 25 apple and 10 peach varieties. For many years they have been commanding premium prices for organic fruits. In recent years, with the general increase in organic production, the food wholesalers have had so much product that they have begun to turn down seconds (fruit with a less than perfect appearance). Steve and Kim concluded that there is absolutely no reason why seconds cannot be turned into first-class fruit wines. "And also," he adds, "we love wine." They produce a growing range of delicious fruit wines.

Committed environmentalists, Kim and Steve also grow 1.2 hectares (three acres) of organic grapes for what they call their Earth Series Wines. "When Kim and I decided to produce several grape wines for the discerning customers, we also wanted to do something special that took our organic and sustainable lifestyle and production practices to a new level," Steve says. Some of the proceeds from these wines—so far

KIM BRIND'AMOUR AND STEVE
VENABLES

a Cabernet Sauvignon and a Sauvignon Blanc—go to groups like the David Suzuki Foundation that address bio-diversity and sustainability issues.

MY PICKS

The wines are as original as the labels. Pomme Desiree is a luscious dessert wine blended with six apple varieties. Crushed Innocence is a delicately pure expression of white peaches. Impearfection is an exotically spicy wine from Asian pears. Adam's Apple is a dry apple wine easily paired with main courses. The tour de force is Cerise d'Eve, a port-style cherry wine with the brilliance of a ruby, flavours of cinnamon, crabapples and Black Forest cake, and a totally florid back label.

OPENED 2005

620 Sumac Road
RR1 Site 33 Comp 9
Cawston, BC V0X 1C3
T 250.499.2649
W www.forbiddenfruitwines.com

WHEN TO VISIT
Open daily 10 am – 6 pm April to October, and by appointment

ACCOMMODATION
Harvest Moon Retreat
Guest House

FOXTROT VINEYARDS

The first four vintages of Foxtrot's superb Pinot Noir were all made at the nearby Lake Breeze winery, giving Torsten Allander and his family time to assess the acceptance of their wines. The winery built its own cellar in 2008, after virtually every top restaurant in British Columbia had Foxtrot on its list and after a New York importer had ordered wine for that market. The new cellar, a domed concrete cave sunk into the earth for natural temperature control, enabled Foxtrot to double its production to 1,000 cases of Pinot Noir in 2009.

An elegantly mannered retired pulp and paper engineer, Torsten Allander extends a lifetime of high achievement to wine growing, his most recent passion. Born in Sweden, he came to Canada in 1973 for a career with NLK Associates, a top pulp and paper consulting firm based in Vancouver and Montreal. The Allander family is as passionate about track and field as they are about wine. Torsten's wife, Elisabeth (the family calls her Kicki), is a champion pentathlete. Torsten was a founding member of the West Vancouver Track and Field Club. Soon after moving to the Okanagan, he became president of the Penticton Athletics Track and Field Club. Son Gustav and daughter Anna-Marie have both been athletes and coaches.

The immaculately tended 1.4-hectare (3½-acre) Foxtrot vineyard had been planted entirely to Pinot Noir in the mid-1990s. The Allanders bought the property in 2002, initially for a country retreat. They sold grapes for several years before striking a technical partnership with the Lake Breeze winery for a three-year winemaking trial, beginning with the 2004 vintage, to see just how good Foxtrot Pinot Noir could be.

"I wanted to convince myself before I invested a lot of money in a winery that we could produce a top wine that could compete on a world level," Torsten says. By the time the 2006 vintage was in barrel, the Allanders had decided to proceed with a winery of their own.

Gustav, who once considered taking up engineering like his father, has become the winemaker and vineyard manager. His wife, Nadine Kinvig, who completed her winemaking studies in New Zealand in 2008, also takes a hand in making Foxtrot wines.

OPENED 2007

2333 Gammon Road
Naramata. BC V0H 1N0
T 250.496.5082
W www.foxtrotwine.com

WHEN TO VISIT
By appointment

MY PICKS

The winery's Pinot Noirs are among the most elegant and suave examples of this variety from any Canadian producer. The winery's Burgundy-styled Chardonnay, first made in 2008, is one of the Okanagan's most sophisticated whites.

TORSTEN AND KICKI ALLANDER

GEHRINGER BROTHERS ESTATE WINERY

From the long uphill sweep of the driveway, neatly bordered by rows of Riesling vines, the Gehringer Brothers winery looks modest and unassuming. This is deceptive, however. Visitors who tour the winery find that substantial cellars, not visible from the parking lot, have been built into, and sometimes buried beneath, the hillside. The space is needed to accommodate the 30,000 or so cases of wine made each year, largely from grapes grown at the winery's 10.5-hectare (26-acre) vineyard.

The deliberate lack of flash reflects the personalities of Walter and Gordon Gehringer, the Oliver-born brothers, sons of German immigrants, who run this popular family winery. When the family conceived of a winery in 1973, Walter, who had just completed high school, was sent to the Geisenheim research institute, Germany's leading wine school, to become its first Canadian graduate. Gordon, his younger brother, got his training at Weinsberg, another good German wine school. While the brothers were studying in Europe their family completed years of climate studies before buying this Golden Mile vineyard property in 1981.

At first Gehringer Brothers produced primarily white wines, such as Riesling, Auxerrois and Ehrenfelser, in an off-dry Germanic style. The brothers added drier wines after 1996 when they bought the vineyard, now called Dry Rock, which adjoins their original Golden Mile vineyard. Dry Rock is planted with non-Germanic varieties, including Chardonnay, Sauvignon Blanc and Cabernet Sauvignon. These choices were dictated in part by the rising demand from visitors for drier wines and for reds. Walter, who spends a lot of time in the tasting room, was noticing. As well, he concluded it was much less risky to grow French varieties today because the Okanagan is measurably warmer than when the family bought their first site in 1981.

WALTER GEHRINGER

The Gehringers make refreshing whites that are free of the excessive alcohols now alarmingly common in South Okanagan wines (another sign of climate change). Their Pinot Gris wines, as an example, are seldom more than 12.5 percent alcohol, as much as 2 percent lower than those of nearby producers. Several years ago, the Gehringers introduced a reserve tier, called Optimum. The whites are textbook expressions of pure fruit. The winemakers capture the fruit flavours of their grapes most strikingly in their ice-wines, made with Riesling, Ehrenfelser and Cabernet Franc.

OPENED 1986

Highway 97 at Road 8
Oliver, BC V0H 1T0

T   250.498.3537
    1.800.784.6304 (toll free)

W www.sunnyosoyoos.com/
   webpages/gehringer_winery
   .htm

WHEN TO VISIT
Open daily 10 am – 5 pm June through mid-October and 10 am – 5 pm Monday through Friday the rest of the year. Open during the May long weekend.

MY PICKS

All the wines are appealingly value-priced. My favourite Dry Rock whites are the zesty Sauvignon Blanc and the citrusy Chardonnay. The elegant Optimum Pinot Gris and all of the Gehringer Rieslings—from dry to icewine— are delicious. The budget-priced find here is Cuvée Noir, a soft, easy-drinking red.

GOLDEN BEAVER WINERY

The Golden Mile bench peters out at or just before it gets to Golden
Beaver Winery and its 2.8-hectare (seven-acre) vineyard, wedged
between Highway 97 and the mountain to the west. Originally known
as Gersighel Wineberg, the winery was opened in 1995 by Dirk De
Gussem, a flamboyant Flemish farmer who brought his family to the
Okanagan in 1986. Soon he ripped the fruit trees from the property and
planted vines. Recognizing that the afternoon shade makes this one of
the cooler vineyards on the Golden Mile, he planted more than a dozen
varieties, including Merlot, Vidal, Pinot Noir, Pinot Blanc, Riesling,
Gewürztraminer and Viognier.

When he decided to sell in early 2006, the winery's roadside location caught the attention of Bruno Kelle and Stella Schmidt, Calgarians
looking for a winery after becoming smitten by the Okanagan lifestyle.
Bruno, a technical college graduate, grew up on a tobacco farm in
Tillsonburg, Ontario. He helped his family diversify into culinary herbs
and, after moving to Calgary in 1996 and working as a sales and marketing executive, even considered opening his own herb farm. Stella
Schmidt, a bookkeeper, grew up in a family that trained dogs, and
shares Bruno's passion for farming. That shared passion showed almost
immediately when they imposed order on what had been a notably
unkempt vineyard.

The Golden Beaver name, originally reinforced by bucolic labels that
subsequently have been toned down, came about when Bruno and Stella
noticed the popularity of the so-called "critter" wines. Indeed, the idea
of putting a beaver on the label came as they were enjoying a bottle of
[yellow tail], the hugely popular Australian brand that launched a flood
of animal labels. It seemed obvious to them that a Canadian winery
should choose a beaver as its critter. As they explained it, they have had
to work like beavers to renovate the fixer-upper winery. The beaver's
nickname is Goldie, of course, and it showed up in the names of two
blends, Goldie's Passion and Goldie's White Passion.

Golden Beaver has carved out a particular niche with tasty dessert wines called Vin de Curé. They are made by air-drying ripe grapes (Merlot and Vidal) to concentrate the flavours and the sugars. The winery makes a fine late-harvest from its planting of Siegfried, a German white that, in the Okanagan, may be unique to this vineyard.

OPENED 1995
(AS GERSIGHEL WINEBERG)

29690 Highway 97 South
RR1 Site 42 Comp 19
Oliver, BC V0H 1T0

T 250.495.4991

W www.goldenbeaverwinery.com

WHEN TO VISIT
Open daily 10 am – 6 pm April 15 to October 15; noon – 5 pm Wednesday through Sunday in winter. Closed first week of December through first week of January.

PICNIC AREA

BRUNO KELLE AND STELLA SCHMIDT (PHOTO BY ALYSSA KELLE)

GRANITE CREEK ESTATE WINES

Granite Creek is a winery that appeals to nature lovers. Situated on a farm at the head of the Tappen Valley, the grounds include seven kilometres (four miles) of hiking trails that have been developed for visitors. In turn, these trails give access to a more extensive equestrian trail system on the mountainside. Riders occasionally tether their horses near the winery while enjoying the warm tasting room hospitality of the Kennedy family.

This is also cougar country. In September 2007 the winery's dog, Shiah, a Golden Labrador/Golden Retriever cross, was attacked by a cougar. Shiah fought it off (but lost most of her ears) and did not come out of the forest for four days. When the story circulated on the Internet, at least one get-well card arrived at Granite Creek and a California family visited the following spring to see Shiah—and, of course, to taste the wines.

Winemaker Doug Kennedy, born in Vancouver in 1972, and his Polish-born wife, Mayka, have pursued careers with an oil field services company. Their schedules have given them enough time off to make wines with a consultant's help. Both were accomplished amateur winemakers, strengthened technically by Mayka's degree in chemical engineering. When they are off in the oil patch, the vineyard and the tasting room are managed by Doug's parents, Heather and Gary, who has a doctorate in agricultural engineering.

The Kennedy family has farmed in the 1,600-hectare (3,954-acre) Tappen Valley since 1959, primarily with a dairy herd. Driven by Doug and Mayka's passion for wine, they planted four hectares (10 acres) of vines in 2003, with considerable room for more. They grow varieties suited to this northern vineyard: Gewürztraminer, Kerner, Ortega, Optima, Siegerrebe and Maréchal Foch, along with a test block of Pinot Noir. Other varieties, including Syrah, Merlot, Pinot Gris and Ehrenfelser (Granite Creek's current flagship white), are obtained

DOUG AND GARY KENNEDY

under contract from Okanagan growers. The Kennedys boldly made almost 2,000 cases in 2003, their debut vintage. The objective is to build production to about 5,000 cases over several years, an ambitious target that should make Granite Creek the largest winery in the Shuswap Lakes region.

MY PICKS

The Ehrenfelser wines, which won Granite Creek's first awards in competition, are classic expressions of this variety's peachy lushness. The bold Syrah has been an award winner for the winery. The Fortified Merlot has the weight of a good ruby port. "I've always been a port lover," Doug Kennedy says.

OPENED 2004

2302 Skimikin Road
Tappen, BC V0E 2X0

T 250.835.0049

W www.granitecreek.ca

WHEN TO VISIT
Open daily 10 am – 5 pm in summer, or by appointment

GRAY MONK ESTATE WINERY

You must visit Gray Monk often because, or so it seems, the winery is evolving all the time. It was once a modest cellar nesting on a vineyard slope. Then it added a restaurant with an open-air deck (large enough for a dance hall), a conference centre and a baronial wine library. When visitors' cars jammed up all nearby public roadsides, a section of the precious Rotberger vineyard was uprooted for a parking lot. That just created a people jam in the tasting room until, in 2009, a large new wine shop was built on top of the old one, magnificently styled like a European château.

Echoes of Europe are hardly surprising here. George Heiss, born in 1939, grew up in Vienna and apprenticed with his father, a world champion hairdresser. His wife, Trudy, was born near Berlin. They met in Edmonton, where both had hair salons. Hugo Peter, Trudy's father, began growing grapes in the Okanagan. George and Trudy followed him there, planting vines in 1972 for the winery they opened a decade later.

Today they count themselves among the rare families with four generations in wine growing in Canada. Son George Jr., their German-trained winemaker, also has taken over Hugo Peter's vineyard. His brothers, Robert and Steven, manage the winery while Robert's son, Kieran, has qualified as a viticulturist.

The Heiss family has had a profound impact on Okanagan wine growing. They were the first to import clones of Pinot Gris, Gewürztraminer and Auxerrois from Alsace. They facilitated the Becker Project, an eight-year trial of German vines that, by its conclusion in 1985, proved the viability of varieties now among the most important in the Okanagan. Among all the wine producers in North America, they alone nurture the hard-to-grow Rotberger grape to make notable rosé.

Now making about 80,000 cases a year, Gray Monk built its reputation with unoaked white wines that are expressive, fruit-driven and juicy on the palate. Winemaker Roger Wong joined the Heiss team in

ROGER WONG AND GEORGE HEISS JR.

2005 to develop sparkling wines. And after making Merlot and Pinot Noir for a decade with purchased grapes, Gray Monk is making a big bet on reds with what it calls its Paydirt Vineyard south of Oliver: five hectares (12 acres) recently planted primarily with Malbec, Merlot and Cabernet Sauvignon.

MY PICKS

The quality of all Gray Monk wines is consistently high, and that includes its popular Latitude 50 wines, now half the winery's production. These are refreshing, easy to drink and affordable. The winery's flagship is Pinot Gris (the German name for that variety translates as "gray monk"). Odyssey is the winery's reserve label, with the Odyssey Pinot Gris, the Odyssey Merlot and the Odyssey Rosé Brut being particularly fine.

OPENED 1982

1055 Camp Road
Okanagan Centre, BC V4V 2H4

T 250.766.3168
   1.800.663.4205 (toll free)

W www.graymonk.com

WHEN TO VISIT
Open daily 9 am – 9 pm July and August; 10 am – 5 pm daily the rest of the year, except January and February (closed on Sundays)

RESTAURANT
Grapevine Patio
Open daily 11:30 am – 4 pm, plus for dinner during summer

GREATA RANCH ESTATE WINERY

This is a historic property, named for George H. Greata (the locals pronounce it gretta), an 1895 emigrant from Britain who planted a 20-hectare (50-acre) apple orchard. After a couple of ownership changes, it was run for many years by John T. Long and his family, some of whose descendants still live in the Okanagan. The Longs turned Greata Ranch into one of the North Okanagan's largest orchards, shipping so much fruit that the ranch had its own dock on Okanagan Lake for barging loads to the nearest railhead. Immediately after the Longs sold the ranch in 1965, a very cold winter killed many of the trees. The property slid into prolonged decline and even had squatters living there before CedarCreek proprietor Ross Fitzpatrick bought it in 1994, cleaned it up and planted vines. The 16-hectare (40-acre) vineyard, besides supporting Greata's wine needs, grows some of CedarCreek's top Pinot Noir, Chardonnay and Pinot Gris.

The Greata Ranch winery answered a popular demand. Motorists, seeing the vineyard on the slope below Highway 97, frequently drove to the vineyard manager's house looking for wine. Finally CedarCreek erected an attractive red-roofed winery with a shaded picnic veranda overlooking Okanagan Lake. Long-term plans call for an elegant lakeside residential development.

The Greata Ranch winery replicated CedarCreek wines until 2006 when Corrie Krehbiehl, who had been associate winemaker at CedarCreek, moved across the lake to Greata. Born in Kelowna in 1975, she has an agriculture degree from the University of British Columbia that includes six months of viticulture and winemaking at Lincoln University in New Zealand. She started working at CedarCreek while in high school, affixing VQA stickers to bottles of CedarCreek wine. The winemaker then was Ann Sperling, another Kelowna native, who gave her eager young protegé more and more to do until, as Corrie recalls, "I got hooked."

When Corrie was moved to Greata Ranch, the Fitzpatricks intended that she would develop a boutique winery producing reserve-level Chardonnays and Pinot Noirs. The primary buyers were to include residents of the planned vineyard community. Corrie did make several exceptional wines but left after the reserve winery project was suspended in 2009, a victim of the global financial crisis and its depressing impact on the sales of Okanagan resort properties.

Greata Ranch continues to produce modest volumes of wine, primarily supplying the tasting room and wine shop, an even more popular stop after the recent widening of the highway introduced safer dedicated turn lanes.

OPENED 2003

697 Highway 97
Peachland. BC V0H 1X9

T   250.767.2768

W www.greataranch.com

WHEN TO VISIT
Open daily 10 am – 6 pm April 1
through October 31

MY PICKS

The original Greata Ranch wines were unpretentious, easy-drinking and attractively priced. The reserve wines, which might still be in private wine shops, are among the best Chardonnay and Pinot Noir in the Okanagan.

HERDER WINERY & VINEYARDS

In 2009 Lawrence and Sharon Herder adopted a "small is beautiful" stance: after making 4,000 cases of wine a year in the two previous vintages, they cut back to the 2,500 cases they were making previously. "We woke up one day and said this isn't as fun as it used to be," Lawrence says. At the lower volume, the Herders run most of the winery, including sales, by themselves. Lawrence now has more time for detail-heavy winemaking. A recent vintage of Josephine, the winery's flagship red, was crafted by evaluating 17 different blends over several days.

Born in San Diego in 1967, Lawrence is a graduate of the winemaking school at Fresno State. In between operating a winery in Paso Robles and the current one in the Similkameen, the Herders owned a Burnaby printing company. The business did not engage Lawrence's interest, unlike winemaking, a passion since he made his first wine at home at age 14. He returned to winemaking at the Jackson-Triggs winery near Oliver for two vintages, and then made one vintage at Golden Mile Cellars while launching his winery near Cawston. When the Herders relocated to Upper Bench Road near Keremeos in 2008, their original winery reopened as EauVivre Winery under new owners.

On Upper Bench, the Herders acquired a property that included a three-floor house spacious enough to accommodate living quarters, a grand tasting room with a breathtaking view of the valley, and a ground floor for wine tanks and a barrel cellar. A sometimes nervous winemaker, Lawrence prefers living in his winery. "Putting the winery downstairs gives me more peace of mind during crush," he says.

The almost six-hectare (15-acre) vineyard was formerly an orchard (the Herders retained a block of pear trees) on a mineral-rich, south-facing slope. It backs against a cliff that shields this sun-drenched property in winter from chill northeast winds. In line with their winemaking ambitions, the Herders have planted about 4,000 Merlot vines, 2,200 Pinot Noir, 1,100 Syrah and just over 900 Cabernet Sauvignon.

LAWRENCE AND SHARON HERDER

To support production of the winery's flagship red blend, Josephine, they also grow Cabernet Franc, Malbec and Petit Verdot. Viognier (2,200 vines) and Chardonnay (450 vines) are the only whites grown here.

The Herders also buy grapes from carefully chosen quality vineyards, notably Bellamay Vineyards of Keremeos, owned by physician Dr. Johan Boshoff and his wife, Helga. The Bellamay Merlot, very good on its own, is the backbone of Josephine as well.

OPENED 2004

2582 Upper Bench Road
Keremeos, BC V0X 1N4
T 250.499.5595
W www.herder.ca

WHEN TO VISIT
Open daily (except Tuesday)
noon – 5 pm May through
October, and by appointment.
Tours by appointment.

MY PICKS

Upon first release, the Herder wines created an immediate buzz in the wine press, including the rich, plummy Merlot, the California-style Chardonnay and the fruity Pinot Gris. The Bellamay Vineyard wines are superb, notably the Pinot Noir, delicious Pinot Gris and terrific Merlot. Herder's complex red Meritage is named Josephine after the artist who designs the winery's labels.

HESTER CREEK ESTATE WINERY

This winery takes its name from the creek flowing by the south side of the winery vineyard peninsula. The creek was christened by Judge J. C. Haynes, the first customs officer at Osoyoos in the 1860s. Legend has it that his daughter, Hester, fantasized about being towed by a mythical lake creature while swimming here. A stylized image of Hester now graces the labels of the wines.

Hester Creek's more recent history is equally colourful. The vineyard was first planted by Italian-born Joe Busnardo in 1968, growing only vinifera when almost every other vineyard grew hybrids. When he could not get a premium for his grapes from other wineries, he opened the Divino Estate Winery in 1983. It was renamed Hester Creek after Joe sold it in 1996 and relocated Divino to Vancouver Island.

After Hester Creek's erratic owners ran out of money, the winery was rescued from bankruptcy in 2004 by Curt Garland, a wine-loving owner of a Prince George trucking company. The property has been almost completely transformed since then, beginning in 2006 when Curt hired veteran Ontario winemaker Robert Summers. The potential of the 30-hectare (74-acre) vineyard at Hester Creek had impressed Robert in 2003 while he was buying grapes for Andrew Peller Ltd., for which he was then the national winemaker.

Born in Ontario in 1962, Rob has been a winemaker in Ontario (except for a brief stint in a distillery) since getting his food sciences degree at the University of Guelph. However, he nursed the ambition to make wine in the west. When the call came from Hester Creek, Rob, as he puts it, just followed his heart. "It was a no-brainer," he says. Soon after arriving, he designed a modern 30,000-case winery, which opened in the fall of 2009. It is partially buried in the hillside but the wine shop's expanse of windows looks over the vineyard and the valley.

ROBERT SUMMERS

"The main thing here is the vineyard," Rob says. "It's a great site for Bordeaux reds and maybe even Syrah." Trebbiano is a legacy of Joe Busnardo, and is one of the several Italian varieties he planted that succeeded here. Each year Hester Creek releases a wonderfully crisp and refreshing white from these vines.

MY PICKS

The signature wines at Hester Creek have been Pinot Blanc, Cabernet Franc and Trebbiano. Rob's capable winemaking now has extended the choices to include superb Pinot Gris, tangy Sémillon Chardonnay and solid Cabernet Sauvignon and Merlot, along with blends of these varieties.

OPENED 1983
(AS DIVINO ESTATE WINERY)

13163 326th Avenue
Oliver, BC V0H 1T0

T 250.498.4435

W www.hestercreek.com

WHEN TO VISIT
Open daily 10 am – 5:30 pm May 1 to mid-October; 10 am – 4 pm mid-October through April

ACCOMMODATION
Six mountainside Tuscan-style guest suites

HIDDEN CHAPEL WINERY

This winery is named for the tiny white chapel, barely large enough for eight people, secluded among trees at the rear of this property and behind the winery cave. The previous owner from whom Deborah Wilde and Lanny Kinrade bought this roadside property (10 minutes north of Oliver) occasionally performed weddings here. Once this winery opens, the Kinrades once again may host small weddings at this bucolic spot.

The winery is based on a 1.2-hectare (three-acre) vineyard of Cabernet Sauvignon that Lanny planted in 2005 after running a turf farm and then growing vegetables. "I got tired of managing the farm," he says. "Most of my friends in Oliver have vineyards and wineries." Lanny was born in Kimberley, where both his father and grandfather worked in the famous Sullivan lead-zinc mine. Perhaps because the mine was nearing the end of production, Lanny's father advised him to find different employment. He became a telephone lineman in Vancouver until he moved to the Okanagan in 1988. He ran his own organic vegetable farm near Oliver for 10 years before selling it in 2006.

With some help from his brother Terry, who recently retired from the Ministry of the Environment, Lanny has an off-season business doing residential renovations. "But I wanted to keep my hands in the dirt," he says.

Even though friends suggested he plant Merlot, Lanny settled on Cabernet Sauvignon, a favourite variety of his. He is considering planting a tiny plot of Orange Muscat in the remaining unplanted area. With no room for more vineyard, he buys other varieties, mostly from neighbouring vineyards, for a range of wines that includes a Bordeaux blend and a Syrah, along with Viognier. "We will be doing more whites because I like whites," promises Deborah, a real estate agent. "I'd like to do Sauvignon Blanc."

The barrel cellar, buried at what was formerly the property's swimming pool, is designed with a capacity of 60 to 90 barrels, depending on how they are stacked. Lanny and Deborah are projecting that Hidden Chapel will open with about 1,000 cases of wine and eventually grow to double that volume.

MY PICKS

No wines were available for tasting.

OPENING PROPOSED 2010/11

9756 382nd Avenue
Oliver, BC V0H 1T0

T 250.488.2188
    250.490.6000

W www.hiddenchapelwinery.com

WHEN TO VISIT
To be established

LANNY KINRADE AND DEBORAH WILDE

HILLSIDE ESTATE WINERY

Much has changed since Hillside opened as the first winery on Naramata Road. No one would have predicted that the twisting two lanes of blacktop would develop such a concentrated winery population. Hillside was established by Vera and Bohumir Klokocka, former employees of the Czech state airline, who defected to the West when they tired of Communism. The original winery was in a modest farmhouse in a postage-stamp vineyard that replaced an orchard in 1984. The tasting room was the size of a large pantry. Parts of the house have been incorporated into the current winery, a roadside fortress with a bell tower, a good-sized tasting room and a 160-seat bistro.

The new winery was built after Hillside was acquired in 1996 by a group of about 90 Alberta investors, who went over budget on the winery and nearly failed. Eventually the ownership was consolidated into the hands of 22 investors, including Calgary-based chair Duncan McCowan, president Bill Carpenter and his wife, Kathy Malone. "I am trained in science and business, with a passion for wine," says Bill, who is a Saskatchewan-born geologist. "Kathy is an accountant and a trained chef, with a passion for food."

Their wine and food interest developed during 25 years of international oil industry postings. When travelling became tiresome, Bill enrolled in the master's program at the University of California's wine school in 1995 and then worked a year with Iron Horse Vineyards. Needing to finance a move into wine, he returned to Alberta to start and then sell a succession of junior oil companies. Some of Hillside's investors asked Bill in 2000 to become involved in improving the quality of the wines. In 2005 the Carpenters moved to the Okanagan to manage the winery.

Now producing about 12,000 cases of wine annually, Hillside owns or controls about 16 hectares (40 acres) of vineyards. This permits Hillside to produce a focused portfolio of well-made wines, reflecting the skills

KATHY MALONE

BILL CARPENTER

of winemakers Kelly Symonds and Kathy Malone, who succeeded Kelly after the 2008 vintage. Born in New York and with a chemistry degree from the University of Victoria, Kathy previously made wine at giant Mission Hill for almost two dozen years before switching to Hillside for a more "hands-on" cellar experience.

Hillside's signature white is Muscat Ottonel, a spicy, floral white, a legacy of the original vineyard and a wine so popular that consumers scramble for their allocations each spring.

OPENED 1990

1350 Naramata Road
Penticton, BC V2A 8T6

T 250.493.6274
  1.888.923.9463 (toll free)

W www.hillsideestate.com

WHEN TO VISIT
Open daily 10 am – 5:30 pm
May through October and on
weekends in April; 10 am –
4 pm Monday through Friday
in winter, and by appointment

RESTAURANT
The Barrel Room Bistro
Open for lunch and dinner
during wine touring season

MY PICKS

The Muscat Ottonel, the Gewürztraminer and the Pinot Gris offer crisp and refreshing flavours. The winery's bold reds include the spicy Old Vines Gamay from quarter-century-old vines, the intense Reserve Merlot, the peppery Syrah and the yummy Pinotage, tasting of black cherries and coffee. The flagship red is Mosaic, a Bordeaux blend first made in 2002.

HOLLYWOOD & WINE
ESTATE VINEYARDS

Seldom explored by wine tourists, the countryside just west of Summerland is a photogenic maze of agricultural valleys where farms grow everything from tree fruits to buffalo. Neil and Betty Massey moved to their 4.5-hectare (11-acre) slice of this paradise in 1998. They chose to replace the apple trees with organically grown vines. Originally they intended to sell juice to home winemakers but changed their minds, developing a winery of their own. They call it Hollywood & Wine because Neil, a truck driver for movie production companies, has spent a lot of time around movie sets and befriended many performers, whose autographed photos are displayed in the wine shop.

The Masseys, who have lived in British Columbia since 1965, come from Prairie farm families. Neil was born in 1940 in Selkirk, Manitoba, into a family with a long tradition—which he adopted—of home winemaking (raspberry, dandelion, chokecherry, plum and whatever else was at hand). He became an independent trucker, first in the grocery industry and then with the movies. Betty, born in Saskatoon in 1941, discovered her talent for art while still a doodling teen in school. Today her superb oils are pastoral scenes or images of the quarter horses she and Neil once raised. The wine labels here feature her paintings.

Well sited on a volcanic slope behind the winery, the vineyard includes Pinot Gris, Pinot Noir, Gewürztraminer, a few Muscat varieties and two early reds, Zweigelt and Léon Millot. "I love Pinot Noir," Betty says. "I love the way you have to treat it, the way you have to be gentle with it." With winemaking help from consultant Christine Leroux, the Masseys offer Pinot Gris, Pinot Noir and Gewürztraminer. Some of the Zweigelt, Merlot and Léon Millot in their three-hectare (7½-acre) vineyard end up in a blend whimsically dubbed Grumpy Old Man.

They were taken by surprise in the summer of 2007 by the crush of visitors to the Hollywood & Wine tasting room. That propelled the decision to dig a wine cellar into a nearby bank, with gravity-flow production and a larger wine shop. Neil also scaled back his hours as a trucker to spend more time on the vineyard tractor and, with Betty, to experiment with products other than table wines. "I would love to have a port of some sort down the road," Betty says.

MY PICKS

The Gewürztraminer and Pinot Gris, superb choices for a Summerland vineyard, are crisp and fresh. The Pinot Noir also has considerable appeal.

OPENED 2007

9819 Lumsden Avenue
Summerland, BC V0H 1Z8
T 250.494.0311
W www.hollywoodandwine.ca

WHEN TO VISIT
Open daily 11 am – 5 pm
July through October,
and by appointment

NEIL AND BETTY MASSEY

HOUSE OF ROSE VINEYARDS

After running this winery for 10 years, Vern Rose began thinking of selling in the 2003 vintage, when he turned 76, because that was one of his toughest summers. The Okanagan Mountain Park forest fire threatened his Rutland neighbourhood three times, forcing evacuation of the winery and sharply curtailing the usual number of visitors. Yet even after such a taxing summer, Vern hoped that a buyer would let him manage the vineyard for five more years. Before a buyer emerged, Vern was incapacitated by a stroke that sapped the energy from one of the wine world's great characters. In 2009 the winery was taken over by his daughter, Aura, and her husband, Wouter van der Hall.

A Saskatchewan native who was born in 1927, Vern acquired his Okanagan vineyard after retiring in 1982 from a career as a school-teacher in Edmonton. A few years later he accomplished his lifelong dream to visit New Zealand. Not one to merely enjoy the sights, he attended a viticultural conference and volunteered at a vineyard. That inspired him to open his winery north of Kelowna. His habit of wearing Tilley hats (a clean one at wine shows, a scruffy one in the vineyard) became his trademark.

He was perhaps the only Okanagan vintner to still back the heritage varieties that most others removed in the 1988 pullout. House of Rose still produces both Okanagan Riesling and De Chaunac in its 2.2-hectare (5½-acre) vineyard, along with Verdelet for icewine and Maréchal Foch, almost the only red hybrid to make a comeback in British Columbia. The vineyard also has Chardonnay and Cabernet Foch. The latter was provided to Vern by Swiss plant breeder Valentin Blattner after the two had become fishing buddies.

Aura, who runs her own health care communications company, became involved with House of Rose in 1996 as the bookkeeper. She and Wouter, a Dutch-born child-welfare consultant, have brought dis-

cipline to the sprawling wine portfolio at House of Rose, with perhaps more focus on the heritage varietals and on Winter Wine, as the trademarked dessert wines are called.

MY PICKS

The Okanagan Riesling is a crisp white with flavours of green apple and citrus. The De Chaunac, which used to be an off-dry red, is worth a second look now that the finish is dry.

OPENED 1993

2270 Garner Road
Kelowna. BC V1P 1E2
T 250.765.0802
W www.houseofrose.ca

WHEN TO VISIT
Open daily 10 am – 6 pm April to October; noon – 6 pm Tuesday through Saturday November to March

VERN ROSE

HOWLING BLUFF ESTATE WINES

In April 2008, nearing his 50th birthday, Luke Smith decided he had juggled two careers long enough. He quit working as a stockbroker, something he had been doing for more than 25 years, to focus on his estate winery. Because he had the resources, he had purchased some of the best winery equipment available, including a $15,000 pump for transferring must from the fermenters.

For the 2008 vintage he retained Chris Carson, a Canadian wine-maker trained in New Zealand—who happens to be a Pinot Noir zealot. Scorning the pump, Chris ordered the very surprised Luke to strip to his underwear, climb into the fermenter and transfer the Pinot Noir gently, a bucket at a time. "That was my introduction to Chris's passion for Pinot Noir," Luke says. "I'm on board now." The experience also changed plans for a future winery. That building now will follow the contour of the hillside so that gravity, not pumps, will move the wine. "I'm trying to make remarkable wine," Luke says.

He began coming to the Okanagan in 2000 to help his friend Paul Gardner develop the vineyard for the Pentâge winery. Three years later, Luke bought a Naramata Bench bed and breakfast on an orchard that soon was transformed into vineyard. A university economics graduate, Luke was unfazed by the challenge of a vineyard and winery. "Every single post put into the vineyard I have touched three times," he says. "I put the irrigation in. There is nothing here that I haven't done." The 15,000 vines include Merlot, Cabernet Sauvignon, Cabernet Franc, Malbec, a little Petit Verdot, Pinot Noir and a single white, Sauvignon Blanc.

The winery's debut 2006 vintage (made by Garron Elmes, the wine-maker at Lake Breeze) included a Pinot Noir that won a Lieutenant Governor's Award of Excellence. When Government House called to tell him of the award, Luke thought for a few moments that his leg was

LUKE SMITH

being pulled. In fact, the award validated his hard work in the vineyard. His 2007 Pinot Noir was even better—but, he says, wait until you taste the 2008!

MY PICKS

The portfolio here is focused: a crisp Sauvignon Blanc, a silken Pinot Noir and a red called Sin Cera. Initially this is a Merlot but it will evolve into a Bordeaux blend as complementary varieties in the vineyard come into production. The Latin name is the root for the word "sincerity," which describes Luke's winemaking goal.

OPENED 2007

1086 Three Mile Road
Penticton, BC V2A 8T7

T 250.490.3640

W www.howlingbluff.ca

WHEN TO VISIT
Open daily 11 am – 5 pm May to October and by appointment

ACCOMMODATION
The Inn at Howling Bluff

HUNTING HAWK VINEYARDS

It is unusual for an entire vineyard to move, but that is what has happened here. It was only 240 vines, along with the posts and the irrigation lines, but it was a move nonetheless that enabled Greg Tippe and Irene Johnson to re-establish Hunting Hawk Vineyards at Salmon Arm after the winery closed its outlet at Vernon's O'Keefe Ranch.

The original Hunting Hawk, now operating as Edge of the Earth Vineyard, was opened in 2002 near Armstrong by Russ Niles. Three years later he leased enough space at the O'Keefe Ranch, a popular tourist attraction, for a wine shop and small vineyard, also operating under the Hunting Hawk name. When the lease expired, Russ sold the business, including the name and the vines, to Greg and Irene, who relocated it to their 2.2-hectare (5½-acre) farm near Salmon Arm. They logged it soon after moving there in 2008. In the spring of 2009 they dug out the vines at the O'Keefe Ranch property—mostly Maréchal Foch and Ortega—and transplanted them successfully. Cuttings from these vines and from Siegerrebe vines (obtained from the nearby Larch Hills winery) are enabling the pair to extend their plantings in 2010.

Born in Vancouver in 1960, Greg is a heavy-equipment operator with a long career in the forests and mines of British Columbia. In Revelstoke, where the couple lived for two decades, Ingrid, a preschool teacher and a licensed esthetician, brought home a wine kit from the local hardware store. After making a few kit wines, Greg moved to fruit wines. Then he joined the Revelstoke Winemakers Guild and began to make wine from grapes. Intrigued, he began looking for an opportunity in the wine business. That came along when Russ put Hunting Hawk on the market.

Greg and Irene were unable to transfer the O'Keefe Ranch winery licence. Having purchased the winery name, however, Greg has been making his wines, starting in the 2008 vintage, with Russ at what is now Edge of the Earth Vineyard. This has enabled him to keep a supply of Hunting Hawk wines in the market while he and Ingrid develop a winery and tasting room of their own.

MY PICKS

Greg says he likes big reds—and the winery's Maréchal Foch is a good example.

OPENED 2009

3171 Lionel Road
Salmon Arm, BC V1E 3J3
T 250.832.3383
W www.huntinghawkvineyards.com

WHEN TO VISIT
Tasting room to be established

INNISKILLIN OKANAGAN VINEYARDS

Sandor Mayer has one of the most enviable jobs among all the wine-makers working for the Vincor group of wineries (which includes Inniskillin). The grapes available to him are the bling in a winemaker's jewel box. In addition to the mainstream varieties, he makes wine for Inniskillin's Discovery Series with Zinfandel, Malbec, Petit Verdot, Tempranillo, Chenin Blanc, Marsanne, Roussanne, Viognier and Grüner Veltliner. The Inniskillin wine shop is a must if you have tired of the "same old, same old." Sandor says that he is offering "different wines for wine enthusiasts and wine lovers . . . but locally grown."

Born in Hungary in 1958, Sandor began making wine with his father when he was 14. After getting a degree in winemaking, he worked with a major research institute there. "In Hungary I was involved in different trials and made wines with many different varieties," he recalls. No winemaking jobs were available when Sandor and Andrea, his wife, came to the Okanagan in 1989, so he took a job replanting what Inniskillin now calls its Dark Horse Vineyard. He ignored advice against planting vinifera and, among other varieties, planted Cabernet Sauvignon. "Cabernet loves this place and I love Cabernet Sauvignon," he says.

The rugged nine-hectare (22-acre) Dark Horse Vineyard is on a hillside just above and behind the winery, easily accessible during any winery tour, except perhaps on very hot days. This is one of the hottest vineyards in the South Okanagan, which is why Cabernet Sauvignon thrives.

The winery itself, although it has been thoroughly updated, is a heritage property. The original owners—the winery has had five sets of owners—tunnelled 11 horizontal wine tanks into the hillside. Perhaps the only buried horizontal tanks in any Canadian winery, they are still in use.

SANDOR MAYER

"We learned how to use them," Sandor says with a chuckle. "They are easy to wash. We have a cooling system inside. They are excellent for malolactic fermentation where the temperature should be more constant. You try to find the advantage in everything."

MY PICKS

All the Discovery Series wines, especially the elegant Zinfandel, the punchy Malbec, the tangy Chenin Blanc and the crisp Marsanne/ Roussanne. Also very fine are the Dark Horse Cabernet Sauvignon, the complex red Meritage and the icewines.

OPENED 1980
(AS VINITERA ESTATE WINERY)

Road 11 West, RR1
Oliver, BC V0H 1T0

T 250.498.6663
   1.800.498.6211 (toll free)

W www.inniskillin.com

WHEN TO VISIT
Open daily 10 am – 5 pm May through October; 10 am – 4 pm Wednesday through Sunday the rest of the year

INTRIGUE WINES

On a flight to the Maritimes for a family vacation, winemaker Roger Wong and his wife, Jillian, were kicking around names for their new winery when someone observed that wine is intriguing. They realized they had found the name for the venture they opened in 2009 with partners Ross and Geri Davis. He owns a Kelowna data centre and she is the controller at Gray Monk Estate Winery.

Roger, who was born in Vancouver in 1965 and has a geography degree, has been intrigued with wine since becoming a home winemaker at 17. When he was 30 he quit a government job to help Tinhorn Creek in the 1995 crush, moving on the next year to the winery's vineyards and cellar. That winery advanced his career, helping him take courses at the University of California. In 1998 Roger took over as winemaker at Pinot Reach Cellars, a Kelowna winery that became Tantalus Vineyards in 2004. In 2005 he moved to Gray Monk to make the red and sparkling wines.

Roger's first independent label was Focus Wines, concentrating on Riesling, a variety he believes is well suited to the North Okanagan. He made the first Focus Riesling in 2002, but the venture stalled after the 2003 forest fires saturated Kelowna vineyards with smoke, ruining the grapes.

The dream was reborn after Roger and Jillian found Ross and Geri to be kindred souls. "We all have the passion," Geri says. On their two properties near Wood Lake (near Oyama), the couples in 2008 planted 6.9 hectares (17 acres) of vines, the majority being Riesling. The winery and tasting room are currently under development at the Davis vineyard. Meanwhile the partners launched Intrigue by purchasing grapes in the 2008 vintage, debuting with 450 cases. The long-term plan is to build production to 10,000 cases.

Crisp and dry, the Riesling is among the best in the Okanagan. The Pinot Gris, fruit-forward but with a hint of oak, is delicious, as is the white blend, Intrigue 8—so called because the number changes with each vintage (9 in 2009, and so on).

OPENED 2009

PO Box 41061 RPOS
Lake Country, BC V4V 1Z7
T 1.877.474.3754 (toll free)
W www.intriguewine.com

WHEN TO VISIT
Tasting room not yet open

GERI AND ROSS DAVIS, AND JILLIAN GARLAND AND
ROGER WONG WITH THEIR SON, GARRETT WONG

JACKSON-TRIGGS VINTNERS

Winery tours are not offered here for a good reason: visitors would get lost amid the towering tanks and stacks of barrels in this sprawling winery. But the elegant hospitality centre, opened in 2006, definitely deserves a visit. Jackson-Triggs has a large portfolio of award-winning wines, many of which can be tasted and purchased here.

The key to all of the awards Jackson-Triggs has won is in its vineyards. Since 1998, Vincor Canada, the parent of Jackson-Triggs, has planted nearly 400 hectares (1,000 acres) of vines, almost all of it either on Black Sage Road or on the Osoyoos Lake Bench. These professionally managed vineyards are among Canada's best.

All of the vineyards produce premium fruit. However, with the experience of several vintages, Jackson-Triggs has been able to pinpoint superior blocks, one of which is now called the SunRock Vineyard. About 40 hectares (100 acres) in size, it lies on a gentle south-facing slope near the north shore of Osoyoos Lake. The defining feature, and the genesis of the name, is a massive cliff at the northern end of the vineyard. It captures the sun during the day, giving the vineyard the hot microclimate preferred by Shiraz and Cabernet Sauvignon vines. A 2004 vintage SunRock Shiraz whipped a tough field of Australian and other New World wines to be judged the best of variety at the 2006 International Wine & Spirits Competition.

The red wine maker at Jackson-Triggs Okanagan is Brooke Blair, who came here in 2004. Born in 1978 at Mount Gambier in Australia, she trained at the University of Adelaide, starting out in commerce before switching to wine, in part because winemakers get to travel. Her favourite grape variety? "I love working with Shiraz," she confides.

The white wines are made by Derek Kontkanen. Born in Midland, Ontario, in 1978, he has a master's degree in enology. His thesis was on icewine fermentation and it shows in the focused purity of the Jackson-Triggs Riesling icewines.

DEREK KONTKANEN AND BROOKE BLAIR (PHOTO BY STUART BISH)

MY PICKS

The top wines from Jackson-Triggs are the gold-label wines (Proprietors' Grand Reserve) and the single vineyard reserves (notably the SunRock label). My favourite reds include Shiraz, Merlot, red Meritage and Cabernet/Shiraz blends. My favourite whites include the Viognier, the Sauvignon Blanc, the Chardonnay and the Riesling. The sparkling icewine is a tour de force for special occasions.

OPENED 1981
(AS BRIGHTS WINES)

38691 Highway 97 North
Oliver, BC V0H 1T0

T   250.498.4500
    1.866.455.0559 (toll free)

W www.jacksontriggswinery.com

WHEN TO VISIT
Open daily 10 am – 6 pm April 2 to October 31 and 10 am – 4 pm November through March. Winery tours by appointment only.

JOIEFARM

According to conventional wisdom, aromatic whites made with Germanic grapes are unfashionable, and hardly anybody drinks rosé wines. Contrarians Michael Dinn and Heidi Noble, the owners of JoieFarm, beg to differ. These were exactly the wines they made in 2004, their first vintage. The 840 cases they released on April 1, 2005, sold out within weeks; the 140 cases of Pinot Noir rosé were snapped up in seven days. After one of the most successful BC winery launches, they produced about 10,000 cases (28 percent was rosé) by their fifth vintage. "That's as big as we're going to get," Michael promises.

When they started their winery, the couple knew everything about wine except how to make it. They repaired that shortcoming cleverly by mentoring with established Okanagan winemakers, including Pentâge's Paul Gardner. Michael, born in Victoria in 1967, is a history major who started serving in restaurants when he was in university. His 14-year career as a server and sommelier in top Vancouver restaurants inspired a burning ambition to make wine in the Okanagan. Heidi, born in Toronto in 1974, began cooking at 14. She has degrees in philosophy and literature but turned down an academic scholarship to attend a chefs school. Like Michael, she also worked in a top Vancouver restaurant. The couple met when she enrolled in a sommelier program. By 2001, when they married, both were working for wine agencies and refining their palates. "If you don't know what good wine tastes like, how can you achieve it?" Michael asks.

The wines have always reflected their taste for the wines of Alsace and Burgundy—"genuine passions of ours," Heidi says. For example, the Gewürztraminer-based wine they call A Noble Blend is inspired by the Edelzwicker blends of Alsace. They started with three varieties in the debut Noble Blend but have increased that to six, making a much more refined and complex wine. There has been a similar rising trajectory of quality across their entire portfolio.

In 2007 Michael and Heidi built a winery of their own, setting it amid a new Naramata Bench vineyard with just under a hectare entirely devoted to Moscato Giallo, supporting the delicate Muscat wine that has become another signature of JoieFarm.

OPENED 2004

2825 Naramata Road
Naramata, BC V0H 1N0

T   250.496.0073
    1.866.422.5643 (toll free)

W   www.joie.ca

WHEN TO VISIT
No tasting room or wine shop

MY PICKS

Every Joie wine is quite simply delicious, with clean, fresh fruit flavours and vivid aromas. Even when a wine has a trace of residual sugar, the wine is so well balanced with acidity that one perceives a dry finish. Almost without exception, alcohol levels do not exceed 13 percent; Michael and Heidi believe wine should be enjoyed without flirting with inebriation.

MICHAEL DINN AND HEIDI NOBLE
(PHOTO BY CRAIG NOBLE)

K MOUNTAIN VINEYARDS

This property gives the Holman Lang group, which has all its other wineries on the Naramata Bench, a strategic foothold in the Similkameen Valley.

In 2008 Keith Holman purchased a popular organic fruit stand on the main street of Keremeos, adding a tasting room, a small winery and a small vineyard. This is the first winery encountered by anyone motoring to the Similkameen or Okanagan valleys on Highway 3 (also known as the Crowsnest Highway). The winery provides an additional attraction to those stopping at one or more of the town's many fruit stands.

Originally Keith was going to call this the Red Bridge Winery, after a famous Keremeos landmark, until he was reminded that the Orofino Winery at nearby Cawston already had registered a wine under the Red Bridge label. So Keith looked around and spotted an even more prominent landmark: K Mountain, which looms above Keremeos. Long debris slides on the mountainside resemble a gigantic letter "K"—hence the mountain's name. Keith jokes that he has the biggest winery sign in the industry.

In the winery's initial years, K Mountain's portfolio has remained small and focused. The whites include an unusual aromatic blend called Proprietor's Reserve: Schönburger, Gewürztraminer, Pinot Blanc, Auxerrois and Chardonnay. The reds include an easy-drinking Merlot and a soft Syrah.

MY PICKS

Current range not tasted.

OPENED 2008

3045 Highway 3
Keremeos, BC V0X 1N1

T 250.499.7052

W www.holmanlangwineries.com

WHEN TO VISIT
Open seasonally. Please call
for hours.

KALALA ORGANIC ESTATE WINERY

Kalala is the town in the Punjab where Karnail Singh Sidhu, this winery's owner, was born in 1968. Translated, Kalala means "miracle place," and Karnail honours this on the winery's labels, which show a wolf and lamb with their heads together affectionately. Legend has it that these animals lived in harmony at this place in the Punjab. To Karnail, the Okanagan has comparable serenity. On the back label of the wines, he points out that the winery's "organic grapes are grown in harmony with their environment and nature's elements."

When Karnail came to Canada in 1993, his diploma in electrical engineering was not recognized, so he turned to his 25 years' experience as a farmer for work in the Okanagan. In 1996 he joined the pruning crew at the Summerhill Pyramid Winery. That was the beginning of a 10-year career there during which he emerged as a leader in organic viticulture in the Okanagan. The company he set up in 1997 with two brothers, Kalala Agriculture, has provided supplies and expertise for the emerging number of organic grape growers in the valley. One of the growers he mentored, Dave Dhillon, opened Chandra, also an organic winery, near Oliver in 2008.

Karnail's winery, which is seeking organic certification, gets fruit from his organic vineyards at Westbank and near Oliver in the South Okanagan. The south-facing Westbank property, one of the highest-elevation vineyards in this part of the Okanagan, is well suited to the cool-climate varieties planted here, including Pinot Noir, Pinot Gris and Gewürztraminer. Karnail also has a significant planting of Zweigelt, an Austrian red that does well in many terroirs. At Kalala, the variety supports both table wines and a full-flavoured icewine.

KARNAIL SINGH SIDHU

MY PICKS

The Pinot Gris, the
Riesling and the
Gewürztraminer are
refreshing whites. The
Merlot, the Pinot Noir and
the Zweigelt, although
aged in barrels, show
attractive fruit flavours
that are not submerged
in oak. Perhaps the most
robust red is Cuvée Noir,
made by blending a
rustic Russian red called
Michurinetz with Zweigelt
and Blaufränkisch
(no wonder it has a
proprietary name!). Wine
prices here are affordable.

OPENED 2008

3361 Glencoe Road
West Kelowna, BC V4T 1M1

T   250.768.9700
    1.866.942.1313 (toll free)

W www.kalalawines.ca

WHEN TO VISIT
Open daily 10 am – 6 pm
April through October, 11 am –
5 pm Wednesday to Sunday
November through March

KETTLE VALLEY WINERY

When they launched Kettle Valley, chartered accountant Bob Ferguson and geologist Tim Watts intended to limit production to three wines: Chardonnay, Pinot Noir and a Bordeaux blend called Old Main Red (named for their Naramata vineyard where the grapes grow). They also believed they would never make more than 5,000 cases a year. Yet today the winery makes about 11,000 cases a year and has almost 30 wines in its portfolio.

What happened? It seems that the partners, former home winemakers who met when they married sisters, seldom refuse well-grown grapes. Meticulous growers in Kettle Valley's own vineyards, Bob and Tim also started buying additional grapes from growers prepared to adhere to their vineyard disciplines. Varieties such as Pinot Gris, Sauvignon Blanc and Schönburger were not in Kettle Valley's original plans, but the partners hesitate to let well-grown fruit go to competitors. "If we work with growers to get the grapes we want, we don't want them doing the same things to the other grapes—and then sending them off to some-body else," Tim explains.

Bob and Tim grow superbly ripe, full-flavoured grapes for their remarkably intense wines. The red grapes are given prolonged skin contact during fermentation. "We spend a lot of time in the vineyard, making sure those skins have a lot of flavour in them," Tim says. "We like to get that out."

The partners often make single-vineyard wines in limited volume. For example, the individual flavours of the superbly ripe Merlot from their McGraw Estate Vineyard in Naramata are highlighted in vineyard-designated wine. In the 2006 vintage only 225 cases were released. One of Kettle Valley's best Pinot Noirs is grown in the Hayman Vineyard, which the partners planted in 1988. Only 80 cases were made in 2006. Now that Kettle Valley has begun getting Similkameen Valley grapes, both from a grower and from the winery's own young planting of

TIM WATTS AND BOB FERGUSON

OLD MAIN VINEYARD

Syrah and Viognier, the partners have kept some Similkameen wines separate from their Okanagan wines.

"In the long term, we expect them to be significantly different in taste," Tim says. "It may turn out to be quite advantageous to have another suite of flavours or characteristics we can use for blending. We will do whatever results in a better wine."

MY PICKS

Old Main Red is a seamless blend of Merlot, Cabernet Sauvignon and Cabernet Franc, touched up with a dash each of Malbec and Petit Verdot. The winery's first-rate Pinot Noirs age like fine Burgundies. The other reds, notably the Merlots, the Malbec and the Shiraz, are bold and rich. In recent vintages the whites have been made in a style that is fresher and more appealing than before. Look for the Gewürztraminer, the Viognier, the Sauvignon Blanc and the Pinot Gris.

OPENED 1996

2988 Hayman Road
RR1 Site 2 Comp 39
Naramata, BC V0H 1N0

T 250.496.5898
  1.888.496.8757 (toll free)

W www.kettlevalleywinery.com

WHEN TO VISIT
Open daily 11 am – 5 pm
May to mid-October, and by
appointment. Groups of more
than eight should book an
appointment.

KRĀZĒ LEGZ VINEYARD AND WINERY

Considering how many wineries have sprung up in the Okanagan over the past decade, it is surprising that none opened at picturesque Kaleden until 2010, when Susan and Gerry Thygesen launched Krāzē Legz (pronounced "crazy legs"). After all, Kaleden was laid out in 1909 and, according to *A Traveller's Guide to Historic British Columbia* (Whitecap Books, 2009), the town's name celebrates the site's pastoral beauty. The name combines the first syllable of *kalos*, Greek for "beautiful," with "Eden."

The Thygesens found their 5.6-hectare (14-acre) patch of Eden in 1995 when they bought an apple and peach orchard with an enchanting view of Skaha Lake. They removed the apple trees so that Susan, an equestrian, could keep horses. However, they did not plant vines until 2007 because they were busy with other careers.

Gerry, who was born in Bonnyville, Alberta, in 1957, came to the Okanagan in 1973 to play junior hockey in Penticton. A hockey scholarship took him to St. Lawrence University in upstate New York where he majored in biology and decided against a hockey career. He came back to Penticton in 1980, married Susan (who is from Golden) and joined Okanagan Dried Fruits, helping to make its fruit leathers for major national brands. In 1996 he took this experience to a similar company, Stretch Island Fruit Company in Seattle. Over the following 10 years, he completed a marketing degree at the University of Seattle and was a marketing vice-president at Stretch Island and two other food companies. Susan leveraged her knowledge of horses to become an equine photographer.

They moved back to their personal Eden in 2006 to open this winery, planting Merlot, Cabernet Franc, Chardonnay and Pinot Blanc. They were mentored by neighbouring grape grower Chris Scott, the former head of Okanagan Dried Fruits and a long-time friend of Gerry's. When the vineyard yielded its first harvest in 2009, the Thygesens sold some of the Merlot but kept enough fruit to produce about 900 cases, with the help of a consulting winemaker.

The winery's whimsical name is meant to suggest the "legs" formed on the inside of a wine glass after the wine is swirled. The labels depict a keyhole in a 1920s speakeasy, with dancers seen through the keyhole. The wines are named for such period dances as the Charleston. "While we take our grape growing and wine crafting very seriously, ourselves not so much so," Gerry says. "You're going to get a good bottle of wine when you open one of our bottles, but there is nothing snooty about what we do."

MY PICKS

No wines were available as this book went to press.

OPENED 2010

141 Fir Avenue
Kaleden. BC V0H 1K0

T 250.497.6957

W www.krazelegz.com

WHEN TO VISIT
Daily 10 am – 6 pm May through early October. and by appointment

GERRY AND SUSAN THYGESEN
(PHOTO COURTESY OF KRĀZĒ LEGZ)

LA FRENZ WINERY

The La Frenz tasting room, a squat building with a corrugated roof, is striking and unusual for the Okanagan because it resembles a farm building in the Australian outback. It is a memory of home for winery owners Jeff and Niva Martin, Australians who have lived in the Okanagan since 1994, when Jeff became the winemaker at Quails' Gate. Jeff grew up in Griffith, the wine farming town that is home to McWilliam's, one of Australia's largest family-owned wineries. Jeff joined McWilliam's in 1977 when he was 20, found time to get a winemaking degree and then rose to senior winemaker before coming to Canada.

He put Quails' Gate on the map and he has done the same at La Frenz, where the wines always show elegance and finesse. "I have come to the opinion [that] there is just no place for average wine," he says. "Why would I want to do average? It's way easier to sell the better wines."

Jeff and Niva established La Frenz (the winery's name comes from his grandfather's surname) on busy Naramata Road, converting an apple orchard to 2.5 hectares (six acres) of vines in 2002. Since then they have planted or contracted vineyards in strategic locations on the Naramata Bench or in the South Okanagan. The aptly named Rockyfella Vineyard south of Oliver is a sun-baked, rock-strewn site planted in 2006 with late-ripening Bordeaux reds, supporting an expanded production of La Frenz Reserve and other red blends.

Like so many other winemakers, however, Jeff cannot resist the challenge of Pinot Noir, which was one of the signature wines at Quails' Gate. In 2008 Jeff and Niva converted another two-hectare (five-acre) Naramata orchard entirely to Pinot Noir, planting five different clones. This gives him two sources of Pinot Noir on the Naramata Bench, one of the best terroirs for this variety.

To give himself more time in his vineyards, Jeff recruited a second winemaker for La Frenz in the spring of 2009. Vancouver-born Scott Robinson, initially trained in kinesthesiology, designed knee braces and

NIVA AND JEFF MARTIN

orthopedic devices before switching in 2005 to the cellar at Township 7 Winery. After three vintages there and one in New Zealand, he got a master's degree in enology at the University of Adelaide. He was ecstatic to be recruited by La Frenz. "This is a place in which I really wanted to work," he says.

OPENED 2000

740 Naramata Road
Penticton, BC V2A 8T5
T 250.492.6690
W www.lafrenzwinery.com

WHEN TO VISIT
Open daily 10 am – 5 pm
May through October,
or by appointment

MY PICKS

They're Australians, mate, so naturally Jeff and Niva know how to make terrific Shiraz. The La Frenz Reserve is a powerful Bordeaux blend that should be in every collector's cellar, probably alongside the tasty Merlot and the elegant Pinot Noir. Jeff also makes tasty Chardonnay, Viognier, Sémillon, Sauvignon Blanc, a fine off-dry Muscat called Alexandria, and two first-rate fortified wines.

LAKE BREEZE VINEYARDS

Lake Breeze was the first Canadian winery to make Pinotage, South Africa's iconic red variety. The vines were brought to the Lake Breeze property by the winery's original owner, a former South African businessman named Paul Moser. He also recruited a young South African winemaker, Garron Elmes, and built a neat white winery with a design straight from the Cape. The winery has changed ownership twice since then, but has not lost its South African character. Garron continues to make the wines, including a Pinotage of ever more impressive quality as the vines mature. The quantity is only 125 cases a year (sometimes less) because the Pinotage block occupies such a small area in the seven-hectare (17-acre) vineyard.

The current owners are two Alberta couples with a passion for wine and with strong financial backgrounds. Gary Reynolds, born in Montreal in 1955, has given up his day job as an accountant to manage the winery. Tracey Ball, his wife, is chief financial officer of Canadian Western Bank. Drew MacIntyre is a Calgary investment banker, and his wife, Barbara, is an accountant. "We should be able to figure things out," Gary says with a laugh.

Lake Breeze is justly renowned for its white wines, which account for about two-thirds of its total annual production of 9,000 cases. The major variety in the vineyard is Pinot Blanc; one of its rarest whites is Sémillon, a wine with a dramatic herbal aroma and grapefruit flavour. Beginning with the 2008 vintage Garron began making an affordable crowd-pleaser called Bench White, an aromatic blend of unoaked Chardonnay, Viognier, Gewürztraminer and Sauvignon Blanc. A Bench Red is sure to follow.

The winery's refined Chardonnay and its top red wines, including Merlot, Pinot Noir, Pinotage and a Bordeaux blend called Tempest, are released under the premium Seven Poplars label, inspired by the stately poplars shading the patio restaurant.

GARRON ELMES

MY PICKS

Bench White is a perfect patio wine. Other favourites include the tangy Sémillon, the zesty Sauvignon Blanc, the refreshing Pinot Gris, the peachy Ehrenfelser, the spicy Gewurztraminer, the juicy Pinot Blanc and the full-bodied rosé. Look for the Seven Poplars Pinotage (tasting of vanilla, cherries and chocolate), the satisfying Merlot and the increasingly finessed Pinot Noir.

OPENED 1996

930 Sammet Road
PO Box 9
Naramata, BC V0H 1N0
T 250.496.5659
W www.lakebreeze.ca

WHEN TO VISIT
Open daily 11 am – 5:30 pm May to October; noon – 4 pm Friday through Sunday in April. Winter visits by appointment.

RESTAURANT
The Patio
Open daily for lunch May through mid-October. Reservations recommended.
T 250.496.5619

ACCOMMODATION
The Artist's View Cottage (unavailable in 2010)

LANG VINEYARDS

One of the original Naramata Bench wineries, Lang Vineyards was acquired in 2005 by Holman Farms, the owner of a cluster of Naramata wineries. The one obvious change is the significantly enlarged tasting room, providing much-needed elbow room in one of the most popular wineries on the tour. Perched high above Naramata Road, this winery offers some of the best views of the Naramata Bench.

German-born Günther and Kristina Lang did not even have a winery in mind in 1981 when they bought this four-hectare (10-acre) property for the beauty of the site. It just happened to come with a vineyard. Nine years later they opened their winery, which looks over vines that grow on the sort of slope one usually sees in the best sites along the Rhine. The vines included some of the oldest Riesling plantings on the Naramata Bench.

Throughout much of Lang Vineyards' history, the winemakers have been German-trained, latterly including Bernhard Schirrmeister, head winemaker for the Holman Lang group until he left in early 2010. As a result Lang has always offered a range of toothsome Rieslings, from icewine and late-harvest to dry table wines.

Traditionally the Lang wines have been fruit-driven wines pristinely made in stainless steel, for Günther (no longer active with the winery) was no great fan of barrels. The exception was the Soaring Eagle brand, oak-aged premium wines that were created for Lang by winemaker Ross Mirko before he moved to New Zealand in 2005. The brand was so successful that it was transformed into a winery of its own in 2006. This returned Lang to its historic focus. It is the only winery in the Holman Lang group that makes Riesling because, as Bernhard once pointed out, "Lang is known for Riesling."

I like dry Rieslings and there are few better ones in the Okanagan than Lang's citrusy, herbal Farm Reserve Riesling. Lang's Maréchal Foch and both the red and white Grand Pinot blends have a strong following.

OPENED 1990

2493 Gammon Road
Naramata, BC V0H 1N1
T 250.496.5987
W www.langvineyards.com

WHEN TO VISIT
Open daily 10 am – 6 pm May to October. Off-season hours vary; please call for times.

LARCH HILLS WINERY

Jack and Hazel Manser made two tours of the Okanagan before buying Larch Hills in mid-2005, a vineyard just beyond the northern end of the Okanagan Valley. "I like a green country," Jack says, explaining why they chose not to settle in the desert landscape of the South Okanagan. Born in eastern Switzerland in 1957, Jack had a 20-year career there as a forester before coming to Canada in 1992. When he could not get a visa to work here as a forester, he bought a small mixed farm in Alberta. When that generated only a modest living, he looked around for an agriculture business with more potential and settled on wine growing.

At 700 metres (2,300 feet) Larch Hills is the highest-elevation vineyard in British Columbia. The non-irrigated five-hectare (12-acre) vineyard was planted by Hans and Hazel Nevrkla. Like the Mansers, they settled on this heavily forested property because of its verdant richness. After clearing some of the south-facing slope, Austrian-born Hans, a prize-winning home winemaker, succeeded as a professional vintner with early ripening varieties chosen to suit this northern location. The three primary white varieties in the vineyard are Ortega, Siegerrebe and Madeleine Angevine. After selling in order to retire, Hans Nevrkla agreed to tutor Jack in winemaking through several vintages. "Hans made really nice wines," Jack says. "And he kept really precise records of what he did."

Jack realizes that managing the vineyard is the easy part of owning a winery. "Driving a tractor is nothing new to me. In forestry I planted thousands and thousands of trees. Putting a plant in the ground does not scare me." In fact he increased the vineyard's plantings of Ortega and Madeleine Angevine. The slope still has more than 25 hectares (62 acres) of land with vineyard potential, provided the forest is cleared.

HAZEL AND JACK MANSER

MY PICKS

The dry Ortega, crisp and fruity, is one of British Columbia's best examples of this variety. Other favourites in this cheery tasting room include the vivid Siegerrebe, the whimsically named Mad Angie (who can get their tongue around Madeleine Angevine?) and Tamarack Rosé. The rosé, a blend of St. Laurent and Lemberger grapes, is a fruity wine smelling of rose petals and tasting of cherries, and is superb summertime picnic fare. Purchased grapes enable the winery to produce good reds with Lemberger, Merlot and Maréchal Foch. Those three varietals also are blended into the winery's big red, called Grandview Bench.

OPENED 1997

110 Timms Road
Salmon Arm, BC V1E 2P8

T 250.832.0155
1.877.892.0155 (toll free)

W www.larchhillswinery.com

WHEN TO VISIT
Open daily 9 am – 5 pm; check road conditions in winter

LASTELLA

This winery has atmosphere to spare. The name, LaStella, was inspired by the twinkling constellations in the clear night sky of the South Okanagan. The wines take their names from Latin musical terms (a former partner was a classical music lover). The secluded Tuscan-style building is nestled at the bottom of a vineyard with 122 metres (400 feet) fronting on Osoyoos Lake. Sean Salem, who owns the winery with wife Saeedeh, becomes lyrical when speaking of the bird songs he has heard while relaxing here.

LaStella and its sister winery, Le Vieux Pin near Oliver, are operated by Enotecca Wineries and Resorts, the Vancouver holding company set up by the Salems to make Okanagan wine. LaStella is meant to have a certain Italian style, with Italian varietals such as Sangiovese in its vineyard. Winemaker Daniel Bontorin was born in Surrey in 1976, but he has dual citizenship and took advantage of that to make a vintage in Italy in 2005, where he has family.

The LaStella wines are among the most intense in the Okanagan, due largely to the extreme viticulture here. The vines are irrigated sparingly to get them producing low tonnages of grapes that are small and packed with flavour. Daniel may make the red wines even more concentrated by draining off a small portion of the juice for rosé. And the rosé wines have lots of personality too.

The result? Wines like the Merlot-based Maestoso; in one recent vintage, the grapes were so ripe that the wine had 15.3 percent alcohol. It also had such luscious flavour that the alcoholic muscle was not noticeable.

MY PICKS

Maestoso is one of the Okanagan's most expensive red wines but also one of the most memorable. Other delicious reds include Allegretto (a Merlot), Fortissimo (a Tuscany-inspired blend) and La Sophia (Cabernet Sauvignon). Rounding out the portfolio are Vivace (Pinot Gris), Leggiero (unoaked Chardonnay) and LaStellina (a Merlot rosé). The vintage dates of all wines are expressed in Roman numerals, underlining the Tuscan theme.

OPENED 2008

8123 148th Avenue
Osoyoos, BC V0H 1V0
T 250.495.8180
W www.lastella.ca

WHEN TO VISIT
By appointment 11 am – 5 pm
Tuesday to Saturday

FOOD SERVICE
Licensed patio

DANIEL BONTORIN

LAUGHING STOCK VINEYARDS

The quality of the wine at Laughing Stock is dead serious. So why the name? Proprietors David and Cynthia Enns are poking fun at themselves: they were successful financial consultants before opening the winery, and some of their friends questioned the wisdom of their career change.

Born in 1957, David grew up in Kelowna but developed an interest in wine by collecting European and California wines. After a tour of Washington wineries in 2001, David impetuously bought a truckload of grapes to make wine at his Vancouver home. When it succeeded, David and Cynthia moved their consulting business (now sold) to wine country in 2003, purchasing vineyard property near Naramata. Two years later they built a gravity-flow winery at the top of the vineyard with one of the Naramata Bench's million-dollar views. The winery has "best in class" equipment that includes a grape-sorting table, the mark of truly conscientious winemaking.

Having been consultants, the couple knew how to tap the expertise they needed as wine growers. A professional viticulturist showed David how to grow grapes. For winemaking he struck a hands-on mentorship deal with Ian Sutherland of nearby Poplar Grove, one of the Okanagan's best winemakers. "I didn't want to hire a fly-in consultant," David says. "I really wanted to learn the industry from the ground up."

This is a smart couple (Cynthia has an MBA) who make good wines and sell them creatively. Portfolio, the winery's flagship red blend, comes in bottles encircled with ticker tape showing the trading value of certain shares on the days when the grapes were picked. During the sickening stock market crash of 2009, David and Cynthia offered refunds on the first 300 cases of Portfolio 2007 if the market slid further by the time the wine was delivered to buyers. The offer generated a lot of chatter, but, happily for everyone, the market recovered.

DAVID ENNS

MY PICKS

Portfolio has justifiably had a cult following since its first vintage, in 2003. As new plantings have matured, the Portfolio blend becomes ever richer and more complex. Its solid little brother is called Blind Trust. Laughing Stock also has terrific Chardonnay and Pinot Gris, and David has been working on Syrah.

OPENED 2005

1548 Naramata Road
Penticton, BC V2A 8T7
T 250.493.8466
W www.laughingstock.ca

WHEN TO VISIT
Open 11 am – 5 pm Wednesday
through Sunday from May to
October, and by appointment

LE VIEUX PIN

The Robert Mackenzie—designed winery at Le Vieux Pin is said to resemble a small French railroad station with its drooping overhang of a roof, which shades the walls from the blistering Okanagan sun. Its French name was inspired by the old pine tree on the ridge overlooking the nearby town of Oliver. The compact winery is designed to produce no more than 3,500 cases a year, for the owners believe it would be difficult to handcraft quality wines at much larger volumes. LaStella, its sister winery, is built for a similar capacity. Both are owned by Enotecca Winery and Resorts of Vancouver.

Enotecca acquired vineyards of its own as well as working with select growers. Sean Salem, who owns Enotecca with his wife, Saeedeh, says, "Because we had such a small volume of production, I could not believe that we would not have our own vineyards. Then we would have our own way of growing grapes. That would allow us to keep the quality where it is today."

Le Vieux Pin's four-hectare (10-acre) property, a former orchard, was planted in 2005, chiefly with Syrah, along with a small plot of Viognier. Recently the winery has added Marsanne and Roussanne vines. As these vines come into production, Le Vieux Pin is converting its portfolio to Rhône varietals. In its initial vintages, this winery's reputation was built with Sauvignon Blanc and Pinot Noir. The final Pinot Noir vintage was 2008. Some of those vines were then grafted over to Syrah. Meanwhile winemaker James Cambridge produced rich, concentrated Syrahs in 2008 with grapes purchased from growers on Black Sage Road. The only Pinot Noir still in the line is the very popular rosé, Vaïla, named for a former vineyard manager's daughter.

The winery has also changed its labels, phasing out such labels as Belle and Périgée (both Pinot Noirs) and Époque and Apogée (both Merlots). For the most part the new releases highlight the varietal name on the labels. Initial prices were aggressive (but justified by the quality of the wines), but the winery has now created a second label, Petit Le Vieux Pin, for value-priced wines.

MY PICKS

The Syrahs here are first-rate. So are the rosé wines—Vaïla and a Syrah rosé released as Petit Le Vieux Pin Sigma Rosé. Sigma means "sum of the parts"; thus the delicious Sigma Blanc is an enigmatic blend of Viognier, Pinot Gris, Sauvignon Blanc and Gewürztraminer.

OPENED 2006

34070 73rd Street and Black Sage Road
Oliver, BC V0H 1T0

T   250.498.8388

W   www.enotecca.ca
www.levieuxpin.ca

WHEN TO VISIT
Open daily 11 am – 5 pm;
appointments recommended

PICNIC PATIO

JAMES CAMBRIDGE

LITTLE STRAW VINEYARDS

Some wineries have given up trying to break down consumer resistance to Pinot Auxerrois, a resistance likely based in its obscure pronunciation, since the grape produces excellent white wines. (It is pronounced OX-er-wah.) Peter Slamka, the winemaker at family-owned Little Straw, remains an Auxerrois stalwart.

The gnarled plants at the top of Little Straw's six-hectare (15-acre) vineyard are Auxerrois vines that were imported from Europe in the 1970s. These provide the grapes for the winery's Old Vines Auxerrois. Peter also has a younger, but still mature, Auxerrois planting for a very special icewine described as "crème brûlée in a glass." These wines are available primarily in the winery where, Peter has found, resistance melts away when the wines are tasted.

The vineyard was established in 1969 by Peter's father, Joe, a machinist who came to Canada in 1948 from what was then Czechoslovakia. The family—Peter, who was born in 1954, has two younger brothers—began planning their own winery after farm gate winery licences were created in 1989. The winery opened in 1996 after Peter had spent nearly a year touring wine regions around the world. In 2004 the winery changed its name to Little Straw, a direct translation of Slamka from the Slovak language.

The current two-level winery, replacing the remodelled farm building that served Peter through a dozen vintages, opened in 2006. "I don't mind working hard, but I don't like hard work," he quipped as he moved into the new winery, which has lots of elbow room. The tasting room is spacious. A second-floor mezzanine, after serving briefly as an art gallery, has become a popular lounge where visitors can enjoy food, wine and great views of the Okanagan.

The choices in the wine shop, besides Auxerrois, include Viognier, Sauvignon Blanc, Riesling, Pinot Noir, Syrah and Maréchal Foch. Beginning in the 2007 vintage, Peter fermented a number of red vari-

PETER SLAMKA

eties together to produce a blend that he proposes to release as La Petite Paille (French for "little straw"). When he has time, Peter prefers to be meeting visitors in the tasting room. "To me, that's the best part of the business," he says. "I like being out front, selling wine."

MY PICKS

The medal-winning Sauvignon Blanc is one of Little Straw's most exciting white wines, rivalling the Viognier and the Auxerrois. The Pinot Noir is always reliable. The Syrah is a surprise—not because it is good, although it is, but because it is surprising to find this varietal so far north in the Okanagan.

OPENED 1996
(AS SLAMKA CELLARS)

2815 Ourtoland Road
West Kelowna, BC V1Z 2H7
T 250.769.0404.
W www.littlestraw.bc.ca

WHEN TO VISIT
Open daily 10 am – 5:30 pm
April through October

FOOD SERVICE
The Barrel Top Lounge
Open daily noon – 4 pm during
high season

MARICHEL VINEYARD

For viewing the extraordinary beauty of the Naramata Bench, few places are better than Richard and Elisabeth Roskell's home, overlooking the three hectares (7½ acres) of Syrah and Viognier vines they have planted since 2000. The sculptured vineyard dips sharply down a slope, pauses for a rise, resumes on the top of the rise and then disappears toward the lake. Richard, an excellent photographer, has posted his calendar-quality images of the vineyard on the winery's website.

The Roskells acquired this magical property after several years of searching Okanagan properties. It belonged to a pair of absentee German investors who were estranged from each other. The Roskells sent several purchase offers to their agent in British Columbia without getting a reply. So Elisabeth, who was born in Germany, worked her way through German telephone listings until she located the reclusive owners. After six months of difficult negotiation, the Roskells finally bought the property late in 1999 and began their career changes to become wine growers.

Elisabeth is the former owner of a dental laboratory. Richard, born in North Vancouver in 1952, was an Air Canada pilot until retiring early in 2005, fed up with jet lag. "The thought of doing another seven years of long-haul flying did not appeal to me," he says. "I really wanted to stretch out into something different."

A niche producer, Marichel (an amalgam of several family names) makes only Syrah and Viognier. "I'll be surprised if we ever make it to 1,000 cases a year," Richard said in his first year. The wines were so well received that in his second year he said that Marichel would expand "all the way up to 1,000 cases [but] we are not going to get big. We are going to stay personally focused on the vineyard and in the winery, and we will stay faithful to the terroir it comes from, and that will be the Naramata Bench."

ELISABETH AND RICHARD ROSKELL

MY PICKS

The Viognier is vibrantly fresh while the Syrah is rich and peppery, with a concentration that reflects Richard's decision to keep his tonnages low.

OPENED 2007

1016 Littlejohn Road
Naramata, BC V0H 1N0
T 250.496.4133
W www.marichel.ca

WHEN TO VISIT
By appointment

MEADOW VISTA HONEY WINES

Think of a bee foraging busily from blossom to blossom and you have an idea of Judie Barta's energetic entrepreneurship. Born in Coburg, Ontario, in 1971, she started her first business, a boat cleaning company in Belleville, when she was 19. She re-created the company in Kelowna in 2006 and ran it successfully for three years before selling it to open the meadery. In between stints polishing yachts, she became a wine consultant as well as a massage therapist and the operator of a Kelowna spa and wellness centre. *And* this self-described Queen Bee has raised two daughters.

Judie came to wine through a job at the wine bar at the Banff Springs Hotel, after having moved to Banff to ski. From there, she worked with several wine agencies and wine stores in Victoria and Calgary; she spent two years in the early 1990s selling wine for Sumac Ridge Estate Winery.

Although she has sketched out two exciting concepts for wineries making grape wines, she judged that there may be a glut of such wineries at this time. Meadow Vista stands out at the Okanagan's first honey winery and one of only four meaderies in British Columbia. "I am entering the market with products that are different," Judie says. For example, Joy is the first sparkling honey wine in the Okanagan made in the traditional method. The wines are all made with organic honey, and because honey has its own preservative properties, the wines are all sulphur free, a boon to consumers sensitive to sulphur, a common wine preservative.

Although she has made small lots of mead since 2002, Judie leaves Meadow Vista's winemaking to Alan Marks. He has a doctorate in the chemistry of sparkling wine and, after starting his career at a Missouri winery, has been a winemaker and consultant in the Okanagan since 1994.

MY PICKS

Don't come looking for a lot of sweet wines. Except for Libra, a dessert wine made with apricots and honey, the wines are dry and food-friendly. Joy, the sparkling wine, is crisp and fruity. Mabon is an exotic and tasty honey wine, flavoured with coriander, cinnamon, cardamom and nutmeg.

OPENED 2009

2229 Sunview Drive
West Kelowna, BC V1Z 4V9
T 250.769.2337
W www.meadowvista.ca

WHEN TO VISIT
Tasting room under
development

JUDIE BARTA

MEYER FAMILY VINEYARDS

Okanagan real estate developer John Meyer (who goes by JAK) jokes that, when he was a stockbroker, he learned to identify good wines by "right-hand-column ordering." That's the column on a wine list with the prices. JAK would run his eye down the column until he spied the expensive bottles, and he would order one of those. His wine knowledge was much more nuanced by the time he and his wife, Janice Stevens, opened Meyer Family Vineyards. However, it is probably no coincidence that, when the winery released its debut Chardonnay wines, one had a price designed to hook the right-hand-column orders, matched with a quality to keep the orders coming.

The winery was conceived in 2004 while JAK, who was born in Calgary in 1958, and Vancouver wine educator James Cluer were discussing their shared passion over a beer. James agreed to mentor him. JAK, after a two-year property search, bought a 1.4-hectare (3½-acre) Naramata Bench vineyard planted with 10-year-old Chardonnay. With these grapes, Road 13 winemaker Michael Bartier produced two vintages of elegantly finessed Chardonnay (2006 and 2007).

The wines were so well received that in 2008 JAK hired his own winemaker, Edmonton-born Christopher Carson, whose wine interest was fired in 1997 while he was a student backpacker in New Zealand and he worked in a vineyard. Since then he graduated in winemaking from Lincoln University and made wine in California and France. He is impassioned about Pinot Noir and Chardonnay. The focus at Meyer is primarily on these varieties. "You specialize," JAK explains. "Pick a couple and you want to be the best at that. I don't think everybody can be the best of everything."

JAK needed a full-time winemaker after he took over a failed winery project just east of Okanagan Falls late in 2008, including 5.6 hectares (14 acres) planted with, among other varieties, Pinot Noir and several

LAURA, TERRY AND JAK MEYER WITH CHRISTOPHER
CARSON (LEFT TO RIGHT)

Bordeaux reds. JAK has a tasting room here. Eventually he will also establish a winery and tasting room at the Naramata Bench vineyard.

MY PICKS

Both the Tribute Chardonnay and the ultra-premium Micro Cuvée Chardonnay are world-class wines. The excellent Pinot Noirs are evidence that winemaker Chris Carson started working with that variety at a top New Zealand winery.

OPENED 2008

965 Old Main Road
Naramata, BC V0H 1T0

T 250.496.5300

W www.mfvwines.com

WHEN TO VISIT
No tasting room

OKANAGAN FALLS WINE SHOP
4287 McLean Creek Road
Okanagan Falls, BC V0H 1R0

T 250.497.8553

WHEN TO VISIT
Open daily 10 am – 4 pm
June through September,
and by appointment

MISCONDUCT WINE COMPANY

On Valentine's Day in 1929 in Chicago, gangsters associated with Al Capone lined up seven associates of a rival gang of bootleggers in a garage and shot them. Seventy-eight years later in the Okanagan, the Misconduct Wine Company made rosé by what is called in French the *saignée* method. That involved "bleeding" juice from newly crushed red grapes. Because the winemaker bled juice from seven varietals, it occurred to Misconduct founder Richard Silva to call the wine Massacre Rosé. As that shows, Richard is an original and Misconduct is a different sort of winery.

Richard, who was born in Oliver in 1971, grew up in a family that had come to the Okanagan from Portugal in the 1950s as agricultural workers. Other than an allusion to being "a shiny suit guy in Vancouver," he is deliberately obscure about his previous career. It contributes to the aura around Misconduct, a winery he says is owned by a clandestine syndicate. "The reason the winery is called Misconduct Winery is that I was a badass," Richard says. "In my early twenties, I was a nightmare to society. I was one of those guys who was a rebel. I have done the full gamut. It was part of growing up in a small town."

All that energy is now channelled into this virtual winery with edgy branding. Misconduct is called virtual because it launched without getting licensed, arranging to have its initial vintages made at a licensed winery that does custom crushing. Others have done it as well, establishing brands in the market without sinking capital into production facilities. "We basically had enough money to buy the grapes and get ourselves going," Richard says of the clandestine syndicate. "I did not see the value of spending $600,000 to $1 million on a facility that would take my grandchildren to pay off."

When Misconduct had wines ready to sell in 2008, Richard handed the job to a well-connected wine agent. The wines, which are reason-

RICHARD SILVA

ably priced, were soon available in private wine stores and restaurants, with a website and back-label stories designed to provoke a buzz. Typical is this comment on the website: "Our clandestine syndicate, 'The Uncrushables,' will not reveal its vineyard sources or what truck their grapes may have fallen off [of]."

Eventually, Misconduct plans to have its own wine shop somewhere in the Okanagan. Don't be surprised if it looks like a 1929 garage.

OPENED 2008

c/o Anderson & Son Wine Brokerage
104 – 2510 Government Street
Penticton, BC V2A 4W6

T 250.493.9412

W www.misconductwineco.com

WHEN TO VISIT
No tasting room

MY PICKS

Even if the wines were not tasty, one might buy them for their edgy labels: Misfit (white blend), Massacre Rosé and The Big Take (Bordeaux blend).

MISSION HILL FAMILY ESTATE

As pure spectacle, Mission Hill, entirely rebuilt since 1999, outshines any winery in British Columbia. The winery's awesome beauty and the attention from well-trained staff sweep visitors away, setting up high expectations for the wines—which they live up to. It is hard to believe there were dirt floors here in 1981 when Anthony von Mandl acquired Mission Hill.

The grand architecture—the winery might be a medieval bishop's palace in Tuscany—is driven by Anthony's ambition to raise Mission Hill to a top 10 rank among world wineries. Perhaps that flame was lit in 1992, when New Zealand–born winemaker John Simes took charge of the cellar. His first Chardonnay at Mission Hill won a major international award; Mission Hill went on to promote it as the "best Chardonnay in the world." On the coattails of that award, Mission Hill bought its first vineyards. Today, Mission Hill owns 385 hectares (951 acres) where, under John's direction, top-quality grapes are grown.

The winemaker, who works in a superbly equipped cellar, taps some leading international winemaking consultants to further the pursuit of excellence. Michel Rolland, the prince of Bordeaux consultants, helps to blend Mission Hill's ultra-premium wines. Similarly Germany's Fritz Hasselbach, the owner of Weingut Gunderloch, has collaborated with Mission Hill in the crafting of a fine Riesling.

Everything here is stage-managed to impress, from the 15th-century Austrian fountain to the tower where four bronze bells mark the hours. There have even been performances of Shakespeare and concerts under the stars in the amphitheatre. VIP guests are greeted by name at the main entrance as well as being announced on a marquee. You can choose between casual or intensive tours, and general tastings are available in the expansive wine shop. You can book private tastings in a room enhanced with Anthony's personal collection of historical wine artifacts or dine on

JOHN SIMES

the mountainside terrace. Few wineries anywhere have put together a comparable experience.

MY PICKS

All the wines are delicious, beginning with ultra-premium Oculus, the flagship Bordeaux blend, and Compendium, its little brother; Quatrain, a red blend including Syrah; and Perpetua, an elegantly polished Chardonnay. Wait for the Fritz Hasselbach Riesling! The wines in the premium Select Lot Collection range and the Reserve range never disappoint. The Five Vineyards wines deliver good value at a modest price.

OPENED 1966

1730 Mission Hill Road
Westbank, BC V4T 2E4

T 250.768.6448
1.800.957.9911 (toll free)

W www.missionhillwinery.com

WHEN TO VISIT
Open daily 10 am – 6 pm
(5 pm in winter). Tour program
includes deluxe tours and
private tastings. Charges apply.
Consult website for details.

RESTAURANT
Terrace
Open daily for lunch May to
October, weather permitting

T 250.768.6467

MISTRAL ESTATE WINERY

Veteran fruit growers Keith and Lynn Holman dipped a toe into the wine business in 2003 with the Spiller Estate fruit winery. In short order they expanded to Mistral and Stonehill, a pair of wineries side by side further along Upper Bench Road. By owning wineries Keith is realizing a dream he has nurtured since the late 1970s, when he and Lynn spent two years in France looking after a house for a friend.

Born in Salmon Arm, Keith took a degree in marine biology but never worked in that field because he really wanted to farm. Lynn, who is a teacher, comes from a pioneer Penticton fruit growing family. The couple bought their first orchard after their French sojourn, ultimately ending up with 61 hectares (151 acres) of cherry and apple trees. They began planning a reduction of orchard holdings in 2004, when they bought the Mistral vineyard early in the year and then the Benchland (now Stonehill) winery and vineyard next door. In the spring of 2005 they purchased a spectacularly sited property at 1775 Naramata Road, planting vines there for the Soaring Eagle winery. That fall they bought Lang Vineyards. Subsequently they opened three more wineries—and in 2009 put several up for sale, having perhaps moved too fast.

The wines have been made under the direction of Bernhard Schirrmeister, the group's Geisenheim-trained winemaker. Born in Germany's Rheingau in 1965, he worked with several wineries there, honing expertise with Riesling, Pinot Noir and sparkling wine. Having been drawn to the Okanagan during an earlier vacation, Bernhard joined Lang in 2005. He left the Holman Lang group in early 2010.

He designed the wines differently for each winery. The Mistral wines, taking a cue from a previous winemaker, are meant to be big, long-lived wines. Keith Holman calls them "main meal wines."

Mistral has been repositioned as one of the Holman wine group's upmarket wineries, focusing on Cabernet Sauvignon, Merlot, Meritage and Muscat.

OPENED 2005

250 Upper Bench Road South
Penticton, BC V2A 8T1

T 250.770.1738

W www.holmanlangwineries.com

WHEN TO VISIT
Open daily 11 am – 5 pm May to
Canadian Thanksgiving Monday.
Closed November through April.

KEITH HOLMAN

MT. BOUCHERIE ESTATE WINERY

Nirmal and Kaldep Gidda, brothers who own this winery with their families, are among the largest non-corporate owners of vineyard in British Columbia, with 85 hectares (210 acres) in the Okanagan and Similkameen valleys. "We are proud of being farmers and growers, first and foremost," Nirmal says. "Having your own vineyards [means that] you can control the quality of the grapes that come into the winery." And it shows in the deep and well-crafted selection of wines offered in the tasting room.

The Gidda saga in British Columbia began with their immigrant father, Mehtab, a one-time Punjabi farmer who bought the family's first vineyard in 1975 near Westbank. He flourished as a farmer but did not let his three sons join in the farming enterprise until they acquired professional education. The eldest, Sarwan, studied business administration. Nirmal got a science degree and Kaldep became a heavy-duty mechanic.

Strategically they acquired or developed vineyards in three different terroirs—Westbank (where the winery was built), the Similkameen Valley and Okanagan Falls. Sarwan left the partnership in 2008, taking some of the Westbank vineyards with him for his own winery, Volcanic Hills. The remaining Gidda brothers more than replaced that acreage by planting a significant new Okanagan Falls vineyard. They grow an alphabet soup of grape varieties, from Bacchus to Zinfandel and Zweigelt, providing their winemakers, Jim Faulkner and Dave Frederick, with an enviable range of options.

After opening in 2001, Mt. Boucherie attracted notice first with its flagship Pinot Gris, its Gewürztraminer and its budget-priced Pinot Noir. The winery has since added big reds and complex white blends under a premium tier called Summit Reserve. Recently a super-premium tier called Family Reserve has been created for wines considered exceptional, such as the 92 cases of 2004 Family Reserve

KALDEP AND NIRMAL GIDDA (PHOTO COURTESY OF
MT. BOUCHERIE)

Cabernet Syrah that was released at $50 a bottle in the fall of 2008, followed by a small release of 2007 Family Reserve Zinfandel. Members of the Mt. Boucherie Wine Club (registration is free) get advance notice when special wines are released.

MY PICKS

Every time I taste the wines here, my list of recommendations grows. The whole portfolio is impressive, including the Chardonnay, the Sémillon, the Pinot Gris and the Gewürztraminer among the whites; and the Pinot Noir, the Cabernet Franc, the Merlot, the Syrah, the Blaufrankisch and the Zweigelt in the reds. Excellent blended reds are released as Summit and Mélange Noir.

OPENED 2001

829 Douglas Road
Kelowna, BC V1Z 1N9

T 250.769.8803
   1.877.684.2748 (toll free)

W www.mtboucherie.bc.ca

WHEN TO VISIT
Open daily 10 am – 6 pm in
summer, 11 am – 5 pm in winter

PICNIC AREA

NICHOL VINEYARD & ESTATE WINERY

When Ross Hackworth wheels through the Naramata countryside in his yellow 1980 Ford pickup, the many friendly waves he receives remind him that, with his 2005 purchase of Nichol Vineyard, he has returned to his roots. The truck originally belonged to his father, Doyle, a former Naramata Bench orchardist. His father took the truck with him in 1987 when he retired to Arizona but drove it back when his son needed a farm vehicle. Naramata locals still remember it.

Born in California, Ross was 10 years old when his parents bought a Penticton-area orchard in 1973. "It was the best thing they could have done for me," he says, crediting his disciplined work ethic to being brought up on the adjoining orchards belonging to his parents, his uncle and his maternal grandparents. A business graduate from the British Columbia Institute of Technology, Ross was previously a sales vice-president in the Vancouver office of a Japanese pulp and paper giant. Corporate entertaining educated his wine palate but he tired of the job's extensive travel.

He rediscovered the appeal of Naramata in 1999 while helping a school friend renovate the community's heritage hotel. "The lifestyle was absolutely appealing," he says. He started looking at vineyard properties in 2002 and bought Nichol from retiring founders Kathleen and Alex Nichol. The winery had a solid reputation for Pinot Gris, Cabernet Franc and, especially, Syrah; this was the first Okanagan winery to release this popular variety. "I knew the Nichol wines," Ross says. "I'd been drinking them for years."

Ross has refined the Nichol wines, which were already very good. A spacious new winery has allowed a doubling of production and the addition of a tasty Gewürztraminer to the portfolio. The tasting room has fine views of the lake.

MY PICKS

The Syrah can be a big, brooding south-of-France red in the best growing years and light and peppery in cooler years. The Cabernet Franc and the Pinot Noir are deep, concentrated wines. The St. Laurent, a lighter red, is hard to find. The pink-hued Pinot Gris, intense in flavour, is a deliciously eccentric take on this varietal. The Gewürztraminer could be from Alsace.

OPENED 1993

1285 Smethurst Road
RR1 Site 14 Comp 13
Naramata, BC V0H 1N0

T 250.496.5962

W www.nicholvineyard.com

WHEN TO VISIT
Open daily 11 am – 5 pm from
May 1 to Canadian Thanksgiving,
and by appointment

ROSS HACKWORTH

NK'MIP CELLARS

This winery, on a hilltop surrounded by eight hectares (20 acres) of vines, recalls a Santa Fe pueblo. Architect Robert Mackenzie has captured two themes in his design: the simulated Spanish style of Osoyoos and echoes of the Aboriginal culture of New Mexico. Nk'Mip (pronounced IN-ka-meep) is North America's first Aboriginal winery, owned by the Osoyoos Indian Band in a joint venture with Vincor. The winery anchors a development of luxury condominiums, a golf course and an interpretation centre where the band shares its culture with visitors.

Winemaker Randy Picton, who acquired his winemaking prowess at CedarCreek before being recruited by Nk'Mip, works in one of the Okanagan's best cellars, assisted by cellar supervisors Justin Hall and Aaron Crey, both members of First Nations bands. They craft wines with grapes from the winery vineyards and from the band's Inkameep Vineyard at Oliver. Since it was established in 1968, the Inkameep Vineyard has become one of the Okanagan's best. Randy is able to get grapes from the vineyard's top sites, hand-tended by the vineyard's most experienced crew. When Randy asks the vineyard for special favours, he gets them—and repays them by making award-winning wines.

You can sample the wines in the winery's exceedingly smart tasting room or sign up for tutored tastings, one of which also features Riedel stemware. Nk'Mip makes both a regular and a reserve tier. Rather than use the term "reserve" for a wine produced on a reserve, Nk'Mip dips into the Salish language to dub its upper-tier wines as Qwam Qwmt, meaning "achieving excellence." How is it pronounced? Even the winery staff uses a shortcut: Q squared.

RANDY PICTON

MY PICKS

Everything. Nk'Mip's regular Pinot Blanc is arguably the Okanagan's best, while the Merlot is rich and chewy. But if I have to limit my choices, I would particularly recommend all the Q squared wines, including the complex, full-bodied Meritage; the peppery Syrah; and the elegant Pinot Noir and Chardonnay—plus one of the outstanding Riesling icewines.

OPENED 2002

1400 Rancher Creek Road
Osoyoos, BC V0H 1V0
T 250.495.2985
W www.nkmipcellars.com

WHEN TO VISIT
Open daily 9 am – 5 pm May to
October (to 6 pm June through
August); 10 am – 4 pm in winter

RESTAURANT
The Patio at Nk'Mip
Open daily 11:30 am – 4 pm
May 1 to September 30 and
until 9 pm Friday and Saturday
in July and August, weather
permitting

NOBLE RIDGE VINEYARD & WINERY

When Leslie D'Andrea began meeting people in the wine business, she found that they were almost always in a good mood. Now running the Noble Ridge tasting room with unaffected effervescence, she epitomizes the good mood. Leslie and husband, Jim, joined the Okanagan wine scene early in 2001 when they bought a 10-hectare (25-acre) property with a small vineyard and a fine view of Vaseux Lake. Born in Welland, Ontario, in 1954, he was a champion football player at Queen's University, where he attended law school. Now a partner in a major Calgary law firm, Jim specializes in employment law. Leslie is a Toronto native with a master's degree in health administration who ran hospitals and had her own consulting firm in Calgary. They caught the wine bug in the 1990s in Europe during a wine touring sabbatical from their busy careers.

The Okanagan Falls property is on a commanding ridge and grows noble varieties, hence the winery name. The vineyard has a sun-drenched south-facing slope planted with Merlot, Cabernet Sauvignon and Pinot Noir, and a cooler north-facing slope for Chardonnay, Pinot Gris and a little more Pinot Noir. Fully planted, the vineyard extends to six hectares (15 acres), with most of the uncultivated land falling away into deep gullies. In 2006 the D'Andreas bought a three-hectare (7½-acre) vineyard just across the road, with a sturdy building, formerly used for truck storage, that they turned into a winery. The elegant wine shop and tasting room, however, are in a separate building on top of the ridge in the original vineyard.

The estate-grown grapes have dictated an admirably disciplined focus to date on five wines: Chardonnay, Pinot Grigio, Pinot Noir, Meritage and King's Ransom, the winery's super-premium red Bordeaux blend. Because some Pinot Meunier is in the vineyard, production of a classic sparkling wine is under consideration.

JIM AND LESLIE D'ANDREA (PHOTO BY PAUL D'ANDREA)

MY PICKS

The winery launched with an impressive quartet of quality wines, especially the Pinot Grigio, the Chardonnay and the Meritage. Philip Soo, a former Peller Estates winemaker, became the Noble Ridge winemaker in 2006.

OPENED 2005

2320 Oliver Ranch Road
Okanagan Falls, BC V0H 1R2
T 250.497.7945
W www.nobleridge.com

WHEN TO VISIT
Open daily 10 am – 5 pm May to
October, and by appointment

PHILIP SOO (PHOTOS COURTESY OF NOBLE RIDGE)

OLIVER TWIST ESTATE WINERY

As newcomers to wine, Bruce and Denice Hagerman knew they had made the right career choice when they discovered how friendly and helpful their competitors are. "Coming from my previous experience—I was a police officer—it wasn't the case," Bruce says. "I usually met people who were not too nice."

Wine is only the latest endeavour of the energetic Hagermans. "I like to do different things," Bruce says. "I once asked an old lady about the things she did in her life and what it was she regretted. She said, 'Sonny, it is not the things I did in my life that I regret, it is the things I didn't do.'" Born in Calgary in 1950, Bruce studied electronics and retail management. By the time he was 25, he was running a large Radio Shack store in Edmonton. He learned to fly so that he and Denice could visit her family in Grand Prairie. He then became a farmer and an auctioneer. The couple went travelling across North America for several years in a motor home, eventually settling in Palm Springs, where Denice worked for a large tennis club while Bruce joined the police force. On the side he learned locksmithing. They also co-authored a hiking guide.

Bruce began making wine as an amateur in 1989. They returned to Canada in 2002 and bought an orchard south of Oliver, on Black Sage Road, with a winery in mind. They replaced the fruit trees in 2006 with seven hectares (17 acres of grapes) and built their winery, with consultant Christine Leroux helping them make the wines.

Bruce and Denice have approached the wine business with the same brio they brought to their other activities. Everyone leaves the Oliver Twist tasting room smiling, especially those favoured with a lesson from Bruce on opening screw-capped wine bottles. All of their wines, which are closed with twist tops, are unblended varietals. "We like keeping everything pure," Denice explains.

BRUCE AND DENICE HAGERMAN

MY PICKS

The whites—Kerner, Pinot Gris, Chardonnay, Viognier—and the Merlot rosé are attractively fresh and fruity. The initial releases of Merlot and Pinot Noir were uncomplicated, fruit-forward reds. These have now been joined by a barrel-aged Merlot and a peppery Syrah.

OPENED 2007

33013 Road 9A
Oliver, BC V0H 1T0
T 250.485.0227
W www.olivertwistwinery.com

WHEN TO VISIT
Open daily 10 am – 5:30 pm May
to October, and by appointment

ORCHARD HILL ESTATE CIDERY

In the midst of wine country, Orchard Hill offers the wine tourist a distinct change of pace. This is the South Okanagan's only apple cidery, making its products with fresh fruit grown right here.

The cidery was established by Gian Dhaliwal and his son, Ravi, who operate a roadside orchard and fruit market. The orchard grows primarily apples, along with cherries and other tree fruits. For some time, the Dhaliwal family has sold its fruits and vegetables at what they called the Sunshine Valley Fruit Market. The cidery opened in 2006, adding value to the apples and giving passing motorists another reason to stop and linger.

Three ciders, all vintage dated, were offered when Orchard Hill opened. Okanagan Bubbly is a semi-sweet cider made refreshing with its effervescence. Summer Sipper is a medium-dry cider with a little more body that the sparkling version. Extra Dry cider, according to the Dhaliwal family, "is unlike any other dry apple cider . . . Usually extra dry means harsh and bitter. Orchard Hill Extra Dry [is] very light and delicate. It is handmade from a blend of the more astringent Okanagan apples." The flagship cider, also sparkling, is called Red Roof.

Modestly priced, the ciders are packaged both in 750-millilitre bottles and, like many competing ciders, in half bottles.

Orchard Hill's Red Roof cider is crisp, with refreshing sparkle to lift the flavours.

OPENED 2006

23404 Highway 97
Oliver, BC V0H 1T0

T 250.689.0240

W www.orchardhillwinery.com

WHEN TO VISIT
Open daily 8 am – 8 pm July and
August; 8 am – 6 pm in June,
September and October

OROFINO VINEYARDS

There is a bit of France in this winery. In 1991 schoolteacher John Weber and his wife, Virginia, a nurse, went wine touring in France. Both were born in 1969 and grew up in Saskatchewan. After the wine tour they returned to Saskatchewan and took up professional careers, but the appeal of the wine lifestyle persisted. In March 2001 they took over a 2.4-hectare (six-acre) producing vineyard near Cawston and immediately had to figure out how to prune vines. "We spent the first year on a huge learning curve," John says. Nevertheless, nothing dimmed their enthusiasm. Four years later the couple opened Orofino—Spanish for "fine gold" and the name of one of the mountains overlooking the vineyard.

While taking wine courses at Okanagan College, John engaged various consulting winemakers, tapping their expertise until he could go solo. "The idea was to hire a winemaker and apprentice right here, on our property, but wean ourselves off, so that eventually Virginia and I—but mainly myself—became the winemakers," John says. They have a growing list of awards to show how quickly they have learned the art of making wine. They have also extended their portfolio by convincing neighbours to plant more of the Bordeaux reds (such as Cabernet Sauvignon and Petit Verdot) that do so well in the Similkameen Valley.

Orofino deserves special notice for the design of its winery. The two buildings—the winery itself and the smaller tasting room separated by a breezeway—constitute British Columbia's only winery built with straw bales. The buildings look conventional except for thick walls that are finished attractively in dusty pink stucco. Orofino rightly promotes itself as "ecofriendly" and John and Virginia are proud to explain the virtues of this design, which is exceptionally energy efficient.

MY PICKS

Thanks to the growing volume of red Bordeaux varietals from Orofino and neighbouring vineyards, the winery in the 2007 vintage began assembling a sophisticated blend called Beleza. It is a solid companion to the other good wines here—Red Bridge Red, Pinot Noir, Chardonnay, Sauvignon Blanc, Riesling and Gewürztraminer. The speciality of the house is the delicate Late Harvest Muscat dessert wine.

OPENED 2005

2152 Barcelo Road
Cawston, BC V0X 1C0
T 250.499.0068
W www.orofinovineyards.com

WHEN TO VISIT
Open daily 10 am – 5 pm May
to October

PICNIC AREA
Tables shaded by almond trees

JOHN WEBER

OSOYOOS LAROSE ESTATE WINERY

Osoyoos Larose offers no public tours and is unlikely to do so until a winery is built on the vineyard sometime in the future. The 32-hectare (80-acre) vineyard is a few kilometres northwest of Osoyoos, on the western slope of the valley and near the Desert Interpretation Centre. It is worth looking through the fence, if only to see how the French grow grapes. The vines are crowded together more closely than is customary in the Okanagan, reducing the quantity of fruit, but forcing them to produce really ripe, full-flavoured grapes.

Osoyoos Larose is a joint venture arranged in 1998 between Vincor International, Canada's largest wine company, and Groupe Taillan, the owner of distinguished Château Gruaud-Larose and five other Bordeaux properties. To learn from the French, Vincor let its partner make most of the big decisions, including picking the vineyard site, deciding what vines to plant (Merlot, Cabernet Sauvignon and three other Bordeaux reds) and appointing the winemaker.

Since the inaugural 2001 vintage, Pascal Madevon has made the wine in the dedicated northeast corner of Vincor's big Jackson-Triggs winery. The grandson of a small Burgundy wine grower, Pascal was born in Paris in 1963 and grew up in the city. His desire to work in the outdoors led him to viticulture and enology at the Bordeaux Wine School. He has made wine for several important Bordeaux producers, notably Château La Tour Blanche, and has written two wine books. He knew little about Canadian wine when he was tapped for Osoyoos Larose, but he has become so enthused about the quality of the wines he makes in the Okanagan that, in 2009, he even became a Canadian citizen.

There are only two wines at Osoyoos Larose. The flagship is Le Grand Vin, an age-worthy blend built around Merlot plus the four other Bordeaux reds. In the 2004 vintage the winery launched its second label, Pétales d'Osoyoos, a softer, earlier-drinking red blend.

MY PICKS

The quality of Le Grand Vin has risen steadily as the vines have matured. No collector of Okanagan wines should be without this wine in the cellar, along with Pétales d'Osoyoos for more immediate pleasure.

OPENED 2004

38691 Highway 97 North
(Jackson-Triggs winery)
Oliver, BC V0N 1T0
T 250.498.4981

WHEN TO VISIT
No tasting room

PASCAL MADEVON (PHOTO COURTESY OF VINCOR)

OVINO WINERY

Legend has it that Yankee Flats Road, not far west of Salmon Arm, was named for the Vietnam-era draft dodgers who once lived in this bucolic farm country between the Salmon River and the Fly Hills. John Koopmans considered it as a name for his winery but decided against it, concerned about attracting anti-American sentiment. He settled on a more generic winery name and jokes that he will just hang an "N" in front of the name when he is sold out.

Born in Holland in 1956, he became interested in wine as a student at a Dutch agricultural college that organized several field trips to French vineyards. "My chemistry professor was fascinated with wine and used it a lot as examples," John remembers. "He had a bit of a club there, messing about with smaller batches of wine."

Discouraged by a perceived lack of opportunity to farm in Holland, he joined an uncle in Canada in 1977. A muscular, sturdily built man, John spent many years both in forestry and in dairy farming before he and Catherine, his wife, bought this 12.5-hectare (31-acre) Yankee Flats farm in 1992 for a dairy herd of their own. Fourteen years later, deciding it was time to do something new, he replaced the cows with a small herd of sheep. (Ovino, in fact, is derived from "ovis," the genus name for sheep.) That gave him time to concentrate on the 1.6-hectare (four-acre) vineyard planted mostly in 2007 and to build a winery large enough to make about 1,000 cases a year. The consulting winemaker is Hans Nevrkla, a former owner of Larch Hills Winery.

The vineyard occupies a dome with exposures to "all sides of the compass," he notes. He grows Pinot Gris, Gewürztraminer, Pinot Meunier and Maréchal Foch, along with an experimental plot of Cabernet Libre (a Blattner hybrid) and Regent, a winter-hardy red grape. John also buys Chardonnay and Lemberger from a vineyard near the Gray Monk winery on Okanagan Lake.

MY PICKS

The winery launched with well-priced Pinot Gris, Gewürztraminer, Blush and two reds from Maréchal Foch.

OPENING PROPOSED 2010

1577 Yankee Flats Road
Salmon Arm, BC V1E 3J4

T 250.832.8463

W www.ovinowinery.com

WHEN TO VISIT
Open daily 11 am – 5 pm from early June to mid-October, and by appointment

JOHN KOOPMANS

PAINTED ROCK ESTATE WINERY

Excitement for the wines of Painted Rock built soon after the winery's first vintage in 2007. The wines, full-bodied Bordeaux reds and a Syrah, had been made at the Poplar Grove winery by a team that included Frank Gigliotti, owner of Vancouver's California Cult Classics winery; Ian Sutherland, Poplar Grove's legendary winemaker-owner; and Gavin Miller, his assistant. Like a proud father, John Skinner soon was tasting barrel samples with wine-loving friends, to great acclaim.

Encouraged by that reception, John hired Gavin as Painted Rock's winemaker. It looks like a dream job. To begin with, the property is on a picturesque bench on the east side of Skaha Lake, just below the famous Skaha climbing bluffs. John bought 24 hectares (60 acres) in 2004 and a neighbouring parcel in 2006. Almost half has been contoured for vines, primarily multiple clones of Syrah and Bordeaux reds, with a small plot of Chardonnay. Not one to cut corners, John has sought the advice of expert consultants, including label designers from Napa and a leading French viticulturist, Alain Sutre, who helps with the critical blending.

John has changed careers, retiring in 2009 after many years in the investment business to devote himself exclusively to the winery. The son of a Canadian Forces pilot, he was born in 1958 in Portage La Prairie and grew up on a succession of military bases. He worked his way through university in a tough sawmill job until he noticed the prosperity of a friend who had become a broker. John soon switched to a financial career, succeeding as an investment advisor while educating himself about wine. "There are also a tremendous number of synergies between the brokerage business and the vineyard business," he says. "A lot of my friends are wine collectors. A lot of my friends own restaurants."

The wines released in the fall of 2009 included a polished Chardonnay, a full-bodied Merlot and elegant examples of Cabernet Sauvignon and Syrah. The flagship wine is a sophisticated Bordeaux blend called, simply, Red Icon, a must-have wine for collectors.

OPENED 2009

400 Smythe Drive
Penticton, BC V2A 8W6
T 250.493.6809
W www.paintedrock.ca

WHEN TO VISIT
Open daily 11 am – 5 pm
May through mid-October

JOHN SKINNER

PARADISE RANCH WINES

Paradise Ranch was the first winery in Canada to make sweet dessert wine exclusively, the idea of Jeff Harries, a Penticton physician, and Jim Stewart, a Vancouver lawyer who roomed with Jeff when they were university students. At the time the winery was launched, Jeff owned Paradise Ranch, a vineyard on the shore of Okanagan Lake north of Naramata. The 261-hectare (645-acre) property was named by its ranching homesteaders for its secluded beauty. In 1975, the physician's late father, Hu Harries, bought the ranch. Since 1981, 40 hectares (100 acres) of vines have been planted. Mission Hill, which had been buying the grapes for a decade, bought the property in 2002, renamed it Naramata Ranch and began converting it to Pinot Noir.

Without its own winery, Paradise Ranch led a gypsy existence. The winery's first two icewines in 1997 were made at the Red Rooster winery and sold under that licence. Expanding to eight icewines the next winter, Jim moved production to larger facilities at the Calona Vineyards winery. After Mission Hill bought the vineyard, Paradise Ranch began buying grapes elsewhere. Jim bought his own press and, for several vintages, stored it at Hester Creek, one of his grape suppliers. Various consulting winemakers have made the wines.

In 2007 Jim settled Paradise Ranch's production in a Kelowna warehouse and purchased a small Naramata property. There, in 2008, the winery planted 3.25 hectares (eight acres) of Chardonnay and Pinot Noir. This is intended to be the first of several vineyard acquisitions.

Icewine is glamorous but risky. By regulation the grapes cannot be harvested unless they have been frozen on the vines to at least −8°C (18°F), and preferably colder to produce the ideal sugar content in the juice. When this freeze happens in November or December, there are still abundant, healthy grapes on the vines. If mild weather delays the freeze to February, many grapes will shrivel or fall to the ground, and

JIM STEWART

icewine production will be uneconomically small. In recent years Paradise Ranch, which markets aggressively in Asia, has reduced the weather risk by having icewines made in Ontario as well.

MY PICKS

Paradise Ranch has icewine vintages available from 1998. Although icewine ages well, I prefer younger, more exuberant icewines, notably those made with Riesling, Chardonnay or Pinot Noir. Paradise Ranch also has a companion label, Whistler Icewines.

OPENED 1998

901 – 525 Seymour Street
Vancouver, BC V6B 3H7
T 604.683.6040
W www.icewines.com

WHEN TO VISIT
No tasting room

PELLER ESTATES

The premium label for Andrew Peller Ltd. (formerly Andrés Wines), Peller has appeared in Calona's Richter Street wine shop since Peller bought Calona in 2005. The merger combines two of the Okanagan's oldest producers.

Now a national company, Peller was launched in British Columbia in 1961 by Andrew Peller, a Hungarian-born brewer from Ontario. After his winery application was thwarted there, he was welcomed by development-hungry British Columbia with a low-priced winery site in the Vancouver suburb of Port Moody. Andrés, as it was then, achieved national stature in no small measure with the amazing success of its grapey Baby Duck sparkling wine that was created in Port Moody in 1971. Baby Duck still has a following, but the Port Moody winery closed at the end of 2005 when the business, now run by Andrew Peller's grandson, John, moved into the Calona winery.

The Peller family's contribution to BC wines includes planting the first vineyard in the Similkameen Valley and giving early backing to Inkameep Vineyards near Oliver. In 1975 Andrés arranged for Riesling, Ehrenfelser and Scheurebe vines to be imported for Inkameep. This was one of the first significant plantings of European vinifera wine grapes in the Okanagan.

Since the 1997 development of the 28-hectare (70-acre) Rocky Ridge Vineyard in the Similkameen Valley, Peller has become the third-largest vineyard owner in British Columbia, including the 81-hectare (200-acre) Sandhill Vineyard and the recently planted 121-hectare (298-acre) vineyard at Covert Farm near Oliver.

MY PICKS

There has been a noticeable rise in the quality of Peller wines since 2005 because the company, controlling its own vineyards, has been delivering superb quality grapes to winemaker Stephanie Leinemann. The whites are all crisply refreshing while the reds—notably the Syrah and the Pinot Noir—show satisfying depth. And none are expensive.

OPENED 1961
(AS ANDRÉS WINES)

1125 Richter Street
Kelowna, BC V1Y 2K6
T   250.762.9144
     1.888.246.4472 (toll free)
W www.peller.com/okanagan

WHEN TO VISIT
Open daily 9 am – 6 pm

STEPHANIE LEINEMANN
(PHOTO COURTESY OF PELLER)

PENTÂGE WINERY

Pentâge Winery is unique in the Okanagan. It is housed in a massive 500-square-metre (5,400-square-foot) cavern dug into the hard rock on the crown of a property with a million-dollar view of vineyards and of Skaha Lake. Paul Gardner and Julie Rennie, his spouse, were enchanted with the site, then a derelict orchard, when they saw it in 1996. Until the Pentâge tasting room opens (possibly in 2010), few people will have seen the winery's dramatic engineering. Access to the winery is expected to be from Valleyview Road above the property rather than by the steep driveway up from Lakeside Road.

Paul and Julie's dream winery is a long way from their initial careers. She has been an executive assistant to a Vancouver financier (and she still works at that job from a home office). Paul, born in Singapore in 1961, spent 20 years as a marine engineer, a background that shows in how well the winery is engineered and equipped.

The winery now produces about 5,000 cases a year, divided into a remarkable kaleidoscope of wines because Paul grows about 20 different grape varieties in this winery's two vineyards, which total 6.5 hectares (16 acres) on the spectacular benches near the Skaha climbing bluffs. Paul has complicated his winemaking life by choice. "I would still rather make small lots of interesting wine than big tanks full of wine," he says. Typical of his small-lot philosophy is that Paul and Adam Pierce, his winemaker, make whites with varieties such as Viognier, Marsanne and Roussanne. He does not grow Chardonnay, but, even though he says there are already too many Chardonnay wines on the market, he could not resist making some when he was able to buy those grapes in 2008.

The winery name, a play on the Latin word for "five," was chosen after Paul planted five red varieties to make his flagship red, called simply Pentâge. The wine is built primarily with Merlot and Cabernet Sauvignon; small amounts of Cabernet Franc, Syrah and Gamay add com-

JULIE RENNIE AND PAUL GARDNER

plexity and personality. Paul is equally original when it comes to icewine, made with five different white varieties. "I do a co-ferment and I end up with an interesting blended icewine," he says.

OPENED 2003

4400 Lakeside Road
Penticton, BC V2A 8W3
T 250.493.4008
W www.pentage.com

WHEN TO VISIT
By appointment

MY PICKS

Everything, including the Pentâge red, the Syrah, the Cabernet Franc, the Gamay and the Merlot. Keep an eye peeled for Zinfandel, Malbec and Tempranillo. The white wines, including Gewürztraminer, Chenin Blanc, Sauvignon Blanc, Sémillon, Pinot Gris and Viognier, are good fruit-forward expressions of these varieties. Some of the winery's Pinot Gris is sold in a three-litre box designed to fit neatly into a refrigerator, convenient for those who prefer wine by the glass.

POPLAR GROVE WINERY

Poplar Grove once was among the smallest of the wineries on the Naramata Bench. It is now becoming one of the largest, with construction just beginning on a new 3,344-square-metre (36,000-square-foot) winery on the side of Munson Mountain with a tasting room overlooking both Penticton and Okanagan Lake. "An era of reinvention" is how the winery's brochure puts it.

For many years winemaker Ian Sutherland was content to make about 2,000 cases of wine a year. Something of a Renaissance man, Ian, who was born in Montreal in 1952, dropped out of university to go trekking in Nepal. Eventually he took up the trade of boilermaking. While he was starting the winery the trade was a means to an end: fixing pulp mill boilers paid for vines and winemaking equipment. A self-taught winemaker, he polished his considerable skills by working several vintages in New Zealand and Australia. During one season in Australia he learned enough about making cheese to start Poplar Grove's own cheese company (now run by his former wife, Gitta).

Poplar Grove's reinvention began in 2007 when Tony and Barbara Holler bought a 75 percent interest in the winery. Tony is a doctor who was born in Summerland in 1951 and has run several successful pharmaceutical companies. A Napa Valley vacation in 2004 spurred him to buy property on the Naramata Bench and to plant a vineyard just south of Poplar Grove. When Tony gets a passion about something, he thinks big. With a consummate winemaker like Ian for a partner, Tony acquired vineyard property throughout the South Okanagan along with the winery site on the mountain. The winery's production increased to 15,000 cases in 2008, and Stephan Arnason joined the winemaking team.

Tony and Ian also launched Monster Wines, Poplar Grove's value label, in 2008. The curious name is inspired by the legend of Ogopogo, the Okanagan's lake monster. "These are fun wines that people can

IAN SUTHERLAND

TONY HOLLER

enjoy on a patio in the afternoon," Tony suggests. "[But] so long as we have the high-quality grapes, the majority of our production will go to Poplar Grove and we'll always produce less of the Monster label."

MY PICKS

Everything, including the $50 Legacy (a top Bordeaux blend), the Cabernet Franc, the Merlot, the Syrah, the Pinot Gris and the Chardonnay. Under the Monster Wines label, the winery releases well-made Riesling, Sauvignon Blanc, Gewürztraminer and Merlot.

OPENED 1997

1060 Poplar Grove Road
Penticton, BC V2A 8T6

T   250.493.9463

W www.poplargrove.ca

WHEN TO VISIT
Open daily 11 am – 5 pm late
spring to early autumn

PROSPECT WINERY

There must be an explanation for this winery's address since no wine-maker, especially someone as lanky as Prospect's Wade Stark, lives in a post office box. Prospect is owned by Artisan Wine Company, a holding company whose best-known property is the Mission Hill Family Estate winery. That is where the Prospect wines have been made by veteran winemaker Wade Stark. Longer-term plans call for a Prospect winery to be built near Oliver.

Prospect was launched as a self-described "tribute to the Okanagan valley." The complete original name is Ganton & Larsen Prospect Winery; those names referred to two of Mission Hill's long-time grow-ers. The name was one device employed to root this virtual winery in the Okanagan.

Another effective device is building each wine label around BC lore and history. For example, Prospect's wildly successful Pinot Grigio is called Ogopogo's Lair. This refers to a bend on the east side of Okanagan Lake where, according to legend, the mythical Ogopogo lake creature has its underwater cave. Another example: the Lost Bars Vidal Icewine refers to the 1896 robbery of three bars of gold from a mine near the Okanagan. Two bars are said to have been buried here, though the loca-tion was lost. Altogether Prospect celebrates Okanagan history on about a dozen different wines.

While there is no tasting room, the wines are widely available in wine stores at very affordable prices.

Prospect's wines overdeliver in quality, considering that all are priced around $15 except for the icewine. The Census Count Chardonnay, the Pinot Grigio, the Sauvignon Blanc, the Riesling and the Merlot Cabernet stand out.

OPENED 2007

PO Box 474
Oliver, BC V0H 1T0
T 604.264.4020
W www.prospectwinery.com

WHEN TO VISIT
No tasting room

WADE STARK (PHOTO COURTESY
OF PROSPECT)

QUAILS' GATE ESTATE WINERY

The Stewart family, who operate Quails' Gate Estate Winery, believe that their father, Richard, put in Canada's first successful planting of Pinot Noir in 1975. The Stewarts, who are from Irish stock that settled in the Okanagan in 1911, are pioneering horticulturists. Part of the 50-hectare (125-acre) Quails' Gate vineyard was planted in 1956. Later it was one of the first vineyards to convert to premium European varieties. Today Quails' Gate is the Okanagan's largest producer of Pinot Noir, with nine clones on 16 hectares (40 acres) in its vineyard on the slope of Mount Boucherie. Pinot Noir comprises one-fifth of the winery's total production, now about 50,000 cases per year.

"I'm a Pinot guy," says winemaker Grant Stanley. Quails' Gate hired him in 2003 precisely because of his Pinot Noir skills. "I probably spend about 80 percent of my time thinking about Pinot Noir." Born in Vancouver in 1967 to parents from New Zealand, Grant became passionate about wine while working in restaurants in Canada and Britain. In 1991 he and his British-born horticulturist wife, Annabelle, moved to New Zealand and took wine industry jobs. After getting professional training, Grant made six vintages with Ata Rangi, a leading Pinot Noir producer.

Until Grant arrived the Quails' Gate winemaking was decidedly Australian because three good Australian winemakers in succession were in command of the cellar from 1994 until 2003. Grant changed the style subtly while focusing production more sharply by reducing the number of wines to 16 from 26. The whites have that exquisite fruit purity for which New Zealand is noted while the reds show more restrained oak. One of the best illustrations of that is the winery's iconic Old Vines Foch (the vines are more than 40 years old). First made in 1994, the wine was modelled on chewy, oak-aged Australian Shiraz. Grant's winemaking technique has revealed attractive black cherry and plum in a remarkably finessed wine. It shows off how effectively Grant uses the other 20 percent of his time at the winery.

GRANT STANLEY

MY PICKS

All the wines are good to superb. Top-tier wines are released as Stewart Family Reserve; Chardonnay and Pinot Noir are especially fine. The regular Quails' Gate tier of wines is also very high quality—notably the Chenin Blanc, the Riesling, the Gewürztraminer, the Chardonnay, the Pinot Noir, the rosé, the Merlot and the Old Vines Foch. And the Botrytis Affected Optima is one of Okanagan's finest dessert wines.

OPENED 1989

3303 Boucherie Road
Kelowna, BC V1Z 2H3

T 250.769.4451
   1.800.420.9463 (toll free)

W www.quailsgate.com

WHEN TO VISIT
Open daily 9:30 am – 7 pm
from July to early September;
10 am – 7 pm in May, June and
September; and 10 am – 6 pm
from October through April.
Check website for extensive
tour schedule.

RESTAURANT
Old Vines Restaurant
Open daily at 11:30 am for lunch
and dinner

T 250.769.2500

QUINTA FERREIRA ESTATE WINERY

John Ferreira jokes that he got his first taste of cork when he was five and growing up in Portugal, where he was born in 1954. It was his chore to take the family's empty wine container for refilling at a nearby shop. Barely tall enough to see over the cork-surfaced counter, he sometimes chewed on it while he was waiting. Today his Black Sage Road winery, on a ridge overlooking Oliver, fulfills the imperative of his heritage. "I believe every man on earth would either like to have a vineyard or a winery," he maintains. "I have always wanted to have a vineyard."

John grew up fast. His parents came to Oliver from Portugal in 1960, working as hardscrabble farm labour. John was driving the tractor when he was seven. Later he (and his sisters) often missed the first few weeks of school because the family was picking apples. Hard work enabled the Ferreiras to lease and then buy this farm, a mere stone's throw from town. Here they carved an orchard from raw sagebrush. In 1979 John and his wife, Maria, bought the orchard. To meet mortgage payments, they had to sell fruit privately. When that got them expelled from the packing house co-operative, the Ferreiras opened their own independent packing house. That packing house, grandly renovated, is now their sandy-hued Mediterranean-style winery.

Beginning in 1999 John replaced his fruit trees with 6.3 hectares (15½ acres) of grapes. "I didn't know the first thing about growing grapes when we put the first one in," John admits. "I was just tired of the fruit business." The grapes—Merlot, Syrah, Malbec, Chardonnay, Viognier and Pinot Blanc—were turned into prize-winning wines by such wineries as Township 7 before John and his winemaker son, Michael, opened the family's winery.

John is thinking of adding Touriga Nacional, the great Portuguese red variety. Indeed, the Ferreiras honour their Portuguese heritage already through some of the proprietary names of their wines. The blends

JOHN FERREIRA

are called Mistura Branca (white) and Mistura Tinta (red). The dessert wine is Vinho du Sól. The flagship red blend is Obra-Prima, Portuguese for "masterpiece." Of course, every wine bottle is closed with natural cork.

MY PICKS

The Obra-Prima lives up to its name. Other delicious wines here include Malbec, Syrah, Viognier, Chardonnay, Pinot Gris, Sauvignon Blanc and the rosé as well as a Chardonnay dessert wine called Vinho Du Sól.

OPENED 2007

34664 71st Street
(Black Sage Road)
PO Box 1064
Oliver, BC V0H 1T0

T 250.498.4756

W www.quintaferreira.com

WHEN TO VISIT
Open daily 10 am – 6 pm

RAVEN RIDGE CIDERY

It is both surprising and delightful to find a place like the Kelowna Land & Orchard Company (KLO) only 15 minutes from downtown Kelowna. Just beyond earshot of the city's traffic, you get to experience an old-fashioned farm complete with market, petting zoo, wagon rides and farm tours—and the Raven Ridge Cidery.

The KLO began in 1904 as a land development company. The agricultural remainder of its lands that escaped development was acquired in 1942 by John Bullock. The property, now 61 hectares (151 acres) in size, became a family farm and orchard now operated by Bullock's son and daughter-in-law, Richard and Jacquie, and their grown children. Their daughter, Nicole, who has a degree in agriculture, runs the cidery.

The Dunster Road property is a busy place during the growing season. Since opening the market and launching education tours in 1995, the farm has begun to attract up to 70,000 visitors a year. The restaurant, called The Ridge, was added in 2000 when a private home was renovated. The ambiance is so romantic that one guidebook included it as one of the best places in which to be kissed.

Raven Ridge's cidermaster is Roger Wong, who is also a winemaker at Gray Monk Cellars and a specialist in sparkling wines. He produces ciders from such apple varieties as Fuji, Braeburn, Ambrosia and Granny Smith.

MY PICKS

The Braeburn Iced Cider, which Nicole once compared to a "good hand-rolled cigar," is my favourite, with its rich caramel and baked apple flavours. But if it is sold out, the other Iced Ciders—Ambrosia, Fuji and Granny Smith—are also delicious. The Fuji Still Cider is a fine, dry cider that tastes like Chenin Blanc, while the True Sparkling Cider is Raven Ridge's nod to Champagne.

OPENED 2003

3002 Dunster Road
Kelowna, BC V1W 4H3
T 250.763.1091
W www.ravenridgecidery.com

WHEN TO VISIT
Open seasonally at the KLO
Farm Market

RESTAURANT
The Ridge
Open daily 11 am – 3 pm late
April through October

ROGER WONG

RECLINE RIDGE VINEYARDS & WINERY

You could say that Recline Ridge extended the Okanagan wine route, opening in 1999 as the most northerly winery in the interior. The winery, with its attractive tasting room in a modern log house, is 14 kilometres (nine miles) west of Salmon Arm in the pastoral Tappen Valley, just off the Trans-Canada Highway.

The actual start of the Okanagan Valley is a 30-minute drive to the south. More and more wine tourists, however, drive the extra distance to the picturesque Shuswap Lake district now that a small cluster of wineries has opened here. In 1997 Larch Hills was the first to open; in 2004 Granite Creek opened just down the road from Recline Ridge; and Ovino Winery is opening in the nearby Salmon River valley. Other wineries are in the wings, something these northern wineries welcome. In the early years owner and winemaker Michael Smith was keenly aware of being somewhat isolated from his peers and from the boom in wine tourism farther south.

A former Salmon Arm cable company manager, Michael was a veteran home winemaker before he and his wife began turning their farm pasture into a vineyard in 1994. Now the Recline Ridge has a three-hectare (7½-acre) vineyard, growing Maréchal Foch, Siegerrebe, Optima, Madeleine Sylvaner, Madeleine Angevine and Ortega, all early varieties suited to the short season this far north. In his early years Michael purchased Okanagan grapes as well, but the recent development of other Shuswap vineyards has provided an adequate supply of grapes from the region.

Since 2008 Michael has been advertising Recline Ridge for sale. "I want to do something different," Michael says. "It's just been a whole lot more work than I wanted." A one-time hobby pilot who sold his airplane in 2008, he plans to team up with friends and sail an ocean-going yacht.

MICHAEL SMITH

MY PICKS

The Siegerrebe is my favourite mouthful here (it is pronounced *Zeeg-er-a-beh*). The winery also has a crisp and refreshing Ortega, a dark, smoky Maréchal Foch and, from Naramata-grown grapes not available to Recline Ridge after 2007, a plummy Pinot Meunier. The winery's tasty port-style wine is called Ridgeport.

OPENED 1999

2640 Skimikin Road
Tappen, BC V0E 2X0
T 250.835.2212
W www.recline-ridge.bc.ca

WHEN TO VISIT
Open daily 10 am – 5 pm July through September; noon – 5 pm April through June and October; or by on-site pager in winter

RED ROOSTER WINERY

As former winemaker Richard Kanazawa once said, the challenge here is to make wines that "fit the building." Both the spacious wine shop and the winery itself are the most baronial of architect Robert Mackenzie's Okanagan winery designs (so far).

This is a far cry from the original Red Rooster's modest winery on a side road near the Naramata fire hall. In 2004 founders Beat and Prudence Mahrer relocated Red Rooster to this "you can't miss it" location right on Naramata Road. Being art lovers, the Mahrers turned the wine shop's second floor into a gallery for local artists. They also found space in the tasting room for *Frank the Baggage Handler*, the controversial nude sculpture that suffered strategic vandalism when it was first displayed in a traffic circle in nearby Penticton. Andrew Peller Ltd. bought Red Rooster in 2005 but, appreciating the attraction of lively irreverence, kept Frank in the rambling tasting room and art in the gallery.

Red Rooster's debut Malbec in the 2006 vintage, from vines adjacent to the winery, did rise to Richard's standard, winning a Lieutenant Governor's Award of Excellence in winemaking. Karen Gillis, who took over when Richard moved to the Blasted Church winery in 2007, has continued making showpiece wines. Born in Vancouver, she grew up in a family of chefs. She initially had the same career in mind when she completed a diploma in food technology at the British Columbia Institute of Technology in 1996. But after three years developing food products, she zeroed in on wine and joined Andrés (as Andrew Peller Ltd. was then called) to become a winemaker.

In the same year that Karen took over, Red Rooster adopted screw cap closures, so important to preserving the fresh fruit-forward flavours of the wines. The decision was first announced to members of the winery's exclusive Adopt-a-Row Club in a test of potential consumer reaction. The members greeted the announcement with a standing ovation!

KAREN GILLIS

MY PICKS

The array of refreshing whites includes Pinot Gris, Pinot Blanc, Riesling, Gewürztraminer, Chardonnay and Viognier. Reserve versions of several whites show even more intense flavours. Bantam is an aromatic easy-drinking white blend based on Müller-Thurgau. The Meritage, the Merlot and especially the Reserve Merlot are excellent. Not much of that superb Malbec is made each year. Members of the Red Rooster Wine Club, which is free to join, get advance notice of special releases.

OPENED 1997

891 Naramata Road
Penticton, BC V2A 8T5
T 250.492.2424
W www.redroosterwinery.com

WHEN TO VISIT
Open daily 10 am – 6 pm April through October; 11 am – 5 pm November through March

FOOD SERVICE
Light lunches on shaded patio

THE RISE CELLARS

The ambitious underground winery originally planned for this spectacular site was derailed by the 2008 bankruptcy of Leona Snider's Okanagan Hills Development Corporation, a victim of the global financial crisis. The vineyards, however, are not part of the bankruptcy and are owned separately by Leona. With her son, Jason Rannelli, she has continued to operate the vineyards, selling some of the grapes to other wineries and offering wines produced for her by other licensed wineries. Leona still proposes to build a winery on this south-facing slope above the north end of Okanagan Lake "as soon as we figure the economy will support it," she says.

An Alberta-born entrepreneur, Leona founded a Whitehorse-based drilling and blasting firm in 1976 and moved into real estate development in the late 1980s. In 1990 she took advantage of a receivership auction to buy a 297-hectare (734-acre) plateau a short drive west of downtown Vernon. There had been a previous effort to run a ranch here. Leona spotted the potential to develop a residential resort with about 1,200 homes, a hotel and a professionally designed golf course. The proposed winery would produce fine wines for residents as well as for general consumers.

Development began in 2004, including the initial 1.8-hectare (4½-acre) vineyard, planted with Pinot Noir and Riesling. Subsequently more of these varieties plus Gewürztraminer were planted on a further four hectares (10 acres), with a final 2.4 hectares (six acres) prepared for more vines in the future. Perched at an elevation of about 700 metres (2,300 feet), this is one of the highest and most northerly Okanagan vineyards. But the vines thrive because the slope is bathed in sun throughout the day.

The golf course was completed by 2008, along with a quarter of the planned homes, before the financial crisis put a halt to further sales and development. Leona's company filed for protection from its

JASON RANNELLI AND LEONA SNIDER (PHOTO
COURTESY OF OKANAGAN HILLS DEVELOPMENT)

creditors in December 2008, seeking
a new owner to complete the grandly
conceived project.

One of the early winery designs involved a cave built into the mountainside. The design will likely now be
more conventional, while still taking
advantage of the breathtaking view that
always impresses.

OPENING TBA

364 Cordon Lane
Vernon, BC V1H 1Z9

T 250.542.5111
  1.866.400.8488 (toll free)

W www.therise.ca

WHEN TO VISIT
To be established

MY PICKS

The vineyard's potential
expressed itself through
a pair of excellent
wines made in 2008 that
incorporated grapes from
Rise grapes—Intrigue
Winery's Riesling and
JoieFarm's Pinot Noir.
Also worth looking
for are the Rise's
2006 Merlot and 2006
Riesling Icewine, made
with purchased fruit.

ROAD 13 VINEYARDS

With its gold-hued parapets gleaming in the Okanagan sun, the Road 13 winery looks like a theme-park castle in a vineyard. It was designed and built by grape grower Peter Serwo, evoking the Europe where he and his wife, Helga, lived before coming to the Okanagan in 1966. When they opened the winery in 1998 they called it Golden Mile Cellars—to the dismay of other wineries along this stretch of vineyards called the Golden Mile.

The original name stayed in place after Mick and Pam Luckhurst bought the winery in 2003, partly in deference to the Serwos, until 2008, when the Luckhursts concluded that it was time to rebrand the winery, which just happens to be at the western end of Road 13. The Luckhursts made amends for their tin ear about the significance of Golden Mile with new labels paying homage to local history. Several popular blends are called Honest John, honouring John Oliver, British Columbia's premier from 1918 to 1927. His government fostered the irrigation project that made orchards and vineyards possible in the South Okanagan. Road 13's reserve wines come out under the Jackpot label, named for one of the many gold and silver mines in the nearby hills that probably inspired the area's Golden Mile tag in the first place.

Previously successful as building supply dealers and developers, the Luckhursts have applied aggressive business skills to achieve fast growth. The winery, which had never made more than 1,000 cases a year before they bought it, now makes about 15,000 cases annually.

As they did in their previous businesses, the Luckhurts hire professionals to get results. Winemaker Michael Bartier came to the winery in December 2004. With a degree in recreation administration, Michael is a keen outdoorsman (tackling rock climbing and any other extreme sport he can find). As a winemaker, he has a natural gift, developed through working in the cellar at Hawthorne Mountain Vineyards begin-

MICK AND PAM LUCKHURST

ning in 1995, doing a crush in Australia, taking courses at the University of California and launching Township 7 in the Okanagan before moving to Road 13. He has also consulted for such wineries as Noble Ridge and Meyer Family Vineyards. He has a particularly adept hand with Chardonnay and at blending.

MY PICKS

Everything, especially Old Vines Chenin Blanc, Fifth Element (a superb red blend), Jackpot Syrah, Jackpot Chardonnay and Road 13 Zinfandel. The moderately priced Honest John wines (a red, a white and a rosé) overdeliver.

OPENED 1998
(AS GOLDEN MILE CELLARS)

13140 316A Avenue (Road 13)
RR1 Site 28A Comp 10
Oliver, BC V0H 1T0

T 250.498.8330

W www.road13vineyards.com

WHEN TO VISIT
Open daily 10 am – 5:30 pm
April 14 to October 31, and by
appointment in winter

MICHAEL BARTIER

ROBIN RIDGE WINERY

The Similkameen Valley's well-known summer attraction is the Grist Mill and Gardens on Upper Bench Road just outside Keremeos. This is a restored flour mill, originally built in 1877, surrounded by gardens dedicated to preserving heritage varieties of grains, apples and vegetables. Robin Ridge's tasting room, wonderfully cool in summer, is located, as owner and winemaker Tim Cottrill puts it, "just kitty-corner from the Grist Mill."

The son of a carpenter, Tim was born in Kelowna in 1966 and grew up in Summerland, where he helped his father build houses. When they tired of the construction industry's boom-and-bust cycles, Tim and his wife, Caroline (who grew up on a peach orchard), switched to grapes. In 1996 they purchased a four-hectare (10-acre) hayfield near the Grist Mill. It took them a full season during 1998 to clear enough of the stones to plant vines. "Grapes don't mind rocks, but farm equipment does," Tim says wryly. He took advantage of that year to take the vineyard management course at Okanagan College.

Tim started by planting a 1.2-hectare (three-acre) block of Chardonnay in 1998, adding Gamay in 1999, Merlot in 2001 and Pinot Noir in 2004. Along the way he also planted small plots of Gewürztraminer, Cabernet Sauvignon, St. Laurent and Rougeon, along with half a hectare (1.2 acres) of table grapes. Tim began selling grapes as the vines came into production, keeping enough so that he and Caroline could make wine for themselves. He picked up some winemaking basics from his instructor at Okanagan College, and he was soon winning awards in local wine festivals, notably with a house blend he crafts from Gamay, Pinot Noir, St. Laurent and Rougeon. This has been the inspiration for the winery's Ridge Red. He launched Robin Ridge with help from a consulting winemaker but was soon flying on his own.

Production at Robin Ridge is approaching 1,000 cases a year, small enough to allow both Tim and Caroline to handle outside jobs as well. They preside over the tasting room with infectious charm.

MY PICKS

The Chardonnay is a satisfying wine, with just the right touch of oak supporting the citrus flavours. Fans of unoaked wine will appreciate the Gewürztraminer. The tasty reds include Gamay, Pinot Noir and Merlot.

OPENED 2008

2686 Middle Bench Road
Keremeos, BC V0X 1N2
T 250.499.5504
W www.robinridgewinery.com

WHEN TO VISIT
Open daily 11 am – 5:30 pm
May through October,
and by appointment

CAROLINE AND TIM COTTRILL

ROLLINGDALE WINERY

Steve Dale certainly knows how to get the best from a perceived liability. When he took over this vineyard in 2004, it included one hectare (2½ acres) of Maréchal Foch, nearly half the total vineyard. Not a fan of Foch table wine, Dale soon began planting Merlot, Syrah and Viognier among the other vines. The Foch continued to produce market grapes while the other vines were young. A vineyard setback in 2005 damaged most of the Foch grapes. In a moment of inspiration, Steve turned what was left into icewine—the Okanagan's first icewine from Maréchal Foch. So small was the production that Steve priced the wine at $850 a half bottle. It is called Portage and it tastes like a fine Christmas pudding. In subsequent vintages, he increased the quantity while rolling the price.

Steve and Kirsty, his wife, come to wine by way of an organic gardening store they once had in Port Moody. Although Steve, born in Ontario in 1971, has a degree in English literature, he became a horticultural consultant based in Switzerland. The Dales took advantage of that locale to explore Italian and French wine regions, nurturing their desire to be in the wine business. In 2003 they returned to Canada and Steve enrolled in the winery assistant course at Okanagan College. To get practical experience at the end of the course, he signed on to prune vines for the Hainle winery in the vineyard that Hainle was leasing. By the end of his first day he had struck a deal to take over the lease. In 2005 he bought the property. A functional metal building serves for a winery. A nearby picnic site has a fine view toward Okanagan Lake.

Rollingdale was the first Okanagan winery to achieve organic certification. Virtually all of the grapes used here are grown organically, and the winemaking process eschews the chemicals routinely used in other wineries for sanitation. Steve is categorically against inorganic products in vineyards. "I don't want to be responsible for poisoning the land,

STEVE DALE

the air, the water or the inhabitants thereof," he vows. "Systemic fungicides, pesticides, chemical fertilizers and herbicides are ugly. I won't handle them and I won't pay someone else to. There is always an organic solution to every problem encountered."

MY PICKS

The wines here are at times eclectic, like the aromatic white blend whimsically called Riewurztrafelseron, and at times as serious as any in the Okanagan. Try the pair ($43 each) of distinguished barrel-aged reds from the 2007 vintage, Merlot La Droite and Cabernet Sauvignon La Gauche. Also recommended: Portage and the icewines.

OPENED 2006

2306 Hayman Road
Kelowna. BC V1Z 1Z5
T 250.769.9224
W www.rollingdale.ca

WHEN TO VISIT
Open daily 10 am – 6 pm
April through October.
and by appointment

PICNIC AREA

RUBY TUESDAY WINERY

The striking Red Rooster Winery, which Beat and Prudence Mahrer built and then sold, has such a terrific location on Naramata Road that wine tourists rarely drive by without stopping. When another great property came on the market just to the north, the Mahrers snapped it up so that no one could erect a competing winery. The irony is that Prudence herself opened Ruby Tuesday Winery on that spot.

She and Beat really intended to retire from winemaking in 2005 when Andrew Peller Ltd. bought Red Rooster. They travelled in the winter and she spent the summers running their 5.6 hectares (14 acres) of vineyard. But Prudence deeply missed having a winery and meeting the public. Had there been a support group for former winery owners, she says, she would have joined it. That is why, at 55 (she was born in Switzerland in 1953), she persuaded her husband to start Ruby Tuesday. "That's the reason why I wanted to start again," she says. "I can easily do another 10 to 15 years."

An effervescent personality, she grew up with the music and culture of the 1960s. That included a Rolling Stones song, "Ruby Tuesday," about a free-spirited young woman following her dream. Prudence identifies with those values. "Some of the songs from the sixties have so much meaning to them," she believes. That explains the winery's name and the free-spirited art on the labels.

Ruby Tuesday, with an annual production between 2,000 and 3,000 cases (all from Naramata Bench fruit), is not nearly as large as Red Rooster (16,000 to 20,000 cases). Beat and Prudence, who had run fitness centres in Switzerland, switched careers in 1990 to grow grapes in the Okanagan, opening the original Red Rooster in 1997 and the grander one six years later.

The Mahrers designed the more modest Ruby Tuesday Winery themselves. (Beat is a highly skilled carpenter and Prudence has a good eye

PRUDENCE MAHRER

for art and design.) Consulting wine-maker Philip Soo made the wines that launched Prudence's tasting room in the spring of 2009. "I want to do what I really loved the most: producing wine—quality wine, of course—watching how the wine develops and then selling it myself to customers," she says.

OPENED 2009

917 Naramata Road
Penticton, BC V2A 8V1

T 250.276.5311

W www.rubytuesdaywinery.com

WHEN TO VISIT
Open daily 11 am – 5 pm
April through October

MY PICKS

The Viognier and the Gewürztraminer are tasty whites. The reds include a full-bodied Merlot, a good Cabernet Sauvignon and a medium-bodied Shiraz.

RUSTIC ROOTS WINERY

The Rustic Roots winery is the most recent enhancement to the high-way-side organic fruit stand operated since the late 1950s by the Harker family. As the winery's name suggests, the family has deep roots in the Similkameen Valley. The current head of the family is Bruce Harker, who has farmed here since 1975. His maternal great-grandfather was Sam Manery, the fourth settler-baby born in the valley after his parents arrived in 1888. The photo gallery on the winery's website includes an image of Sam, a crusty-looking cowboy on a spirited horse.

Bruce and Kathy, his wife, developed a flourishing business in the valley, growing their own organic fruit and wholesaling the fruit of other producers. As they reached their 60s, they had just begun to think of retiring and travelling when sons Jason and Troy returned to the farm and the business. This brought a fifth generation into Harker Organics, with a sixth in the wings. And that was the incentive to add a winery to the business.

The winery is the project of daughter-in-law Sara, Troy's wife. Born in Oliver in 1982, she is a member of a family that emigrated from Hungary in 1956. She comes to wine through the restaurant business. After studying science for a year at Langara College and then business administration at Okanagan College, she spent eight years working at various positions at the Fairview Mountain Golf Club. Troy worked in heavy construction in Alberta for several years until the couple decided to return to the Harker family farm.

Sara equipped herself for the winery by taking Okanagan College's winery assistant program. To launch the winery the Harkers have enlisted Christine Leroux, a consulting winemaker for, among others, Elephant Island Orchard Wines. Sara plans to spend several years mentoring with Christine.

SARA AND BRUCE HARKER

In keeping with the theme, the wine labels all include an image of a tree with immense roots. This is the 110-year-old Snow Apple still growing on the Harker farm.

MY PICKS

Start with the refreshing dry Peach Nectarine wine or the spicy Apple Pear, made with five varieties of apples and three varieties of pear. The Cherry wine, fermented deliberately on the pits, is dry with a nutty undertone. Dessert wines include a delicious Santa Rosa Plum wine and a delicate Iced Apple wine.

OPENED 2008

2238 Agar Road (Highway 3)
Cawston, BC V0X 1C2

T 250.499.2754

W www.rusticrootswinery.com

WHEN TO VISIT
Open daily 10 am – 5 pm spring
and fall; 10 am – 6 pm Monday
through Thursday in summer
(to 8 pm on weekends)

RUSTICO FARM & CELLARS

The Okanagan has seen several virtual wineries come and go, with names like Calliope and Bumblebee. Such producers sell their wines under the licence of existing wineries and may even make the wine at those wineries. This saves sinking a small fortune into property before the winery name is established. D'Asolo Vineyards, the previous name for this winery, was the 3,000-case label with which Vancouver businessman Bruce Fuller set out to create an Italian village south of Oliver. It was named for the Venice-area village called Asolo that had intrigued him ever since he sipped grappa with the locals in 1978.

The D'Asolo wines, made by Tinhorn Creek in 2001 and in several subsequent vintages by Mt. Boucherie, were sold primarily to restaurants in Vancouver and Whistler. However, a lack of financing and a falling-out with a partner ended the Italian village project. Bruce regrouped in 2007, buying a Golden Mile vineyard that came with an eccentric log cabin and an almost-completed new winery.

"I don't think there is any winery that has the story to tell like this one does," Bruce asserts. The 3.6-hectare (nine-acre) vineyard was begun in 1968 by a debonair individual named John Tokias who came to British Columbia from Hungary in 1951 and who purchased this property, then raw crown land, in 1963. He worked for about 17 years in the silver mines near Beaverdell. As mines started to close, he acquired a log cabin bunkhouse. He relocated it log by log to his Okanagan property, apparently using his Volkswagen truck and a trailer to transport the logs gingerly around the mountain highway curves. When he put the cabin back together, he added a massive sod roof. Over the years he hung bleached animal skulls on the exterior, a bizarre decoration only removed recently as Bruce prepared to welcome winery visitors. (The rustic appearance inspired the winery's name.)

BRUCE FULLER (ON THE SOD ROOF)

Four years after John's death in 2000, his family sold the property to Don and Bonnie Bradley. A former brewer, Don had almost completed a new winery before he and his wife changed their minds and sold it to Bruce. With silent partners backing him, Bruce launched the winery in 2009 as Canada's "most romantic winery." The portfolio reflects the major varieties in the vineyard: Merlot, Gewürztraminer, Zinfandel and one of the few remaining blocks of Chancellor in the Okanagan.

OPENED 2009

31238 123rd Street
Oliver. BC V0H 1T0

T 250.498.2739

W www.rusticowinery.com

WHEN TO VISIT
Daily 10 – 6 spring through fall

MY PICKS

The wines are tasty and all bear labels elaborating on (perhaps creating) the property's history: Farmer's Daughter Dry Gewürztraminer, Isabella's Poke Pinot Gris, Doc's Buggy Pinot Noir, and Last Chance (red blend).

BRUCE FULLER

ST. HUBERTUS & OAK BAY ESTATE WINERY

No tours are offered here, but visitors are free to stroll the 31 hectares (76½ acres) of vineyard. Visitors might also get this good-humoured suggestion: "If you see some work, just finish it." Owners Leo and Andy Gebert, who patrol the vineyard with Andy's radio-controlled model helicopter, always bring a sense of humour to the job.

Leo, a banker by training but a farmer by avocation, acquired the vineyard shortly after coming to Canada from Switzerland in 1984. A decade later his younger brother, Andy, formerly a yacht skipper in the Caribbean, joined the partnership to run that part of the property called the Oak Bay vineyard. It is a family business in every way: the brothers are married to sisters who are also active in the winery.

In the summer of 2003 the terrifying Okanagan Mountain Park forest fire swept through their hillside property in early August, destroying both their winery and Leo's heritage home (circa 1930). Fortunately the fire missed their new warehouse, where the freshly bottled 2002 vintage had just been stored. The Gebert brothers added a wine shop to that warehouse and were selling wine within 10 days. Properly insured—"Leo is very religious about that," Andy says—they had a new winery and new house under construction before winter.

One of the Okanagan's earliest vineyards, the St. Hubertus property was planted in 1928 by J. W. Hughes, the valley's first commercial grower of wine grapes. For many years it was called the Beau Sejour vineyard. The arched gate at the entrance to St. Hubertus, which surprisingly survived the fire, still has the Beau Sejour name visible on the back of the St. Hubertus sign. None of the original wine grapes remain, but St. Hubertus has one of the Okanagan's oldest plantings of Riesling, dating from 1978.

The current winemaker, Hooman Haft Baradaran, joined St. Hubertus in 2008. Born in Germany in 1973 of Iranian parents, he came to wine

HOOMAN HAFT BARADARAN

after a degree in hotel management and while working as a sommelier in leading European hotels, among them Claridge's in London. While taking a winemaking degree at Brighton University, he did vintages in Greece, Germany and Washington state—where he discovered the Okanagan wine region. "As for my approach to winemaking," Hooman says, "I am a diverse person. I lived in different places. That reflects in my winemaking. I am not forcing anything."

OPENED 1992

5225 Lakeshore Road
Kelowna, BC V1W 4J1

T 250.764.7888
1.800.989.WINE (9463)
(toll free)

W www.st-hubertus.bc.ca

WHEN TO VISIT
Open daily 10 am – 5:30 pm May through October; noon – 4 pm Tuesday to Saturday, November through March; 11 am – 5 pm Monday to Saturday in April

MY PICKS

St. Hubertus has made its mark with crisp and fruity whites, notably Riesling, Gewürztraminer, Pinot Blanc and a remarkable Chasselas, the variety widely grown in Switzerland but rarely in the Okanagan. The winery's top reds include Maréchal Foch, Gamay Noir and Pinot Noir. Pinot Meunier is now primarily used for sparkling wine.

ST. LASZLO ESTATE WINERY

St. Laszlo is a winery marching to an entirely different drummer. It makes wine from, among other varieties, Clinton and Interlaken, two American labrusca hybrids found at no other winery in British Columbia. When he planted this vineyard in 1976, Slovenian-born Joe Ritlop worried about vine survival in cold winters and chose many hardy hybrids. However, his test plots also included vinifera such as Chardonnay, Riesling and Gewürztraminer.

His son, Joe Ritlop Jr., who manages the winery now, has added Merlot, Gamay, Pinot Noir and Pinot Gris to the vineyard. As if that were not a broad enough selection, Joe Jr. added fruit wines after he scored popular success in the tasting room with a trial batch of raspberry wine. The most exotic is the occasionally produced rose petal wine. The wine-making, which eschews sulphur, is unadorned and traditional. "We are from the old school of thought," Joe Jr. has said.

The generous family usually has most wines available for sampling, sometimes even the red and white icewines. If you want to touch a moderately sore point, ask who made the first commercially available icewine in Canada. Credit usually goes to the late Walter Hainle, the German-born textile salesman who started Hainle Vineyards at Peachland. As a hobbyist, he made icewine in 1973 and continued to do so for years. His first vintage that was available commercially was 1978—but it was not on sale until 1988 when the Hainle winery opened. The elder Ritlop did not make icewine as early as Hainle but he did have one available in his wine shop in 1985. He had taken advantage of a snap frost in his vineyard to crush frozen grapes. Although he entered it in a Vancouver wine competition that fall, he got no recognition because there was no icewine category.

JOE RITLOP JR.

MY PICKS

St. Laszlo's sulphur-free wines are a boon for that minority of consumers with sulphur allergies. The limitation is that unsulphured wines, especially grape wines, may maderize and should be consumed young. The sherry-like character that comes with age is rather tasty in St. Laszlo's apricot and plum wines.

OPENED 1984

2605 Highway 3 East
Keremeos, BC V0X 1N0
T 250.499.2856

WHEN TO VISIT
Open daily 9 am – 5 pm and
later if you knock

SANDHILL WINES

On the Sandhill Estate Vineyard on the Black Sage Bench (next door to Burrowing Owl Estate Winery), two plots have been left free of vines. Sometime during the next several years a Sandhill winery will rise on one of these sites—after a gestation period of almost two decades.

Sandhill's first vintage in 1997, and every vintage since, has been made in the sprawling Calona winery in downtown Kelowna. Sandhill was launched as Calona's premium label. Then, winemaker Howard Soon stamped such an individual personality on the wines that it became imperative for Sandhill to have its own winery. The project was delayed largely because Andrew Peller Ltd., which bought Sandhill and Calona in 2005, decided first to invest in additional vineyards. John Peller, the president of the company, assures us that there will be a Sandhill tasting room on the Black Sage.

To make the Sandhill wines stand apart, Howard makes only single-vineyard wines: wines whose quality expresses the terroir where the grapes are grown. Each vineyard delivers its own flavours. For example, the Phantom Creek Vineyard Syrah is rich, soft and full-bodied. Yet the Syrah from the Sandhill vineyard on the other side of Black Sage Road has a firmer structure. The four or five Okanagan vineyards that supply Sandhill are all identified on the labels. Howard makes blended wines from grapes within a vineyard but he never makes multi-vineyard blends because that would obscure the terroir. This is a tough self-imposed discipline that has never stopped him from making superlative wines. The pride in the wines shows in the back labels, which are always signed by both the winemaker and the grower.

Sandhill was the Okanagan's first successful proponent of Sangiovese and Barbera, two distinctive Italian red varietals rarely grown by anyone else in the valley. These have been released from nearly every vintage since 1999 as part of Sandhill's Small Lots program, so called because production of individual wines seldom is greater than 500 cases and

sometimes is less than 100 cases. Howard even bottles separate blocks in a vineyard if there are distinctive flavours. "Small is where it is at as far as quality goes," he declares.

Handcrafted wines are not all that Sandhill makes. The winery produces almost 40,000 cases a year, all of it of premium quality. "To make a living, you have to be pretty big to achieve economies of scale," Howard admits.

OPENED 1999

1125 Richter Street
Kelowna, BC V1Y 2K6

T 250.762.9144
1.888.246.4472 (toll free)

W www.sandhillwines.ca

WHEN TO VISIT
See Calona Vineyards

MY PICKS

I admire all Sandhill wines, especially those in the Small Lots program. *Sandhill one* and *Sandhill two* are among the Okanagan's best Meritage reds while *Sandhill three*, a blend incorporating Sangiovese and Barbera, recalls a fine super-Tuscan red. Syrah, Petit Verdot and Malbec are real treats. The winery's Pinot Blanc, with grapes from 25-year-old vines, might be the best oak-aged example of this varietal in the Okanagan.

SEE YA LATER RANCH AT
HAWTHORNE MOUNTAIN VINEYARDS

This is a winery with a wonderful story, reflected both in its name and those of several wines—Nelly, Ping, Rover and Jimmy My Pal, formerly the names of dogs. This picturesque property on a mountainside above the vineyards of Okanagan Falls was owned for about 45 years by Major Hugh Fraser. Over that time he owned Nelly, Ping and numerous other dogs. Each was buried under headstones which, in recent years, have been placed at the base of a tree near the vintage home (circa 1902) now serving as the charming tasting room.

According to one legend, the major brought an English bride with him when he moved to this farm after service in the First World War. She could not handle the isolation and returned to England, leaving a note signed "See Ya Later." The real explanation, or so it is said, is that the major, a prolific correspondent, scrawled "See Ya Later" at the end of his letters. This has become the third name for this winery.

An entrepreneur named Albert LeComte launched the winery in 1986 under his own name. It became Hawthorne Mountain Vineyards when Sumac Ridge founder Harry McWatters bought it in 1995. A few years after Vincor purchased the winery in 2000, it was rechristened to take advantage of the history and the canine legacy. The winery honours that legacy by welcoming visitors travelling with dogs and by contributing to the major's favourite charity, the SPCA.

This 40.5-hectare (100-acre) property is the highest-elevation vineyard in the South Okanagan, rising to 536 metres (1,760 feet) and sloping to the northeast, an unusual exposure for the northern hemisphere. However, this cool location makes it one of the Okanagan's best sites for Gewürztraminer, Pinot Gris and Ehrenfelser. Its Gewürztraminer block, at 26 hectares (64 acres), is the single largest planting of this aromatic variety in North America. The other grapes for See Ya Later wines come from Vincor's extensive plantings in the South Okanagan.

If you make the short but steep drive to this winery from Okanagan Falls, consider continuing south to Oliver by Green Lake Road. This

quiet back road cuts through a land-scape of ranches that retain the feeling of remoteness so unappealing to the major's wife (if he really had a wife).

MY PICKS

The entire range of See Ya Later Ranch wines is appealing—notably Ping (a red Meritage), Riesling, Gewürztraminer, Pinot Gris and Pinot 3 (a white blend based on three Pinot varieties). The Ehrenfelser Icewine has lovely ripe pineapple flavours. And winemaker Mason Spink's See Ya Later Ranch Brut is as good a bubbly as anyone makes in British Columbia.

OPENED 1986
(AS LECOMTE ESTATE WINERY)

Green Lake Road
PO Box 480
Okanagan Falls, BC V0H 1R0
T 250.497.8267
W www.sylranch.com

WHEN TO VISIT
Open daily 9 am – 6 pm in summer, 10 am – 4 pm in winter

MASON SPINK (PHOTO BY STUART BISH)

SERENDIPITY WINERY

In 1975 Judy Kingston helped found Canada's first computer law practice with a national law firm in Toronto. That was serendipitous, she says, just like her Naramata winery.

Born in Toronto in 1953, she set out to be a mathematician, majoring in both math and computer science after taking a math-heavy computer course. At the suggestion of her thesis supervisor, she researched the field of computer law and found it virtually undeveloped. "The law had not evolved to take computers into account," she says. "And the judges were always wrong, in my mind." She enrolled in law school, caught the eye of a big firm and began a successful 25-year career in this specialty.

An automobile accident triggered a decision to retire from law. Passionate about food, she gave some thought to running a bed and breakfast. However, she and her husband, David, a telecommunications consultant, have friends who operate a California winery. That lifestyle also appealed to the Kingston family. During an Okanagan vacation in 2006 they impulsively bought an orchard next door to Therapy Vineyards and converted it the next year to three hectares (7½ acres) of vineyard.

The sort of person who always seizes opportunities, Judy enrolled in both the viticulture and winemaking programs at Okanagan College. In 2009 she went to New Zealand to work the crush with Palliser Estate Winery, a four-week crash course that left her with an appreciation for Sauvignon Blanc (which Serendipity grows) and Pinot Noir (not yet planted). One-third of her Naramata vineyard is planted to Merlot; she also has Cabernet Franc, Malbec, Syrah and Viognier.

A skilled networker, Judy has tapped numerous talented Okanagan wine experts to help launch Serendipity. Purchasing grapes in 2008, Judy and winemaker Jason Parkes made two reds (Cabernet Sauvignon and Cabernet Franc). With the winery construction not scheduled until 2010, Judy and Jason extemporized, making wine in other licensed facilities or, in the case of Serendipity's 2009 whites, in their garage. The winery, ready for the 2010 crush, will have the capacity to produce 7,000 cases a year.

MY PICKS

Wines were not available for tasting.

OPENED 2010

990 Debeck Road
Naramata, BC V0H 1N0

T 250.496.5290

W www.serendipitywinery.com

WHEN TO VISIT
Open 10 am – 6 pm Friday through Sunday and by appointment in 2010; check website for updates on hours in future years

JUDY KINGSTON

SEVEN STONES WINERY

Newcomers to the Similkameen Valley, George Hanson and his Quebec-born wife, Vivianne, have embraced its history by naming their winery after seven massive rocks freighted with Aboriginal history. Speaking Rock, for example, was a First Nations meeting place, while Standing Rock—Highway 3 jogs around it—is associated with a tale of a woman who rode her horse to the top. These and other stories are destined for this winery's labels.

Born in Alberta in 1957, George spent 25 years with a telephone company in the Yukon. Home winemaking fired his resolve to retire on a vineyard. When the phone company gave out golden handshakes, he invested his severance in the Similkameen. Since 2000 he has planted eight hectares (20 acres). Most of the vines are the big reds suited to the Similkameen's hot summers: Cabernet Sauvignon, Cabernet Franc, Merlot, Pinot Noir, Syrah and (in 2008) Petit Verdot. Acknowledging a demand for white wine, he also planted one hectare (2½ acres) of Chardonnay.

"This is an exceptional place to grow grapes," George affirms. "We have been selling to four or five other wineries and they are all making premium wines." He had a consultant make a small volume of red Meritage in 2003 but skipped winemaking in 2004 because the newly married couple were too busy building a house. Vivianne, a herbalist who previously owned a Prince George health food store, says wryly that other spouses of wine growers warned that if the house (which she designed) did not precede the winery, she might be waiting for it a long time.

George quickly mastered growing grapes and then the art of making wine. Seven Stones, which now makes about 2,300 cases a year, has a growing collection of medals to prove it. The highway-side wine shop, which Vivianne hosts with irrepressible joie de vivre, is the best place to find the wines.

MY PICKS

I admire all the wines here, including the Chardonnay, the rosé, the Pinot Noir, the Cabernet Franc, the Meritage and especially the Syrah, which is often limited to two bottles to a customer. You can try going back twice in one day but chances are they'll remember you.

OPENED 2007

1143 Highway 3
Cawston, BC V0X 1C3

T   250.499.2144

W www.sevenstones.ca

WHEN TO VISIT
Open daily 10:30 am – 5:30 pm
except Tuesday May through
October, and by appointment

GEORGE HANSON (PHOTO COURTESY
OF SEVEN STONES WINERY)

SILKSCARF WINERY

Roie Manoff spent 20 years flying combat jets for the Israeli Air Force, hence the name of the winery the Manoff family opened in Summerland in 2005. Son Idan draws a parallel between aviation and wine: both involve "meticulous work, day in and day out."

Roie, who was born in Argentina in 1951 but grew up in Israel, has had a long love for wine. He began technical wine studies somewhere between his pilot's career and subsequent ownership of a Tel Aviv software firm. "My dream when I became a winemaker was to make a good Cabernet Sauvignon," he says. The Silkscarf portfolio is now much longer that that, including even a Malbec, the signature Argentinean variety.

When the family decided to leave Israel, a study of wine growing regions brought them in 2003 to the Okanagan and the quiet beauty of a Summerland orchard, most of which has been converted to 3.4 hectares (8½ acres) of vines. While Roie was settling business affairs in Israel, Idan was sent ahead to start the vineyard.

Born in 1976, Idan is a computer science and business graduate. But his more relevant experience for Silkscarf includes growing fruit crops in Israel and working in the Margalit Winery, one of Israel's finest boutique wineries. "The farming part here is not different from what I know," Idan says of the Gartrell Road orchard. The varieties planted include Pinot Gris and Gewürztraminer. Almost a third of the vineyard has been planted to Shiraz, a surprising choice since the variety is usually planted in hotter terroirs than Summerland. The Manoffs have succeeded with the variety, producing both a full-bodied red and a juicy rosé.

Because wine is best appreciated with food, the Manoffs have a small kitchen next door to the Silkscarf wine shop. The intent is that visitors can order wine by the glass and small dishes from the kitchen to pair with the wines. They note that they are not operating a full restaurant but a more casual tapas bar. "We keep our wines as the focus," Roie says, "but the dishes are fantastic."

IDAN AND ROIE MANOFF

The winery's fruity whites include an excellent Viognier and a refreshing Riesling Muscat blend. Among the reds I particularly like the Shiraz Reserve, the Merlot Reserve and the Cabernet Sauvignon.

OPENED 2005

4917 Gartrell Road
Summerland, BC V0H 1Z4
T 250.494.7455
W www.silkw.net

WHEN TO VISIT
Open 10 am – 5:30 pm
weekends in May and June;
daily July through October

FOOD SERVICE
Tapas selections and wine by
the glass 11:30 am – 4:30 pm
weekends; reservations
recommended

SILVER SAGE WINERY

The eclectic choices in Silver Sage's baronial tasting room range from intensely flavoured fruit wines to original table wines. Among the latter is Sage Grand Reserve. This is a Gewürztraminer turbocharged by fermenting the wine with sage that grows in the South Okanagan, resulting in a unique white with the herbal aroma and flavour of rosemary.

Another singular offering is The Flame, a fiery dessert wine with a red pepper in each bottle. Such unusual wines sprang from the imagination of Victor Manola. Both he and Anna, his wife, had managed vineyards and made wine in Romania before coming to Canada about 1980. After successful business careers, the couple returned to their roots in 1996, purchasing a 10-hectare (25-acre) property beautifully situated beside a meandering valley-bottom river. The winery stands peacefully amid vineyards with the aplomb of a French château, a testament to Victor's skills as a builder. Sadly, Victor died in a winery accident in 2002 as the building neared completion.

Anna, a former mathematics teacher with a sure touch with fruit wines, operates the winery and is often behind the tasting room bar. On occasion the sorrow of her loss has even been expressed in the wines. She takes particular pains with Silver Sage's Pinot Noir, leaving the fruit on the vines long into the autumn to develop ripe flavours, then focusing all her winemaking skills on it. The result is a supple red called "Pinot Noir . . . the Passion." The label is a deep clerical mauve, the colour of a widow's garb in Romania.

MY PICKS

The Pinot Noir and the Pinot Blanc are tasty. Sage Grand Reserve must be tried, to be enjoyed, perhaps like Retsina, with Greek cuisine. Then go to the fruit wines, all with room-filling aromas and intense flavours, and to the blends of grape and fruit wines. The peach and apricot–flavoured Pinot Blanc dessert wine is a particular delight.

OPENED 2001

32032 87th Avenue
Oliver, BC V0H 1T0
T 250.498.0310
W www.silversagewinery.com

WHEN TO VISIT
Open daily 10 am – 6 pm

ACCOMMODATION
Three guest suites in the winery

ANNA MANOLA

SKIMMERHORN WINERY & VINEYARD

Until Skimmerhorn opened, wine tourists just whipped through Creston on the way to the Okanagan (unless they paused to tour the Columbia Brewery). Now Creston, with two wineries and counting, could call itself the wine capital of the Kootenays. The bistro at this winery, with veranda tables overlooking the vines, is a delightful stop for lunch from May to October.

Skimmerhorn's owners, Al and Marleen Hoag, grew tree fruits here from 1984 until selling their orchard in 2005. Al first considered opening a cidery but decided they were more likely to succeed with a mainstream beverage like wine. Beginning in 2003 they planted 5.6 hectares (14 acres) of vines on a sunny slope at the south edge of Creston, intelligently choosing varieties that will ripen here (Pinot Gris, Gewürztraminer, Ortega, Pinot Noir, Maréchal Foch).

Knowing it would be difficult to attract Okanagan expertise to Creston, the Hoags went to New Zealand to find a winemaker willing to spend his off-season in the northern hemisphere. They knocked on winery doors across New Zealand's South Island until they found Mark Rattray, the Geisenheim-trained owner of (at that time) Floating Mountain Winery in Waipara. The 2009 vintage was his fourth at Skimmerhorn. Each year he comes in September, bottles the red wines from the previous year and makes the current vintage before going home, all the while mentoring Al in managing the wines.

Al made his first solo wine in the summer of 2009 after a sudden rainfall rendered some cherries too blemished for the fresh market. A nearby orchard offered Al cherries for the cost of picking them and he made Skimmerhorn's first cherry wine. "We don't know if there is any market for fruit wine," he admitted as he dumped juicy cherries into the crusher.

MARLEEN AND AL HOAG

MARK RATTRAY

MY PICKS

The whites—Pinot Gris, Ortega, Gewürztraminer—and the rosé are packed with fruit flavours. Autumn Tryst is an off-dry white blend aimed for consumers who prefer a touch of sweetness. The Maréchal Foch is a bold, rich red, a counterpoint to the light Pinot Noir.

OPENED 2006

1218 27th Avenue South
Creston, BC V0B 1G1

T 250.428.4911

W www.skimmerhorn.ca

WHEN TO VISIT
Open daily 11 am – 5 pm July
and August; 11 am – 5 pm
Wednesday to Sunday May, June
and September – December

RESTAURANT
Bistro in wine shop
Open 11 am – 3 pm Wednesday
to Sunday May – October

SLEEPING GIANT FRUIT WINERY

Thousands visit the specialty fruit manufacturer Summerland Sweets each year, attracted by the fruit products and, in summer, by the generous ice cream parlour. The fruit winery, which opened here in 2008, was a logical extension to the business started in 1962 by the legendary Dr. Ted Atkinson.

He was one of the Okanagan's leading scientists, head of food processing at what was then called the Summerland research station. When he was near retirement, he created a line of fruit candies for a Rotary Club fundraiser. Frustrated that no company would take on the product, he set up Summerland Sweets to commercialize a range of fruit-based products that has grown to include syrups and jams that are sold domestically and exported.

Ted Atkinson's family still operate Summerland Sweets. His granddaughter's husband, Len Filek, was a young commerce graduate when he joined the company in 1984. Today he is the general manager. He spearheaded the addition of a fruit winery with a tasting room inside the Summerland Sweets store. "It's been a thought in the family for quite a while," he says. "With the other projects we had, we just kept putting it off." The winery went ahead after Sumac Ridge founder Harry McWatters urged Len to give the stream of visitors to Summerland Sweets another reason to visit.

Len retained Ron Taylor, a veteran winemaker already working with numerous fruit wineries in British Columbia. "My dad was a home winemaker but I am not interested in making wine," Len admits frankly. "I am interested in wine and I am interested in a good product. That's why we have someone making it for us."

LEN FILEK

MY PICKS

More than a dozen fruit wines are available here, ranging from dry examples made from pear and apple to delicious off-dry wines made from cherry and raspberry. Recent additions (there's a waiting list for them) are pumpkin table wine and "pumpkin pie" dessert wine. All are notable for aromas and flavours that could be fresh from the tree.

OPENED 2008

6206 Canyon View Road
Summerland, BC V0H 1Z7

T   250.494.0377
    1.800.577.1277 (toll free)

W   www.sleepinggiantfruitwinery.ca

WHEN TO VISIT
Open daily 9:30 am – 8:30 pm

SOARING EAGLE ESTATE WINERY

This is a premium brand that grew into a winery. The brand was launched by Lang Vineyards in 2003 with a barrel-aged Merlot, the first of a family of barrel-treated wines. Günther Lang, who founded Lang in 1990, did not age wines in oak until he hired winemaker Ross Mirko in 2002. New Zealand–trained, Ross convinced Günther to add oak-aged wines to the portfolio. Because the style differed from the other Lang wines, the wines were released under the Soaring Eagle label. They were made in limited volumes because the jam-packed Lang winery offered scant space to make and cellar many such wines.

That changed after Holman Farms bought the Lang winery in 2005. Earlier that summer, Keith Holman had purchased a largely derelict property on Naramata Road for a vineyard. It is a property with a curious history, having once belonged to a wealthy German businessman who built a mansion with a fine view of the lake. Shortly after his death in the early 1980s the mansion was gutted by fire, leaving little but the graceful Lombardy poplars still lining the driveway.

The property's well-built tractor barn was easily transformed in 2006 into a well-equipped winery, including a tasting room for the Soaring Eagle winery. Winemaker Bernhard Schirrmeister, who took over when Ross moved to New Zealand in 2005 and who left Holman Lang five years later, scaled up the production at Soaring Eagle. But the wines remain consistent with Ross's style. "The Soaring Eagle wines will be lightly barrel-aged, like they have been before," Bernhard said. He believed the flavours of fruit should be paramount, not what he calls the taste of "the carpenter shop."

The large and ever-changing portfolio includes good Gewürztraminer, Pinot Gris, Viognier, Merlot and Syrah.

OPENED 2007

1751 Naramata Road
Naramata, BC V2A 8T8

T 250.490.4965

W www.holmanlangwineries.com

WHEN TO VISIT
Open daily 10 am – 6 pm May to October. Off-season hours vary; please call for times: 250-490-4965, ext 108.

SONORAN ESTATE WINERY

The Sonoran Desert is a vast arid region extending from Mexico's Sonora State through California, Arizona and into the northern United States. The desert's northernmost finger reaches into the Okanagan Valley. Whether it reaches as far as Summerland is debatable, but the dry slope below Highway 97 is sufficiently like a desert that the Smits family took the desert's name for their winery.

The winery is a family affair, run by Arjan and Ada Smits, their son Adrian, born in 1979, and his wife, Sarah. Emigrants from Holland in 1982, the Smits grew flowers both in Ontario and in British Columbia's Fraser Valley before moving to the Okanagan in 2000. Here they planted 2.3 hectares (5½ acres) of vines. While waiting for the vines to come into production, they operated their Windmill Bed and Breakfast, a landmark beside Highway 97 north of Summerland.

The winery was established initially at this lakefront property, about two kilometres (1¼ miles) north of Sumac Ridge Estate Winery. In 2006 the Smits families moved the winery to a Summerland vineyard they had acquired and planted the year before. While the new facility lacks the breathtaking lake views of the first winery, it is well located at the beginning of Bottleneck Drive, as the Summerland wineries like to call their busy wine route.

The Smits grow a broad selection of varietals, including Merlot, Pinot Noir, Chardonnay, Riesling, Gewürztraminer, Ehrenfelser and Pinot Blanc. "I really like reds," says Adrian, who recently added a small planting of Malbec. With their two properties, they now have 5.6 hectares (14 acres) under vine. Mentored by consultants Gary Strachan and Christine Leroux, Adrian completed the winery assistant course at Okanagan College. He previously worked with a company providing computer technical support, an office job that lost its appeal once his parents involved him in the winery.

ARJAN SMITS

MY PICKS

Look at the winery's new Jazz series wines, which feature regional bands. The debut wine is a Cabernet Sauvignon. Sonoran is one of the rare Okanagan wineries whose portfolio includes Oraniensteiner, a fruity German white with bright acidity. The Oraniensteiner icewine is a consistent award winner. Sonoran also makes a dry white with this variety of grape as well as a dessert wine called Orani Late Harvest.

OPENED 2004

5716 Gartrell Road
(corner of Happy Valley)
Summerland, BC V0H 1Z7

T 250.494.9323

W www.sonoranestate.com

WHEN TO VISIT
Open 10 am – 5:30 pm Monday
through Saturday and 11 am –
5:30 pm Sundays May 1 to
October 31, and by appointment

RESTAURANT
Full Moon Bistro
Open 11:30 am – 2 pm

ADRIAN SMITS AND HIS WIFE, SARAH
WILLARD (PHOTO BY SARAH WILLARD)

SPERLING VINEYARDS

The history of North Okanagan grape growing and winemaking lives here. This winery has been launched by the Sperling family, whose Casorso ancestors planted Kelowna's first vineyard in 1925 and were among the original investors in what is now Calona Vineyards.

The story began when Giovanni Casorso came from Italy in 1883 to work at Father Pandosy's mission, subsequently succeeding on his own. (He was once the Okanagan's largest tobacco grower.) His sons planted several vineyards. Formerly known as Pioneer Ranch, the 18.2-hectare (45-acre) Sperling Vineyards was first planted in 1931 with grapes and apples by Louis and Pete Casorso. When Pete retired in 1960, Bert Sperling, his son-in-law, switched the entire property to vines, both wine grapes and table grapes. The grapes here include a 45-year-old (in 2009) planting of Maréchal Foch, a 35-year-old planting of Riesling and a planting of indefinite age of Pearl of Csaba, a Muscat variety once grown widely in the Okanagan. Current plantings also include Gewürztraminer, Pinot Gris, Pinot Noir and Chardonnay.

Undoubtedly the Sperling family has been thinking about a winery of its own ever since Bert's daughter, Ann, born in 1962, began her winemaking career in 1984, first with Andrés Wines and then with CedarCreek Estate Winery. She moved in 1995 to Ontario, where she helped launch several stellar wineries. She and Peter Gamble, her husband, now consult internationally. Their BC clients include Sperling Vineyards and nearby Camelot Vineyards, where the initial Sperling wines are being made until a winery is developed, either at Pioneer Country Market (run by Velma Sperling, Ann's mother) or on the Casorso Road vineyard.

Even though it is backed by a large vineyard, the Sperling winery has begun small, making less than 1,000 cases.

Look for the Old Vines Riesling and the Old Vines Foch, the Pinot Gris and the affordable Riesling Icewine. Coming soon: a traditional-method sparkling wine.

OPENED 2009

3897 Casorso Road
Kelowna, BC V1W 4R6

T   250.764.1767

W www.sperlingvineyards.com

Tasting room planned at
Pioneer Country Market
1405 Pioneer Road
Kelowna, BC V1W 4M6

WHEN TO VISIT
Tasting room hours to be
determined

ANN SPERLING

SPILLER ESTATE WINERY

The wine shop at Spiller Estate, the first winery on the road to Naramata after leaving Penticton, shares a hilltop location with the heritage home (circa 1930) that is the four-unit Spiller bed and breakfast. The name commemorates the late Elbert Spiller, a pioneer orchardist.

Keith and Lynn Holman purchased the property from the Spiller estate in the 1990s and, being entrepreneurial, grandly restored the old house, added a farm market, then launched a fruit winery. The Holmans have grown fruit in the Okanagan for more than 25 years; Lynn's family, the Sworders, were pioneering Penticton orchardists.

The Holmans acquired their interest in wine long ago, during two years spent house-sitting in France. Since opening the fruit winery they have added five grape wineries and a distillery to their modest empire. Two of these—Stonehill and Mistral—are farther along Upper Bench Road, almost within walking distance of the fruit winery, hence convenient for wine touring. The short commute is also handy for Laurent Lafuente, the winemaker who looks after the distillery within the Stonehill winery.

Spiller's initial vintage of fruit wine was made by veteran Vancouver winemaker Ron Taylor, who, after his first career with Andrés, developed a second career as a vintner of fruit wines. He stamped on Spiller a mainstream fruit wine style: many of the wines have a touch of sweetness, and some are rich dessert wines with ripe fruit flavours that fill the mouth.

MY PICKS

I agree with the judges in wine competitions who awarded several medals to the peach, apricot and port-style cherry dessert wines. These are luscious on their own or over ice cream. The apple wine, light and crisply tart, is versatile, pairing well with many main-course dishes.

OPENED 2003

475 Upper Bench Road North
Penticton, BC V2A 8T4

T   250.490.4162

W www.holmanlangwineries.com

WHEN TO VISIT
Open daily 11 am – 5 pm May to
Canadian Thanksgiving Monday.
Closed November through April

FOOD SERVICE
Baked goods and beverages
available during summer

ACCOMMODATION
Four bed-and-breakfast units

LYNN AND KEITH HOLMAN
(PHOTO COURTESY OF HOLMAN
LANG WINERIES)

STAG'S HOLLOW WINERY

One of the popular tasting room wines here is a fruity white called Tragically Vidal. The tragedy, in the view of proprietors Larry Gerelus and Linda Pruegger, is that so little Vidal remains in the Okanagan. When they left business careers in Calgary to buy this four-hectare (10-acre) vineyard in 1992, Vidal was the largest planting. Three years later Larry grafted Chardonnay onto the Vidal trunks, leaving less than half an acre of Vidal. Subsequently almost half of that block was sacrificed for the new 7,500-case Stag's Hollow Winery. So Larry removed some of the Chardonnay grafts—"It is easy to buy Chardonnay," he says—and has let the Vidal roots grow Vidal grapes again, keeping tasting room patrons happy.

There is more depth to the Stag's Hollow portfolio than Vidal, including the reserve-tier Chardonnay, Merlot and Pinot Noir, released under the winery's Renaissance label. In recent vintages the Stag's Hollow Sauvignon Blanc, made with purchased grapes, has gained so much acclaim that Larry has also added the variety to his vineyard. Influenced by the Rhône tastes of winemaker Dwight Sick, who joined Stag's Hollow in 2008, Larry contracted Syrah, Viognier, Grenache and Marsanne grapes as well.

Stag's Hollow, beginning in 2001, is among the very few Okanagan wineries to offer "futures" on some of the wines. Long practised in Bordeaux, this win/win deal involves the consumer paying for a wine a year before it is released and being rewarded with a discount. The recent vintage of Renaissance Merlot, as an example, could be purchased for $25.50 a bottle, a discount of almost $5 from its retail price when released. Considering how quickly Stag's Hollow wines sell out, a futures order is one way to be sure of getting a case of the flagship Merlot.

LARRY GERELUS

MY PICKS

The Renaissance range, notably the buttery Chardonnay, the deep and brooding Merlot and the Pinot Noir, are always impressive. Heritage Block 1 is a fine Bordeaux blend. The Estate Merlot is good value. The recently added Syrah, Viognier and Quattro IV (a blend of Rhône varietals) are excellent. The Sauvignon Blanc's zesty freshness is retained well under a screw cap closure. And do not leave without savouring the juicy flavours of Tragically Vidal.

OPENED 1996

2237 Sun Valley Way
RR1 Site 3 Comp 36
Okanagan Falls, BC V0H 1R0

T 250.497.6162
   1.877.746.5569 (toll free)

W www.stagshollowwinery.com

WHEN TO VISIT
Open daily 10 am – 4:30 pm May
to October, or by appointment

DWIGHT SICK

STONEBOAT VINEYARDS

The name of this winery recalls this country's agricultural roots. Perhaps you know that the sardonically named stoneboat was actually a sled used by homesteaders to lug rocks off virgin land. Lanny Martiniuk, when conceiving this family-owned winery, wanted to honour the pioneers who hauled the abundant river rock from the six-hectare (15-acre) former orchard beside the Okanagan River that he and Julie, his wife, purchased in 1979.

Born in Vancouver in 1949, Lanny pursued numerous careers (electrician, stone mason, prospector, nuclear medicine technician) before becoming a farmer. Julie, a pharmacist, grew up on an Oliver farm down the road from where they now live. After the Martiniuks bought an orchard on the Okanagan River, Lanny planted almost two hectares (five acres) of experimental vines in 1984 for Brights winery (now Jackson-Triggs). He also learned to propagate vines in a greenhouse and is still a major supplier of vines to other vineyards.

Since 1991 Lanny, who now operates 20 hectares (50 acres) of vineyards, has stuck mostly to mainstream varieties, notably Pinot Gris, Pinot Blanc, Pinot Noir, Cabernet Sauvignon, Cabernet Franc and Merlot. Stoneboat is also one of the few wineries growing Pinotage, the South African red. However, since Lanny is reluctant to pull out any vines, less-familiar varieties generally end up in tasty blended wines. For example, a complex white called Chorus includes Viognier, Oraniensteiner, Kerner and Schönburger.

The Martiniuks launched their small winery to secure their future as grape growers. Ultimately winemaking will be in the hands of Jay Martiniuk, one of their three sons. Jay, who is pursuing a degree in winemaking, has mentored with Pascal Madevon at Osoyoos Larose and with Lawrence Herder, Stoneboat's initial consultant. "The long and short of it is, I'm a grower," Lanny says. "I can't be a winemaker. I appreciate wine but I love the plants."

The winery won back-to-back Lieutenant Governor's Awards for Excellence in BC Wines with Pinot Noir and then with Pinotage. The winery also has excellent Pinot Gris and Pinot Blanc, and Chorus is downright delicious.

OPENED 2007

7148 Orchard Grove Lane
Oliver, BC V0H 1T0

T   250.498.2226
    1.888.598.2226 (toll free)

W www.stoneboatvineyards.com

WHEN TO VISIT
Open daily 10 am – 5:30 pm
May through mid-October,
and by appointment

THE MARTINIUK FAMILY FROM LEFT TO RIGHT: LANNY,
TIM, JAY, JULIE AND CHRIS

STONEHILL ESTATE WINERY

Klaus Stadler, who started this winery, called it Benchland Vineyards. A German brewmaster, Klaus planted this Okanagan vineyard in 1998 and opened the winery when the vines began producing. A stickler for the latest technology, he installed the best winery equipment money could buy, except for barrels. He considered barrels, which are harder to clean than stainless steel tanks, to be obsolescent winery appliances.

Businessman Keith Holman, who was developing the neighbouring Mistral winery in 2004, was delighted to buy Stadler's spic and span winery that fall when the brewmaster returned to Germany. He only needed to supplement the winemaking equipment already there with barrels. The Stonehill winery is big enough to handle the crush for both wineries, while the adjoining vineyards comprise 16 hectares (40 acres).

Stadler intended to add a distillery to Benchland but never got around to it. Keith, who has been interested in spirits since living in France about 30 years ago, believes it is a good idea. Okanagan fruit farmers, often struggling with depressed prices, would benefit by selling fruits for distilling. And the spirits market has yet to be exploited by Okanagan wineries, Keith argues. For that reason, he installed two stills in the Stonehill winery in 2005 and sought a novel licence for a land-based distillery. He also hired Laurent Lafuente, a French winemaker who graduated in 1999 from a Swiss winemaking school. Laurent spent the next five years working in rum distilleries in the Caribbean, becoming the master blender at Antigua Distillery. Laurent won back-to-back gold medals for rum at a San Francisco spirits competition before coming to the Okanagan.

Laurent crafts several port-style wines that have become a specialty at Stonehill. Since the use of the term "port" is now limited to Portuguese wines, these are released as, for example, Esprit de Gamay, Esprit de Cabernet Sauvignon and Esprit de Gewürztraminer.

KEITH HOLMAN

MY PICKS

Stonehill is the winery in the Holman Lang group with the most esoteric wines, including Optima, Schönburger and Zweigelt and, of course, the Esprit line.

OPENED 2001
(AS BENCHLAND VINEYARDS)

170 Upper Bench Road South
Penticton, BC V2A 8T1

T   250.770.1733

W www.holmanlangwineries.com

WHEN TO VISIT
Open daily 11 am – 5 pm May to
Canadian Thanksgiving Monday.
Closed November through April.

SUMAC RIDGE ESTATE WINERY

When Sumac Ridge's latest expansion a few years ago gave the winery the same Tudor design found elsewhere in Summerland, one wag compared it to a Super 8 Motel. That is unkind. What is under the skin—superb wines, VIP tastings and a triple diamond winery restaurant—draws crowds that most motel managers would die for. Now producing more than 100,000 cases a year, popular Sumac Ridge is the granddaddy of Okanagan estate wineries, and one of the most innovative.

Harry McWatters and then-partner Lloyd Schmidt founded the winery in 1979, planting vines on the fairways of a struggling nine-hole golf course just north of Summerland. They kept the clubhouse, making wine in the basement and feeding golfers and customers upstairs. The clubhouse, now called Cellar Door Bistro, enabled Sumac Ridge to run a winery restaurant for many years before other wineries were allowed to serve food in 1995.

Harry McWatters, who retired in 2008, drove innovation at this winery and in the industry. Sumac Ridge made the Okanagan's first Chardonnay in 1981, and in 1984 was one of the first Canadian wineries to produce icewine. Winemaking trials led in 1985 to the development of Steller's Jay Brut, the Okanagan's first successful sparkling wine made in the traditional Champagne method. The cellar, deep in the rock below the former clubhouse, a popular stop on winery tours, is aging at least 250,000 bottles of Steller's Jay at any time.

Other firsts here include the 40-hectare (100-acre) Black Sage Vineyard. Planted in 1993, it was then the single largest planting of French (Bordeaux) grape varieties in Canada. A few years later, Sumac Ridge released Canada's first Meritage wine. And the Okanagan's first $50 table wine was Sumac Ridge's Pinnacle, first made in the 1997 vintage.

MY PICKS

The wines, made by Mark Wendenburg and Jason James, are consistently good. The Private Reserve Gewürztraminer is Canada's bestselling Gewürztraminer. My personal favourites include Steller's Jay, the white Meritage (one of the Okanagan's best white wines), Sauvignon Blanc, Pinot Blanc, Chardonnay, the red Meritage and all the Black Sage wines. The Pinnacle wines (a red blend, a white blend and a sparkling wine) are absolutely world-class wines.

OPENED 1980

17403 Highway 97 North
PO Box 307
Summerland, BC V0H 1Z0

T   250.494.0451

W www.sumacridge.com

WHEN TO VISIT
Open daily 9:30 am – 6 pm
July and August; 10 am – 8 pm
early September through to
June. Tasting bar closes at
6 pm in summer, 5 pm during
other months.

RESTAURANT
Cellar Door Bistro
Open daily for lunch and
dinner. Closed December 21
to January 14.

MARK WENDENBURG

SUMMERHILL PYRAMID WINERY

Summerhill owner Stephen Cipes is an idealist and a mystic, and that is reflected in this winery, one of the most interesting stops on the wine tour. Before you enter the tasting room, linger at the World Peace Park in front of the winery. Towering over a globe encircled with flowers is Summerhill's Peace Pole. Inscriptions exhort "May peace prevail on Earth" in 16 languages.

Stephen's spiritual side is represented by the gleaming white pyramid that dramatically dominates the grounds here, which is employed to age wines. He believes that the pyramid's rejuvenating energy improves good wine as well as improving the spirit and well-being of those who spend time inside. Tours of the pyramid, when available, are not to be missed.

Stephen, an engagingly mercurial personality, was born in New York in 1944 and succeeded in real estate before moving to the Okanagan in 1986 in search of a more environmentally positive lifestyle for himself and his family (son Ezra is now general manager). Steve lives his convictions. Summerhill grows grapes organically in its 20-hectare (50-acre) vineyard and has begun to adopt biodynamic practices. Most of the winery's contract growers also have been converted to organic production. And in 2007 the winery itself achieved organic status for its winemaking methods.

"The idea is to become a model of permaculture," Stephen says. "It is my thought that we should give something back to nature. Let the birds and bees enjoy their lives here instead of being pesticided away."

Winemaker Eric von Krosigk shares those objectives and is currently developing sulphur-free wines. "For me, it is the Holy Grail," he says. "I'm getting more sulphur-sensitive." Born in Vernon in 1962, the son of a ranch manager and brewery founder, Eric spent six years studying at Geisenheim, the great German wine school. On his return he was the

ERIC VON KROSIGK

initial winemaker at Summerhill in 1991 before moving on to other Okanagan wineries. He returned in 2005 to follow his consuming passion for the sparkling wines that are Summerhill's signature.

MY PICKS

The array of sparkling wines includes the elegant Cipes Gabriel, made from Chardonnay and aged in the bottle on its yeast for three and a half years, in the style of top Champagne. Cipes Blanc de Noirs and Cipes Pinot Noir Brut are delicious and complex sparkling wines. Cipes Ice is a highly original cranberry-hued sparkler with just a dash of icewine. Cipes Brut, made with Riesling, Chardonnay and Pinot Blanc, is the winery's bread-and-butter sparkler.

OPENED 1992

4870 Chute Lake Road
Kelowna, BC V1W 4M3

T   250.764.8000
    1.800.667.3538 (toll free)

W www.summerhill.bc.ca

WHEN TO VISIT
Open daily 9 am – 7 pm May
1 to October 14; 11 am – 5 pm
October 15 to April 30

RESTAURANT
Sunset Organic Bistro
Open daily 11 am – 9 pm for
lunch and dinner

SYNERGY WINERY & VINEYARDS

Synergy released its first wines in the fall of 2009, well in advance of building the stunning winery that is proposed for this Munson Mountain location overlooking Penticton. The strategy of the people behind Synergy is to develop the brand over three years. Only then will its winery— a fairy-tale design by Robert Mackenzie—rise from the mountainside.

The lead partners are three Penticton businessmen: Larry Lund, Ron Bell and Jim Morrison, all wine lovers who have also succeeded in other fields. (Larry and Ron already own 40 percent of Blasted Church Vineyards.) Larry, who was born in Penticton in 1960, is a member of the BC Hockey Hall of Fame. He earned that honour through an 18-year career in professional hockey, including six seasons with the Houston Astros of the World Hockey Association. He also operated the Okanagan Hockey Camps and Academy, training young players, from 1963 to 2004.

Ron is a developer, a hotelier and the owner of liquor stores, a pub and a restaurant and, more crucially, a 2.6-hectare (6½-acre) vineyard south of Blasted Church where he grows superb Syrah and Sauvignon Blanc. Jim is a professional engineer, president of Wildstone Construction and Engineering, formed in 1991.

The three partners own this 3.6-hectare (nine-acre) winery site on Lower Bench Road, where Pinot Gris has been planted. Larry and Ron operate 36-hectare (90-acre) Blind Creek Ranch Vineyards near Cawston in the Similkameen Valley, a leased property planted to vines (mostly red varieties) in 2009. Until this vineyard comes into production, Synergy is also contracting Okanagan grapes.

The winemaker is Lawrence Herder. He and his wife, Sharon, who have helped launch at least five other wineries including their own, have a three-year contract to get Synergy going. Using facilities at the Herder Vineyards winery, they made 1,000 cases for Synergy in 2008 and double that in 2009. For the next several years, Synergy will plateau at 2,400 cases, establishing a presence in the market before resuming growth to a target of 20,000 cases a year.

MY PICKS

Synergy's debut wines from 2008—a Syrah, a Pinot Gris and a Sauvignon Blanc—are exceptional. Watch out for the Meritages still to be released.

OPENED 2009

134 Lower Bench Road
Penticton, BC V2A 5E6

T 250.499.9489
250.493.9412

W www.synergywinery.ca

WHEN TO VISIT
Tasting room delayed for several years

LAWRENCE AND SHARON HERDER

TANGLED VINES ESTATE WINERY

This winery began when four friends, all with restaurant backgrounds, were seduced by the Okanagan lifestyle after a summer weekend in 2003 at the Quails' Gate Estate Winery guest house. Their drive home to Vancouver gave them time to flip through real estate listings and to figure out the role each would have in a proposed winery.

The driving force is Craig McKenzie, a Dalhousie law school graduate who preferred restaurant management to law and was operations manager at Bridges Restaurant in Vancouver until the winery opened. The other partners are Craig's brother, Clark, and John and Maxine Hill. All have worked at or managed at Bridges, crediting their initial interest in wine to the knowledge picked up in the restaurant. "We all started in the restaurant business in our teens," John says. "We are lovers of food and wine. It has always been part of our lives."

In 2000 Craig took time off to go to Australia, acquiring winemaking skills by working the crush at Tintara, a historic McLaren Vale winery. "I was at that point in my life where I was looking for something that I was passionate about," he remembers. "The camaraderie of the people in the industry surprised me." The weekend at Quails' Gate just confirmed his Australian experience. The foursome spent a couple of years looking at vineyards. Finally, in the summer of 2005, they found this 1.2-hectare (three-acre) Okanagan Falls vineyard just across the road from Wild Goose and Stag's Hollow wineries. Additional plantings have since tripled the vineyard.

The vineyard is dedicated to white varieties, including Pinot Blanc, Pinot Gris, Sauvignon Blanc and Gewürztraminer. "The aspect of our land is more suited to whites," Craig believes. "And the style of our wines is suited to the foods we eat in British Columbia." Sparkling wines and possibly reds will be added in due course.

CRAIG MCKENZIE

The partners believe that wine should be fun. Accordingly they released the winery's first Gewürztraminer as Premier Goo and the second as GEW II. The popular dry rosé is called Tickled Pink. The winery also offers good Riesling and good Pinot Blanc.

OPENED 2006

2140 Sun Valley Way
Okanagan Falls, BC V0H 1R0
T 250.497.6416
W www.tangledvineswinery.com

WHEN TO VISIT
Open daily 10 am – 5 pm
May to October

TANTALUS VINEYARDS

When Tantalus built the Okanagan's first LEED-certified winery in 2009, the many forward-looking firsts included a charging station for electric cars. LEED is short for Leadership in Energy and Environmental Design, a sustainability certification governed by the Canada Green Building Council. So far the only other LEED winery in Canada is the Niagara Peninsula's Southbrook Vineyards, certified in November 2008.

It just seems right to find a green ethic at work on one of the Kelowna area's most historic vineyards, planted in 1927 by pioneering grower J. W. Hughes. His foreman, Martin Dulik, bought it in 1948 and it remained in the Dulik family for 56 years. In 1997 Martin's granddaughter, Sue, opened a winery that she called Pinot Reach Cellars. In 2004 the Dulik family sold the vineyard and winery to Eric Savics, a Vancouver investment dealer. The winery's new name, Tantalus, originates in Greek mythology. Tantalus was an errant son of Zeus whose punishment was to be "tantalized" by food and water placed out of his reach.

"We have a great setting," says Eric. "It is a good piece of dirt. If we plant the best Riesling and Pinot Noir, maybe we can really make something that would stand out." There is no maybe about it. The Riesling vines that the Duliks planted in 1978 and those planted more recently produce finely structured and widely praised wines. (The vineyard also has a little Chardonnay, Syrah and Viognier.) Jancis Robinson, the influential British writer, calls the Tantalus Riesling one of the 10 best wines in Canada.

There is not a large quantity available yet, for Tantalus has been making only about 2,000 cases a year. However, the new winery, erected on the footprint of the previous building, has capacity to produce up to 10,000 cases of estate wines. Says general manager Jane Hatch, "Nobody builds a winery without thinking of expansion."

DAVID PATERSON AND JACQUELINE KEMP
(PHOTO BY JANE HATCH)

The winery's tasting room here features an entire westward-facing wall of floor-to-ceiling glass, offering a stunning view over the vineyard to the city in the distance. The extensive use of glass in the design admits natural light into the entire winery and gives visitors a look into the barrel hall and, as Jane puts it, "the guts of the winery." Winemaking in the new building is handled by Jacqueline Kemp, a consultant from New Zealand, and David Paterson.

OPENED 1997
(AS PINOT REACH CELLARS)

1670 Dehart Road
Kelowna, BC V1W 4N6

T 1.877.764.0078 (toll free)

W www.tantalus.ca

WHEN TO VISIT
Open daily 11 am – 5 pm in summer, and by appointment

MY PICKS

The Tantalus Old Vines Riesling and the regular Riesling share the same laser beam brightness of aromas, tangy flavours and mineral backbone. The fresh, racy Riesling icewine is intense in its taste, as fine as any top German Eiswein. The silky Pinot Noir is also headed to the front ranks of Okanagan Pinot Noir, and the Chardonnay has a Chablis-like crispness.

THERAPY VINEYARDS

Therapy Vineyards might seem overly cute as a winery name until you experience the effects of sipping Pinot Gris here while watching the sun set over the vineyards of Naramata. The property was the original Red Rooster winery. When Red Rooster moved to its Naramata Road location in 2004, a group of investors (some of them members of the Opimian Society) relaunched the property as Therapy Vineyards.

The winery's name inspired a series of clever labels. Many of the wines are labelled provocatively with what resemble Rorschach ink blots, a psychoanalytical tool. Before you start psychoanalyzing yourself with a bottle of Therapy wine, remember that authentic Rorschach blots (there are only 10) have been guarded carefully by the professionals who use them (although that protection has been breached in recent years, over the objections of many psychoanalysts). Take these colourful labels for the fun they are meant to be. For its first Malbec in 2008 Therapy inaugurated a new series of artist labels: this wine has a hockey player on the label.

Perhaps the most famous name in the history of psychoanalysis is Sigmund Freud. The winery has appropriated his name in the labels of such wines as Super Ego, Freud's Ego (both are red blends), Freudian Sip (a blend of Riesling, Kerner and Pinot Gris) and Pink Freud, obviously a rosé. These names add to the fun of visiting Therapy's tasting room without taking anything from the fact that these are very well-made wines.

Therapy's first winemaker, Marcus Ansems, put the stamp of his native Australia on the wine styles, notably the full-bodied, peppery Shiraz. He was succeeded in late 2008 by Steve Latchford. Born in Ontario's Prince Edward County in 1982, Steve once worked on a dairy farm and believes the transition to a winery is not a big leap. "I worked with pumps in the dairy barn too," he says with a laugh. A 2004 graduate of Niagara College's wine program, he started his winery career at the Jackson-Triggs winery in Ontario.

At Therapy Steve took over a superbly equipped winery. Completed in 2009, it has an underground cellar now housing about 500 barrels, with room for twice as many. Therapy makes about 10,000 cases a year and plans to reach 15,000 cases.

MY PICKS

Therapy wines are excellent across the range, notably the Shiraz, the Merlot, the Chardonnay, the Pinot Gris, the rosé and the Freudian Sip. Freud's Ego is an affordable red blend for drinking now while you cellar the bold Super Ego blend, which is 62 percent Cabernet Sauvignon filled out with Merlot, Petit Verdot, Cabernet Franc and Shiraz.

OPENED 2005

940 Debeck Road
RR1 Site 2 Comp 47
Naramata, BC V0H 1N0
T   250.496.5217
W www.therapyvineyards.com

WHEN TO VISIT
Open daily 10 am – 5 pm May through October (to 6 pm on Friday and weekends)

ACCOMMODATION
Guest house with two bed-and-breakfast units

STEVE LATCHFORD

THORNHAVEN ESTATES WINERY

With its Santa Fe architecture, the Thornhaven winery is an Okanagan jewel. Tucked away behind Summerland's Giant's Head Mountain, the adobe-hued winery is at the top of a slope covered with about 3.2 hectares (eight acres) of vines. The patio affords picture-perfect views, but the best view is from the bottom of the undulating vineyard, preferably when the late-afternoon sun paints the winery and the hillside behind it with a golden tint.

The vineyard was planted by Dennis Fraser, a former grain farmer from Dawson Creek who sold his farm, almost 1,000 hectares (2,500 acres), in 1989 and then began converting a Summerland orchard to vines (Pinot Noir, Chardonnay and Gewürztraminer, with a bit of Sauvignon Blanc and Pinot Meunier). Winemaking began here in 1999, with Dennis planning a modest tasting room in the basement of his home. Then a farmer's habit of thinking big took over and he built a picturesque winery.

The winery was purchased in 2005 by Dennis's cousin, Jack Fraser, who was changing careers after 24 years working in overseas oil fields (mostly in Libya). Thornhaven is now managed by Jack and his wife, Jan, a tasting room hostess with a vivacious personality. Son Jason, who mentored with consultant Christine Leroux, is the winemaker.

Now making about 5,500 cases a year, Thornhaven has a portfolio of 13 to 15 wines, several of which resulted from taking advantage of planting errors. The supplier of vines did not have enough Pinot Noir to fill the Thornhaven order and stretched it with Pinot Meunier. Thus this is one of the few Okanagan wineries with a varietal Pinot Meunier. The winery also offers an unusual Sauvignon Blanc/Chardonnay blend because the varieties are interplanted in the vineyard. The grapes are picked and fermented together, yielding a delicious wine tasting of peaches and citrus.

MY PICKS

Thornhaven has made its reputation with award-winning Gewürztraminer, solidly backed by good Pinot Gris and the refreshing Sauvignon Blanc/Chardonnay. The Pinot Meunier has jammy strawberry flavours and a lovely silken texture. The rosé combines Pinot Noir, Pinot Meunier and Merlot in a tangy wine with character. The tour de force here is the delicate dessert wine, Nectar del Sol, made with Riesling, Orange Muscat and Viognier grapes.

OPENED 2001

6816 Andrew Avenue
RR2 Site 68 Comp 15
Summerland, BC V0H 1Z7

T 250.494.7778

W www.thornhaven.com

WHEN TO VISIT
Open daily 10 am – 5 pm
May 1 to October 14, and by
appointment

RESTAURANT
Patio offers wine by the glass
and deli food. Picnics welcome.

JASON FRASER

TINHORN CREEK VINEYARDS

Aptly named, Tinhorn Creek's Panorama Deck offers visitors one of the best views of the South Okanagan's vineyards. You can linger here as long as you want because the winery's self-guided tour lets you set your own pace. The tasting room experience is also unrushed. If you are reasonably fit, you can find an even better view of the winery and valley by hiking uphill to the rear of the vineyard to the Golden Mile Trail. Developed by Tinhorn Creek, the trail winds along the flank of mountains, amid sagebrush and under the shade of pine trees. One spur gives access to the ruins of the Tin Horn Creek mine's stamp mill. For those not ready for this brisk climb into the hills, the stone arch at the winery's entrance grandly echoes the stamp mill.

With the winery's Fischer Vineyard and the larger Diamondback Vineyard, across the valley on Black Sage Road, Tinhorn Creek, which makes a total of 35,000 cases of wine annually, is self-sufficient in grapes. From the start the winery focused its plantings to produce six table wines: Merlot, Cabernet Franc, Pinot Noir, Chardonnay, Pinot Gris and Gewürztraminer. Icewine is made from Kerner because that variety was already in the Fischer Vineyard when Alberta oilman Bob Shaunessy bought it in 1993 for a winery site.

Recent changes in the vineyard have added such varieties as Syrah, Cabernet Sauvignon, Sémillon, Viognier, Sauvignon Blanc and Muscat, largely to support Tinhorn Creek's premium-tier wines under the Oldfield Series banner. The series is named for winery partner Kenn Oldfield and his wife, the California-trained winemaker Sandra Oldfield. The first wine in the Oldfield's Collection (as it was then called) was the 2001 Merlot, the Okanagan's first premium wine with a screw cap closure. Since the 2005 vintage all Tinhorn Creek table wines have screw cap closures.

That was also the year the winery launched its Crush Club, an idea that the Oldfields brought back from a visit to California. In the first year 800 people joined. That is hardly surprising: it costs nothing to join

BOB SHAUNESSY, AND SANDRA AND KENN OLDFIELD

but members get discounts on wines as long as they commit to buying a couple of cases every year. Membership is often the most reliable way of getting wines, including the premium wines, before they are sold out. Club members also move to the front of the line for personal winery tours and access to the guest suites in Tinhorn Creek's vineyard.

MY PICKS

There are a lot of good wines here. The whites—Gewürztraminer, Pinot Gris, Chardonnay and 2Bench White—are refreshingly fruit-forward. Among the reds, Merlot is the flagship but is often overshadowed by the spicy Cabernet Franc. The Oldfield Series wines show well-crafted elegance, notably the Syrah, the Merlot, the Pinot Noir and the 2Bench Red.

OPENED 1995

32830 Tinhorn Creek Road
PO Box 2010
Oliver, BC V0H 1T0

T 250.498.3743
   1.888.484.6467 (toll free)

W www.tinhorn.com

WHEN TO VISIT
Open daily 10 am – 6 pm May through October, 10 am – 5 pm November through April

RESTAURANT
Scheduled to open in 2011

TOWNSHIP 7 VINEYARDS & WINERY

Township 7 is the British Columbia wine industry's version of siblings: two wineries in two locations but with the same name.

The original Township 7 was opened in 2001 on a heritage farm south of Langley by Gwen and Corey Coleman. Although they had worked in the Okanagan for six years, they chose to open near their wine market rather than near the vineyards. The strategy worked. When they sold Township 7 in 2006, the Langley winery accounted for 85 percent of sales, with the remainder coming through the second Township 7 winery, which opened in 2004 in the Okanagan.

The winery's current ownership is headed by Mike Raffan, an amiable restaurateur. Born in North Vancouver in 1954, he is a former owner of both The Keg and Milestones restaurants. Already a fan of Township 7 wines, he has found his new career in wine as captivating as his former life in restaurants. "I love it," he says. "When I was young the restaurant business was very much that way—I just couldn't get enough of it." Substantial enhancements to the Penticton winery—some as simple as paving the parking lot—have attracted many more visitors and sales to the Okanagan winery, now producing about 10,000 cases a year.

Winemaker Bradley Cooper began making wine in 1997 at Hawthorne Mountain Vineyards with Michael Bartier, Township 7's first winemaker. Born in New Westminster in 1958, Brad is a journalism graduate from Langara College. After several years as a writer and photographer with community newspapers, he switched to working in restaurants and then to winemaking. He honed his experience by working the 1999 vintage at Vidal Estate in New Zealand and the 2000 icewine harvest at Stonechurch in Ontario. In 2002 he joined the winemaking team at Mount Baker Vineyards in Washington state. He returned to the Okanagan in 2003, making two vintages at Stag's Hollow before coming to Township 7 in the summer of 2005.

MY PICKS

Mike Raffan was drawn to Township 7 by the quality of the wines. I can see why. My favourites include the rich, barrel-fermented Chardonnay, the unoaked Chardonnay, the bold Syrah, the Bordeaux reds and a very elegant sparkling wine called Seven Stars.

OPENED 2004

1450 McMillan Avenue
Penticton, BC V2A 8T4
T 250.770.1743
W www.township7.com

WHEN TO VISIT
Open daily 11 am – 6 pm April through October, and noon – 5 pm on Friday, Saturday and Sunday in winter

MIKE RAFFAN

TWISTED TREE VINEYARDS & WINERY

Planted in 2005, the two-hectare (five-acre) Twisted Tree vineyard replaced a cherry orchard so old that the trees were gnarled and twisted. The trees are now gone, remembered only in the name of this highway-front winery on the outskirts of Osoyoos. The owners are Chris and Beata Tolley. When they decided to become wine growers, they prepared themselves by spending 2003 at Lincoln University, New Zealand's top wine school. "Chris and I are risk averse," explains Beata, a chartered accountant and the daughter of a Polish engineer who brought his family to Canada in 1982. Chris, a software engineer, was born in Ottawa in 1966.

In 2004, after successful business careers in Calgary, the couple bought the Twisted Tree property, a former fruit stand, and made their first vintage with purchased grapes (Syrah, Pinot Noir, Cabernet Sauvignon and Riesling). The fruit stand, located beside the highway, has been replaced with a well-equipped winery. The tasting room, with the ambiance of a cozy private club, looks over the vineyard and Osoyoos Lake.

Having decided to purchase mainstream varieties, the Tolleys dedicated their own vineyard to varieties seldom grown in the Okanagan. They grow three white Rhône varieties, Viognier, Roussanne and Marsanne. The reds include Carmenère, Tempranillo and several firsts for the Okanagan. One is Tannat, a vine grown primarily in southwest France and Uruguay, which Twisted Tree has released on its own and in red blends. The other is Corvina, the Italian red variety for a wine called Amarone. Chris emulates the Amarone style, partially drying bunches of grapes to concentrate the flavours and the alcohol of this rich and warming wine.

For future growth Twisted Tree owns a 4.5-hectare (11-acre) orchard nearby, producing peaches at least until 2011. Expect to see more unusual grape varieties planted here.

Twisted Tree crafts two crisp and complex wines from its Rhône whites: a Viognier/Roussanne blend and Trio, a blend of those two along with Marsanne. Bordeaux varieties are combined in an excellent blend called Six Vines. The Syrah is bold and peppery. The Tannat is dark and muscular; the Carmenère is a spicy red; and the Tempranillo is full-bodied. The winery also offers excellent wines under its value-priced Second Crossing label.

OPENED 2006

3628 Highway 3 East
Osoyoos, BC V0H 1V6
T 250.495.5161
W www.twistedtree.ca

WHEN TO VISIT
Open daily 10 am – 5 pm
May through October,
and by appointment

CHRIS AND BEATA TOLLEY

VAN WESTEN VINEYARDS

Every wine Rob Van Westen releases has a name that begins with "V"—sometimes with a hilarious result. The winery's first Cabernet Franc is being released in 2010 as Vrankenstein because the variety is usually harvested on Halloween. But even if some of the names are light-hearted, the wines always deserve to be taken seriously.

Rob and his father and brother (both named Jake) are some of the best farmers on the Naramata Bench. The family, now with 21 hectares (52 acres) of cherries, apples and grapes, has farmed on the Naramata Bench ever since Jake Sr. emigrated from Holland in 1951 after graduating from agriculture school. Rob, tall enough to tower over his vines, was born in 1966. He left school after the 10th grade and worked at construction in Vancouver until 1999, when he returned to help with the family's newly planted vineyard. He embraced viticulture with a passion, studying at Okanagan College and, when he began making wine, spending nearly four months at wineries in Australia and New Zealand.

CedarCreek Estate Winery began buying Van Westen grapes. Impressed with the quality of the fruit, CedarCreek winemaker Tom DiBello encouraged Rob's desire to be a winemaker by giving him six barrels in 2003. Rob launched the winery two years later. Since then he has moved winemaking into a hulking apple-packing plant on one of the family's properties. In 2009 he installed an informal tasting room here as well. When it is open, either Rob or Tammi, his wife, and sometimes both, preside over lively informal tastings. The spirit of the wine shop is mirrored aptly by the name Rob has assigned to the new Merlot: Vivre la Vie.

The Van Westens have five hectares (12 acres) of vineyards, with another hectare or two slated for planting. They grow Merlot, Cabernet Franc, Pinot Gris and Pinot Blanc and plan to add Pinot Noir and

ROB VAN WESTEN

Cabernet Sauvignon—but no Chardonnay. "I've never been a Chardonnay drinker," Rob admits. Conveniently, considering the winery's "V" theme, he does grow Viognier.

MY PICKS

The wines, like the delicious Viognier, all have names beginning with "V." Vino Grigio is a tasty Pinot Gris; Vivacious, a crisp and remarkably complex Pinot Blanc; Voluptuous is a chewy, age-worthy Bordeaux blend. Vrankenstein and Vivre la Vie are eagerly awaited.

OPENED 2005

2800B Aikens Loop
Naramata, BC V0H 1N0

T 250.496.0067

W www.vanwestenvineyards.com

WHEN TO VISIT
Open Tuesdays and Saturdays
by appointment

THE VIEW WINERY & VINEYARD

The owners of this winery, Jennifer and Kent Molgat and Chris Turton, Jennifer's father, have delayed opening a tasting room until a totally new winery is built on the slope of the nearby vineyard. The vineyard location has a million-dollar view, hence the name of the winery. The heritage packing house now used for a winery, surrounded since 2006 by monstrous stainless steel tanks for making apple wine, just lacks the appropriate aesthetics. The apple wine, however, is the engine behind the winery.

The Turton family have been fruit growers here since Chris's grandfather, George Ward, settled these East Kelowna slopes. Chris began replacing some of the apple trees with vines in 1994 and now has 16 hectares (40 acres). Almost a quarter is planted to Pinotage, ably farmed by South African vineyard manager Willem Semmelink. The other varieties grown here are Baco Noir, Gewürztraminer, Riesling, Ehrenfelser and Optima.

About the same time he started planting grapes, Chris began producing Rock Creek Premium Dry Cider, a pub-style cider that has been turned into a huge success by Alberta's Big Rock Brewery. The tanks inside and outside the View's packing house support the production of about one million litres a year.

"I am new to apple wine," says winemaker Marie-Thérese Duarte with a laugh (she is a native of Cahors in France). With a master's degree in winemaking from a university in Toulouse, she came to Canada via California in 2007 in time to make icewine. "That's why I came here—to get some knowledge at making icewine," she says. After working at Rollingdale winery, she stepped in at The View when the first winemaker, of German origin, drew the line at making apple wine. Marie-Thérese has her ego under control and also knows how to make solid grape wines.

MY PICKS

After debuting with a rather light Pinotage from the 2007 vintage, The View has mastered this variety: the 2008 is dark, rich and spicy. Try as well the Gewürztraminer and the late-harvest Optima.

OPENED 2008

#1 – 2287 Ward Road
Kelowna, BC V1W 4R5
T   250.215.1331
W   www.theviewwinery.com

WHEN TO VISIT
No tasting room at this time

JENNIFER MOLGAT

VOLCANIC HILLS VINEYARD & CELLARS

Sarwan Gidda believes he has learned from mistakes. When he and his two younger brothers built the Mt. Boucherie Estate Winery in 2000, they erected a very large winery but a very compact wine shop. They had not anticipated the throngs of wine tourists that now come to taste and purchase wine. In 2008 Sarwan left that partnership to build the 1,400-square-metre (15,000-square-foot) Volcanic Hills winery. Designed by Sarwan's son, Bobby, this winery, literally a stone's throw downhill from Mt. Boucherie, has one of the largest wine shops in the Okanagan. Today Sarwan figures the winery might sell as much as 90 percent of its wines at this shop on busy Boucherie Road. He did not build there to provoke his brothers, Sarwan says. "I built where the business is. You need to be on that road to sell wine."

Born in India in 1953, Sarwan came to Canada with his family as a child. His father insisted that the brothers all get educated before he allowed them to farm tree fruits and grapes. Sarwan thus became an accountant. And he made sure his children also received good educations. Bobby, who was born in 1985, graduated from Okanagan College with a degree in business administration and worked in the finance department there while taking the college's winery assistant and winery sales courses. As part of the coursework, Bobby, who previously worked in the Mt. Boucherie cellar, designed Volcanic Hills, a $2.3-million winery with geothermal heating and cooling. The wine shop is above the processing cellars, with a view of Okanagan Lake.

Sarwan's 30.3 hectares (75 acres) of vineyard, primarily around Westbank, will support substantial production. The intent is to move rapidly to about 10,000 cases a year. Volcanic Hills began making wines in 2007 at nearby Kalala Organic Estate Winery with consultant Alan Marks, a former Mt. Boucherie winemaker. For the 2009 vintage Sarwan recruited Elias Phiniotis, an Okanagan winemaker so experienced that

Volcanic Hills is the 20th winery he has helped. Born in Cyprus in 1943 and trained in Hungary, Elias has worked in the Canadian wine industry since 1976. One of his roles at Volcanic Hills will be mentoring Bobby in winemaking.

MY PICKS

The winery launched with Gewürztraminer, Pinot Noir, Merlot, Gamay and Cabernet Sauvignon plus a 2007 Chardonnay icewine. The other varieties in the vineyard, such as Zweigelt, Michurinetz and Maréchal Foch, are expected to become the basis of interesting blends.

OPENED 2010

2845 Boucherie Road
West Kelowna, BC V1Z 2G6
T 778.755.5550
W www.volcanichillswinery.com

WHEN TO VISIT
Open daily 10 am – 6 pm April through October, and 11 am – 5 pm November through March

BOBBY AND SARWAN GIDDA

WILD GOOSE VINEYARDS

It seems hard to believe that Riesling's popularity fell so far in the late 1990s that Wild Goose dropped the variety for about five years. Now that Riesling has roared back into fashion, the variety comprises a third of this boutique winery's production. That fully justifies Adolf Kruger's decision to plant Riesling (along with Gewürztraminer) in 1983 when he, with sons Hagen and Roland, developed the winery's initial four-hectare (10-acre) vineyard. When Adolf first walked these rock-strewn, sage-covered slopes, he frightened a flock of geese, a memory that inspired the winery's name seven years later.

The Krugers confounded a pessimistic bureaucrat's prediction that they would not even sell 2,000 bottles a year. The winery now sells more than 100,000 bottles a year. Such is the demand for the Wild Goose award-winning wines that Roland, who markets the wines, once lamented that the orders for the winery's Gewürztraminer stretched two vintages into the future.

To support growing sales, Wild Goose has developed three additional vineyards. The Mystic River Vineyard planted in 1999 near Oliver (also the location of the winery's comfortable guest cottage) produces exceptional Pinot Gris, Pinot Blanc and Gewürztraminer. The Kruger's Claim Vineyard was planted in 2005 just east of Okanagan Falls, and the Secrest Road Vineyard was planted in 2008 just northwest of Oliver. Both include Riesling and Gewürztraminer and, significantly, Merlot and Malbec as well. Hagen, who took over winemaking from Adolf in the late 1990s, has chalked up an incredible list of awards for white wines but admitted that he would not feel "complete" until the Wild Goose reds also began stacking up the awards. Estate-grown grapes is one way to assure prize-worthy quality.

The appeal of visiting the Wild Goose tasting room is not just the tasty wines but also the presence of family members throughout the winery. Hagen's two sons are now in the business—Alexander in viticulture,

HAGEN AND ROLAND KRUGER

ADOLF KRUGER

while Nik has emerged as the next generation's winemaker after studying at Okanagan College and apprenticing at wineries in the Okanagan and overseas. In 2008 Nik did a vintage at Bremerton Wines, a red wine specialist in Australia's Langhorne Creek area. This is all part of the family's strategy to take its red wines to the same high level as its whites.

MY PICKS

The white wines— Gewürztraminer, Riesling, Pinot Gris and Pinot Blanc—are simply outstanding. In fact, Autumn Gold, the winery's entry-level white blend and the Kruger family's house wine, is so well made that it alone accounts for an impressive list of awards, including a Lieutenant Governor's Award for Excellence. The reds are catching up fast. Black Brant is the winery's delicious port-style red.

OPENED 1990

2145 Sun Valley Way
Okanagan Falls, BC V0H 1R0
T 250.497.8919
W www.wildgoosewinery.com

WHEN TO VISIT
Open daily 10 am – 5 pm
April 1 to October 31,
and by appointment
November through March

LICENSED PICNIC AREA

ACCOMMODATION
Mystic River guest cottage

WILLOW HILL VINEYARDS

The focus here is on the rarest wine that Lanny Swanky and Patricia Venables, his wife, can produce from the Merlot in their two-hectare (five-acre) vineyard: icewine. He may change his mind, but for now Lanny has decided not to enter the crowded red table wine field, but to stick to the much less competitive dessert wine category. "I'm always looking for an edge," he confides. "I've been self-employed most of my life, so I haven't accumulated any pension to amount to anything. This vineyard and icewine operation will fund my retirement."

A big-framed man who speaks with a slow rumble, Lanny was born in Prince George in 1947, the son of a sawmill owner. He began studying engineering on a scholarship but dropped out to work as a logger, ultimately running his own contract logging business for about 18 years. He closed that to take over what he remembers as the "roughest hotel in Prince George" before selling that business to move to the Okanagan.

Lanny and Patricia took over the dome-shaped Willow Hill property in 1997. Then raw land, it is well located beside the road to the Gehringer Brothers and Hester Creek wineries. In the first vintage, 2001, Willow Hill produced a mere 600 half bottles of icewine. In 2002 Lanny and Patricia made only a late-harvest Merlot because it had not become cold enough for icewine by the end of January 2003, when they had scheduled a vacation in Mexico. They have had good conditions for icewine in every vintage since then. The target is to produce a total of about 5,000 half bottles a year while selling the rest of the vineyard's grapes to other wineries.

Lanny, now retired after managing a large Vincor vineyard near Oliver, was steered through his first two winemaking vintages by consultant Michael Bartier. In 2003 Lanny took the Okanagan College winemaking course and now makes wine independently.

MY PICKS

Red icewine is rare, justly prized by the cognoscenti. With their beautiful colour, the Willow Hill wines sparkle in the glass like jewels and deliver luscious fruit flavours. The select late-harvest Merlot is also delicious. Willow Hill also makes a tiny, tiny quantity of tasty Riesling icewine.

OPENED 2005

12315 326th Avenue
PO Box 597
Oliver, BC V0H 1T0
T   250.498.6198
W www.willowhillwines.com

WHEN TO VISIT
No wine shop at this time

LANNY SWANKY

WORKING HORSE WINERY

Ask to meet Meagan, Gretta and Merle at this winery and be prepared for an experience. Meagan and Gretta are sturdy Suffolk Punch draft horses and Merle is a semi-retired logging horse. Together they work the vineyard for owners Tilman Hainle and Sara Norman. The Suffolk horses, each as heavy as a small car, are examples of a heritage horse developed in 16th-century England that became almost extinct after farming was mechanized. (Merle is a Belgian draft horse, a breed with a history also reaching back to medieval times.) By bringing horses into their vineyard, Tilman and Sara take a stand for sustainable agriculture. Working Horse Winery is the idealistic expression of their green values.

Tilman's green values are deeply rooted. Born in Stuttgart in 1958, Tilman grew up in Canada after his parents, Walter and Regina, moved to British Columbia in the early 1970s. He studied computer science and worked a year as a customs officer, then studied winemaking in Germany before helping his family at their Okanagan winery. Walter, a home winemaker, had made Canada's first icewine in 1973 and, with the help of his son, scaled up to commercial quantities in 1978. They opened Hainle Vineyards a decade later. The family sold the winery in 2002 but kept the 2.4-hectare (six-acre) vineyard, now the home for Working Horse.

Tilman, who worked as a consulting winemaker in the Okanagan before opening Working Horse, has carried on the family tradition of making icewine. Planned attractions at this winery include an icewine interpretation centre.

Tilman and Walter were early organic grape growers and Hainle Vineyards became Canada's first producer of organic wines. By adding horses to the vineyard, Tilman and Sara are taking organic practices to the next level. The objective is to make high-quality wines with the lightest possible footprint on the environment.

MY PICKS

You need to ask? The icewine, of course. As well, the winery's Rare Breeds White is a blend of six varieties (names are not revealed) grown in the Working Horse vineyard. The winery's full-flavoured Merlot is aged in once-filled barrels purchased from the Opus One winery in California.

OPENED 2009

5266 Coldham Road
Peachland, BC V0H 1X2

T 250.448.5007
1.877.448.5007 (toll free)

W www.workinghorsewinery.com

WHEN TO VISIT
By appointment

ACCOMMODATION
The Inn at Working Horse

SARA NORMAN AND TILMAN HAINLE

YOUNG & WYSE COLLECTION WINES

Steve Wyse and Michelle Young, his wife, planned to call this the Black Sheep Winery until discovering that a British brewer had once registered the name for a cider and a Canadian distiller wanted to use it for a rum. So they came up with a bulletproof name—their own names.

"I kind of always have been the black sheep of the family," Steve explains. He is referring to the family that started Burrowing Owl Estate Winery, one of the Okanagan's leading producers: his parents, Jim and Midge Wyse, and his older brother, Chris, who now manages Burrowing Owl. Steve, who was born in 1967, set out to become an airline pilot but earned his commercial licence just as layoffs were sweeping through the Canadian airline industry. He tried real estate sales before moving with Michelle to Whistler, where she managed a major restaurant and they both worked as mountain guides.

The Okanagan caught Steve's attention when his parents began planting the Burrowing Owl vineyard in the mid-1990s, and he and Michelle moved to the Okanagan. He began working with vineyard manager Richard Cleave until construction started on the Burrowing Owl winery. Steve became a project manager and then began mentoring with consulting winemaker Bill Dyer. When Bill left in 2004, Steve, who had also taken Brock University winemaking courses, became Burrowing Owl's winemaker. After three vintages there, Steve helped Burrowing Owl recruit a winemaker from outside the family, having decided, he says, that "it was time for me to spread my wings and find my own identity."

In the summer of 2008 Steve and Michelle purchased a highway-side farm south of Osoyoos, almost at the US border, and quickly converted a former fruit cold storage building into a winery. Their first vintage, totalling 110 barrels, was made with purchased Syrah and Merlot grapes (they started the project too late in the season to get good-quality white grapes). The fruit trees on the property were replaced in the spring of

STEVE WYSE

2009 with four hectares (10 acres) of vines, mostly Malbec, Zinfandel and Viognier. Steve also has contracted for grapes from other growers.

It is hardly surprising that the wines echo the styles that succeeded so well at Burrowing Owl. Steve has learned all of Bill Dyer's tricks and has added a few of his own.

MY PICKS

Initial releases included a full-bodied Merlot and a bold Syrah.

OPENED 2009

9503 12th Avenue
Osoyoos. BC V0H 1V1

T   250.495.3245

W www.youngandwysewine.com

WHEN TO VISIT
To be established

ZERO BALANCE VINEYARDS

This tiny winery is located next to the grandest winery in the Holman Lang group, Soaring Eagle. Although it shares some production facilities and a winemaker with Soaring Eagle, Zero Balance also has a separate winery in a humble metal-clad hut. The winery thus recalls the rustic hut, now demolished, that for seven years served as the production centre for Black Hills Estate Winery. Wine tourists in the Okanagan learned from Black Hills not to judge a winery on its looks. In any event, the wine shop at Zero Balance is in a cozy house across the yard from the winery, with a patio overlooking vineyards and Okanagan Lake.

The wines at Zero Balance are made primarily with estate-grown fruit. The 5.6-hectare (14-acre) vineyard grows enough varieties to give the winemaker plenty of options: Cabernet Franc, Merlot, Malbec, Syrah, Petite Sirah, Pinot Gris and Viognier. Some of the blocks are fairly small: the first release of Malbec was less than a barrel of wine.

The early signature wine at Zero Balance, a multiple medal winner, is a white blend called Project 743 that came about by chance in 2007. As former winemaker Bernhard Schirrmeister recounts, the winery once received a load of grapes from one grower that consisted of seven bins of Sauvignon Blanc, four bins of Muscat and three bins of Sémillon. (Typically, a bin contains 162 kilograms or 400 pounds of grapes.) To make the best use of the tanks, Bernhard crushed and fermented the varieties together—and created a delightful aromatic white.

According to winery owner Keith Holman, Zero Balance refers to wines that are in perfect balance. However, the winery has also come up with wine labels that poke fun at the financial definition of Zero Balance. There is a Bordeaux blend called In the Red, a rosé called In the Pink and an icewine called Frozen Assets. There is no rule against having a little fun in a winery.

Project 743 and the Viognier are attractive whites. In the Red is a big Cabernet Sauvignon—based wine structured for long cellaring, while the Malbec is for more immediate drinking.

OPENED 2008

1865 Naramata Road
Penticton, BC V2A 8T8
T   250.493.3470
W www.holmanlangwineries.com

WHEN TO VISIT
Open daily 10 am – 6 pm
May through October. Closed
November through April.

USEFUL BC
WINE FACTS

IN THE SUMMER OF 2008, WITH SPONSORSHIP OF the British Columbia
Wine Institute, consultants Lynn and John Bremmer, who operate Mount
Kobau Wine Services in Oliver, published their fourth periodic vineyard
census. It is reproduced here as the current snapshot of vineyards and
grape varieties in British Columbia. The Bremmers tallied 3,626 hectares (8,960 acres). This was up dramatically from the 2,653 hectares
(6,555 acres) of grapes two years earlier. They also projected that as
much as another 607 hectares (1,500 acres) would be planted in 2009
and 2010. The slowdown in the economy likely reduced the enthusiastic
pace of new plantings. Even so, the area under vines in British Columbia,
while small in the scale of most world wine regions, has experienced
sevenfold growth in the past two decades.

WHERE THE GRAPES GROW

REGION	HECTARES	ACRES
Oliver/Osoyoos	1,945	4,806
Penticton/Naramata/Kaleden	386	954
Kelowna/Westbank	338	836
Similkameen Valley	235	580
Okanagan Falls	222.5	550
Vancouver Island	140	347
Peachland/Summerland	136	336
Fraser Valley	82.5	204
Lake Country/Vernon	64	159
Gulf Islands	46.5	115
Spallumcheen/Shuswap	30.75	76
Other BC regions	42	104.5

RED GRAPE VARIETIES (2008)

VARIETY	HECTARES	ACRES	PERCENTAGE OF RED	PERCENTAGE OF TOTAL GRAPES
Merlot	641.63	1,585.46	34.31 %	17.49 %
Pinot Noir	321.09	793.41	17.17	8.75
Cabernet Sauvignon	275.54	680.87	14.73	7.51
Syrah (Shiraz)	208.93	516.27	11.17	5.70
Cabernet Franc	158.31	391.18	8.46	4.31
Gamay Noir	58.15	143.69	3.11	1.59
Maréchal Foch	49.19	121.55	2.63	1.34
Malbec	29.08	71.87	1.55	0.79
Petit Verdot	22.53	55.69	1. 20	0.61
Zweigelt	17.45	43.23	0.93	0.47
Blattner Reds	17.19	42.50	0.92	0.47
Pinot Meunier	6.52	16.13	0.35	0.18
Pinotage	5.68	14.05	0.30	0.16
Zinfandel	4.88	12.06	0.26	0.13
Baco Noir	4.33	10.70	0.23	0.12
Chancellor	4.05	10.01	0.22	0.11
Tempranillo	4.01	9.92	0.21	0.11
Lemberger	3.88	9.59	0.21	0.11
Dunkelfelder	3.28	8.11	0.18	0.09
Agria	3.03	7.51	0.16	0.08
Mourvedre	2.69	6.66	0.14	0.07
Sangiovese	1.97	4.87	0.11	0.05
Grenache	1.86	4.60	0.10	0.04
Castel	1.54	3.82	0.08	0.04
Léon Millot	1.41	3.50	0.08	0.04
Barbera	1.34	3.32	0.07	0.04
Rotberger	1.19	2.95	0.06	0.03
Dornfelder	0.99	2.47	0.05	0.03
Michurinetz	0.92	2.28	0.05	0.02
St. Laurent	0.59	1.48	0.03	0.02
Carmenère	0.16	0.40	0.01	0.00
Miscellaneous Reds	17.26	42.65	0.92	0.47
TOTAL RED GRAPES	1,870.84	4,622.80	100.00 %	50.99 %

WHITE GRAPE VARIETIES (2008)

VARIETY	HECTARES	ACRES	PERCENTAGE OF WHITE	PERCENTAGE OF TOTAL GRAPES
Pinot Gris	376.08	928.29	20.89 %	10.24 %
Chardonnay	350.57	866.26	19.49	9.56
Gewürztraminer	260.53	643.77	14.49	7.10
Sauvignon Blanc	177.56	438.76	9.87	4.84
Pinot Blanc	149.39	369.14	8.31	4.07
Riesling	148.58	367.14	8.26	4.05
Viognier	66.56	164.48	3.70	1.81
Ehrenfelser	29.81	73.66	1.66	0.81
Sémillon	29.10	71.91	1.62	0.79
Bacchus	21.16	52.30	1.18	0.58
Ortega	20.47	50.60	1.14	0.56
Auxerrois	17.28	42.72	0.96	0.47
Blattner Whites	17.19	42.50	0.95	0.47
Muscats	15.96	39.44	0.89	0.44
Siegerrebe	15.19	37.55	0.85	0.41
Kerner	13.15	32.51	0.73	0.41
Schönburger	11.13	27.51	0.61	0.30
Chenin Blanc	7.32	18.10	0.41	0.20
Vidal	7.11	17.57	0.39	0.19
Madeleine Sylvaner	6.48	16.03	0.36	0.18
Müller-Thurgau	5.88	14.55	0.33	0.16
Scheurebe	5.69	14.08	0.32	0.16
Optima	5.85	14.46	0.32	0.16
Madeleine Angevine	5.43	13.42	0.30	0.15
Chasselas	5.20	12.87	0.29	0.14
Reichensteiner	4.65	11.50	0.26	0.13
Sovereign Opal	2.83	7.00	0.16	0.08
Roussanne	2.66	6.59	0.15	0.07
Marsanne	1.95	4.84	0.11	0.05
Trebbiano	1.63	4.03	0.09	0.04
Verdelet	1.41	3.50	0.08	0.04
Traminer	0.70	1.74	0.04	0.02
Miscellaneous Whites	14.16	35.00	0.79	0.39
TOTAL WHITE GRAPES	1,798.00	4,443.52	100.00 %	49.01 %

HOW MUCH BC WINE ARE WE BUYING?

The Vintners Quality Alliance (VQA) program began in 1990 to identify those wines made entirely with BC grapes. Because the program is voluntary, some producers (primarily small wineries) do not submit wines to the VQA tasting panel. Nevertheless, VQA wine accounts for the majority of wine grown in British Columbia. This table from the British Columbia Wine Institute reveals the steady growth in sales and value of the wines.

YEAR TO MARCH 31	SALES	PERCENTAGE INCREASE	SALES IN LITRES	AVERAGE PRICE / 750 ML BOTTLE
1991/92	$6,846,183		748,196	$6.86
1992/93	10,559,586	54 %	977,030	8.11
1993/94	15,306,430	45	1,289,672	8.90
1994/95	23,666,799	57	1,775,580	10.00
1995/96	31,321,592	22	2,035,877	11.54
1996/97	32,397,296	3	2,093,324	11.61
1997/98	39,758,907	22	2,324,068	12.83
1998/99	42,143,199	6	2,420,599	13.05
1999/00	48,740,017	16	2,585,217	14.16
2000/01	57,638,465	18	2,999,807	14.41
2001/02	70,418,708	22	3,717,452	14.21
2002/03	83,051,239	18	4,233,458	14.72
2003/04	91,998,327	11	4,728,612	14.60
2004/05	114,891,745	25	5,571,100	15.47
2005/06	141,390,804	23	6,472,816	16.38
2006/07	151,220,894	7	6,783,234	16.72
2007/08	156,730,109	4	6,594,213	17.83
2008/09	160,881,514	3	6,637,387	18.18

WINE-SPEAK: A GLOSSARY

ACIDITY
The natural tartness in grapes and other fruit that contributes to vibrant flavours.

APPELLATION
The geographical definition of a wine region. British Columbia's current appellations are the Okanagan Valley, the Similkameen Valley, the Fraser Valley, Vancouver Island and the Gulf Islands.

BIODYNAMIC VITICULTURE
An extreme form of organic grape growing. Growers not only avoid artificial fertilizers, pesticides and herbicides, they make their own compost and cultivate beneficial bacteria for the soil, culturing it in such media as stags' bladders. It sounds weird but some of the best French wineries do it.

BOTRYTIS
A fungus that attacks grape skins. In favourable conditions (misty mornings, dry afternoons) it dehydrates grapes, allowing the production of intense dessert wines. In unfavourable conditions (too much rain) it rots the grapes. Because the climate is generally dry in the Okanagan and Similkameen valleys, botrytis is rare, and botrytis-affected wines are rarer still.

BRIX
A measure of sugar in grapes: one degree Brix equals 18 grams of sugar per litre. Mature grapes are

typically 21 to 25 Brix, which converts to 11 to 13 percent alcohol after fermentation.

CELLARED IN CANADA

This is a phrase that commercial wineries put on the label of wines made with, or blended with, imported wine. These are sometimes taken to be authentic Canadian wine because, until recently, they have been sold in the same area of liquor stores as wines, such as VQA wines, made entirely from Canadian grapes. Labels and marketing practices are now changing to create a more obvious distinction between wines grown in Canada and wines bottled here with imported wine.

CIDERY

An establishment that makes apple cider.

CLONE

The mutation of a species. Growers select and propagate grape clones chosen for such desirable qualities as early ripening, vivid flavour and deep colour. Several clones of the same variety are often planted in the same vineyard. Because flavour and texture of the wine from each clone will be a little different, wines blended from several clones are likely to be more complex.

COLD SOAK

A procedure that happens before fermentation, in which the grapes are crushed and the resulting stew of skins and juice is cooled and left for several days before fermentation begins. The object is to extract colour and flavour. *See also* Maceration.

COMMERCIAL WINERY

A BC winery that has a commercial licence and is therefore permitted to bottle and sell wine made with imported wine or grapes.

CORKED WINE

The term describes a wine that is chemically contaminated with TCA (2,4,6-Trichloroanisole). TCA contamination is usually caused by faulty corks but can also come from barrels, other cooperage or even, apparently, from wood within a cellar cleaned with chlorine solutions. Such wines smell and taste musty, a bit like an old earth cellar. While cork producers are coming to grips with the problem, some wineries now use either synthetic corks or screw cap closures.

ESTATE WINERY

A winery with vineyards of its own. A 1978 regulation, now obsolete, required estate wineries to have at least eight hectares (20 acres) of vines. Under current regulations, these wineries are licensed as land-based wineries. They use only BC grapes or fruit. Many wineries still call themselves estate wineries, an indication that they are based on vineyards of their own.

FARM GATE WINERY

Licence created in 1989, and now obsolete, for wineries with vineyards too small to qualify as estate wineries. These are now included with the land-based wineries.

FERMENTATION

The natural process in which yeast converts sugar to alcohol.

FLINTY

A generally positive descriptor for the crisp, mineral edge noted in some unoaked white wines, such as a bone-dry Sauvignon Blanc.

FRUIT WINE

A wine made from fruit other than grapes.

GRASSY

A descriptor for the zesty, clean vegetative aromas of grapefruit or gooseberry in certain white wines, notably Sauvignon Blanc and Sémillon. Although such aromas are okay in those varieties, they are not acceptable in red wines, being the result of slightly under-ripe grapes.

HERBACEOUS

A snooty word for "grassy."

HYBRID

Grape varieties typically developed by crossing European varieties with native North American varieties. The plant breeder's objectives include developing varieties that ripen early or resist disease or are winter-hardy.

LABRUSCA

A family of grapes native to North America and not suitable for table wines. The best-known labrusca variety is Concord.

LAND-BASED WINERIES

The new legal jargon for estate and farm gate wineries. Generally it means they grow some of the fruit needed for their wines.

MACERATION

The process of leaving the juice or wine sitting on crushed grape skins, typically red grapes, for days at a time to draw colour and flavour from the skins into the wine.

MADERIZE

When wines take up oxygen while they age, they gradually acquire flavours resembling Madeira, a deliberately aged Spanish wine.

MERITAGE

A word (rhymes with *heritage*) created in California to identify blends made with Bordeaux grape varieties. White Meritage is a blend of Sauvignon Blanc and Sémillon; red Meritage is a blend of Merlot, Cabernet Sauvignon, Cabernet Franc and sometimes Malbec, Petit Verdot and Carmenère. Wineries using the Meritage label subscribe to quality standards of the Meritage Association.

MICRO-OXYGENATION

A fairly recent winemaking technology in which small quantities of air are bubbled deliberately through vats of fermenting red wine. The main benefits include healthier fermentations (which need oxygen) and wines that are softer and ready to drink earlier.

MUST

Unfermented grape pulp or juice. There is no relationship between this term and the word "musty," which describes mouldy aromas.

OLD VINES

Various wineries release wines labelled as "old vines." There is no strict rule defining how old vines must be for such wine. As a rule, the vines should be at least 25 years old. A new vineyard only produces its first full crop in its third year. The majority of vineyards in the Okanagan are no more than 10 to 15 years old. Fruit from old vines is prized because it can yield wines of intense flavour and great character.

ORGANIC

A technique for growing grapes (and other plants) or making wine without using chemicals such as pesticides, herbicides or commercial fertilizers. To maintain their organic certification, vineyards and wineries must be regularly audited by industry associations.

OXIDIZED

Wines that have been exposed to too much air for too long and have become flat and stale; the colour becomes dull, turning to a tired gold with white wines. It is rare to come across such wines these days, but if you do, it means the bottle on the tasting bar has been open for several days or, even worse, the winemaking techniques are dodgy.

PUMP-OVER

During red wine fermentation, the skins are buoyed by the escaping carbon dioxide and float to the top of the wine vats. This is called the cap. Several times each day, wine is pumped over the cap. The main objective of submerging the skins periodically is to make sure colour and flavour are extracted. It also prevents bacteria from growing in the cap.

SCREW CAPS

Replacing corks in wine bottles with screw caps still upsets the traditionalists, who equate caps with plonk. If that is what you think, get over it. There are few better closures for keeping white wines crisp, fresh and clean-tasting. There is still some debate as to whether screw caps are also best for red wines, but the evidence is encouraging.

SPITTING

Wineries are probably the only place where spitting is acceptable. (Okay, maybe in baseball dugouts as well.) In the interest of remaining sober, both winery staff and guests who taste wines are not obliged to swallow them. Winery tasting bars provide spittoons. In the winery itself, it is okay to spit into the drainage grates. Off-target spitters should practise before touring.

STELVIN

The trademarked name for a French design of screw cap closures for wine bottles.

TANNIN

A substance in the skin and seeds of grapes that is essential in providing backbone to red wines. When there is excessive tannin, wines are hard on the palate and have a bitter aftertaste, not unlike overly strong tea. Harsh tannins will soften during several years of bottle aging or when young reds are decanted before serving.

TERROIR

The French term that encompasses the entire environment, including the soil, climate and exposure, that defines the particular character of each vineyard.

TOASTY

A descriptor for a slightly burnt note in the aroma and sometimes the flavour of a wine that has been aged in a barrel whose interior was deliberately charred. This is generally considered positive in Chardonnay and Pinot Noir because, like a pinch of salt, it adds an extra note of interest.

VARIETAL

A wine for which the constituent grape variety is named on the label (such as Chardonnay or Merlot). Such wines must contain a minimum of 85 percent of the named variety.

VINIFERA

The species of classic wine grapes that have spread from the vineyards of Europe to wherever fine wine is made.

VQA (VINTNERS QUALITY ALLIANCE)

All BC wines bearing the VQA seal must be made from BC grapes. The wines are all screened by a professional tasting panel. Wines found faulty cannot be sold as VQA wines. More than half of BC wineries—including very competent producers—have chosen, for various reasons, not to submit wines for the VQA seal.

WINERY LISTINGS

NOTES